Charity and Poverty in Advanced Welfare States

This book conceptualises the role of charity to people who are poor in wealthy countries and outlines a set of practical and conceptual ideas for how it could be reimagined.

Despite professionalised welfare states and strong economies, in many advanced industrialised nations, charity continues to play a major role in the lives of people who are poor. Extending what we know about how neoliberalism drives a decayed welfare state that outsources welfare provisioning to charities and community initiatives, this book asks how can we understand and conceptualise society's willingness to engage in charitable acts towards the poor, and how can charity be reimagined to contribute to justice in an unjust society? Through interrogating multiple data sources, including government datasets, survey datasets, media analyses, and ethnographic data, this book shows that charity is not well-suited to addressing the material dimension of poverty. It argues the need for a revised model of charity with the capacity to contribute to social solidarity that bridges social divisions and is inclusive of the poor. Presenting a model for reimaging charity which enables reciprocity and active contributions from recipients and providers, this book shows how power imbalances flowing from the unidirectional provision of charity can be reduced, allowing opportunities for reciprocal care that foster both well-being and solidarity.

This book will be of interest to all scholars and students of social policy, public policy, social welfare, sociology, and social work.

Cameron Parsell is Professor of the Social Sciences at The University of Queensland, Australia. He is the author of *The Homeless Person in Contemporary Society*. His research focuses on understanding the experience of poverty and what societies do to address it. With an Australian Research Council Future Fellowship, Cameron's recent work examines charity and the Australian welfare state, with an aim of improving both.

Andrew Clarke is an urban sociologist and Research Fellow at The University of Queensland, Australia. He researches urban governance, homelessness, and other forms of housing-related poverty. Andrew has written on the networks of agencies, interventions, and policies that are assembled around urban problems, such as homelessness or antisocial behaviour, and the ways in which these can be reconfigured to better support disadvantaged people.

Francisco (Paco) Perales is Associate Professor of Sociology at The University of Queensland, Australia. His research uses longitudinal and life-course approaches and quantitative methods to enhance our understanding of social stratification in contemporary societies. Paco's recent work has concentrated on identifying the drivers of socio-economic inequalities by socio-economic background, gender, and sexual orientation within Australian society.

Routledge Advances in Health and Social Policy

Research and Evaluation in Community, Health and Social Care Settings
Experiences from Practice
Edited by Suzanne Guerin, Nóirín Hayes and Sinead McNally

Critical Discourses of Old Age and Telecare Technologies
Gizdem Akdur

Aging Veterans with Disabilities
A Cross-National Study of Policies and Challenges
Arie Rimmerman

Creative Arts-Based Research in Aged Care
Photovoice, Photography, and Poetry in Action
Evonne Miller

Inciting Justice and Progressive Power
The Partnership for Working Families Cities
Edited by David Reynolds and Louise Simmons

Death, Grief and Loss in the Context of COVID-19
Edited by Panagiotis Pentaris

Charity and Poverty in Advanced Welfare States
Cameron Parsell, Andrew Clarke and Francisco Perales

For more information about this series, please visit: https://www.routledge.com/Routledge-Advances-in-Health-and-Social-Policy/book-series/RAHSP

Charity and Poverty in Advanced Welfare States

Cameron Parsell,
Andrew Clarke and
Francisco Perales

Routledge
Taylor & Francis Group
LONDON AND NEW YORK

First published 2022
by Routledge
2 Park Square, Milton Park, Abingdon, Oxon OX14 4RN

and by Routledge
605 Third Avenue, New York, NY 10158

Routledge is an imprint of the Taylor & Francis Group, an informa business

British Library Cataloguing-in-Publication Data
A catalogue record for this book is available from the British Library

Library of Congress Cataloging-in-Publication Data
A catalog record has been requested for this book

ISBN: 978-0-367-71381-2 (hbk)
ISBN: 978-0-367-71383-6 (pbk)
ISBN: 978-1-003-15057-2 (ebk)

Typeset in Times New Roman
by codeMantra

Contents

Figures

Boxes

Acknowledgements

We have written this book with significant support and resources from many colleagues, people, and organisations.

We have been supported with funding from the Australian Research Council, through a Future Fellowship (FT180100250) awarded to Cameron Parsell and by the Centre of Excellence for Children and Families over the Life Course (CE200100025). Some of the research drawn on was funded by a grant from the St Vincent de Paul Society Queensland and a Development Fellowship from The University of Queensland.

Dr Ella Kuskoff provided an enormous intellectual contribution through her research towards Chapter 6. Acknowledgement and thanks also go to Sarah Ball and Charlotte ten Have (who assisted with ethnographic data collection), to Karina Kersh (who transcribed the 85 in-depth interviews), and to Peter Whiteford, Bruce Bradbury, and Hal Pawson (for sharing their data). Thanks to Richard N. S. Robinson for helping us understand the meaning of charity.

Many people accessing charity generously gave their time. They willingly, and often with great humour, shared their experiences with and reflections on charity and their life circumstances. We are indebted to them for their contributions. Our hope is that this book conveys some of their experiences in ways that reflect how they make meaning of using charity, and what they would like changed.

We also had the great fortune of receiving support from volunteers and staff at the St Vincent de Paul Society Queensland. Although this book is not a study of the St Vincent de Paul Society, or even a study of the work they do, we have drawn on many insights we have learned through conducting research alongside the Society.

1 The endurance of charity

Introduction

> It must be easy to point to a non-existent long term solution [to homelessness] that will likely never occur without legislation and government funding. Because [charity's] not THE perfect solution, it must [be] … a waste of time, right? Do we have a responsibility to do better as a society? Absolutely. [Charity] is at least bringing awareness, visibility, and activism to the issue and starting conversations like this one. Or we can keep waiting around for someone else to make the perfect solution for us. That seems to be working wonders so far.
>
> The problem is only the Government has the resources to provide this [affordable housing, adequate income], and they don't. Nor, it seems, do they have sufficient appetite to do so. Our national housing shortage has been growing for years. What the [charities] provide is short-term amelioration, not a long-term solution. That's all that's within their reach. If I were on the street myself, I'd be glad for their efforts.
>
> It's easy to criticise [charity to the poor]. Harder to suggest an alternative.

These comments were posted to respond to a 2019 online news article written by the first author of this book (Parsell 2019). The comments speak to widely held public sentiment about the role – and indeed value – of charity as a response to poverty in contemporary and wealthy societies. Individual acts of charity towards people experiencing poverty, and collectively what charity is understood to represent for society, are widely perceived as necessary and positive. As Rose Lindsey and colleagues point out, voluntary charity is seen as a good in its own right, without the need for further scrutiny (Lindsey et al. 2018).

Engaging in charitable care – for example, giving food and money to people who are hungry and poor, or volunteering to provide temporary pop-up accommodation to people who otherwise sleep on the streets – embodies a form of civic action that many believe we ought to celebrate. People interpret these acts of charity optimistically, seeing them as a sign that society has not descended into a selfish dystopia. The well-off providing their resources, time, and money to the poor is taken as evidence that a caring society does in fact still exist; its antithesis would be a good indicator of nihilistic individualism. Our political leaders – conservative and progressive alike – are unequivocal in drawing a direct connection between volunteering in charities that help the marginalised and a caring society. Lord William Beveridge (1948, p. 10), a key architect of the post-war British welfare state, described the presence of voluntary groups to better others' lives as "distinguishing marks of a free society," in contrast to what is found in a "totalitarian society." For Richard Titmuss (2019), altruism and the desire to help each other is evidence of solidarity within society.

Despite the self-evident appeal of, and public support for, charity, the online article reflected upon its limitations. Specifically, the article addressed a charity that temporarily transforms commercial city carparks into pop-up accommodation by installing inflatable mattresses for homeless people to sleep on overnight. In the article, Parsell criticised the charity for soothing the consequences of homelessness and poverty, rather than addressing the problems with evidence-based solutions. The pop-up accommodation charity model received unanimous praise. The media even reported a waitlist of volunteers who wanted to set up mattresses in the carpark and spend time with "the homeless." Parsell's critique asked why we celebrate such inadequate responses, given that there is significant evidence that rough sleeping can be permanently ended (rather than temporarily ameliorated) through the provision of affordable housing and professional services, and the profound wealth that exists in Australia to act upon that evidence.

At their core, the comments introducing this book – consistent with the numerous emails, letters, and criticism the authors receive when they questions the worth of charity – convey three connected sentiments. First, charity is an acceptable response to people in poverty as an "in the meantime" response (Cloke et al. 2017). Yes, supporters agree that charity is not perfect. Charity is not all that is required, but its limitations are not a sufficient reason to discount charity out of hand. The first defence of charity relies on accepting its limitations to deal with the fundamental problem, but stresses that, until those fundamental problems are addressed, charity is justified in the meantime. This justification is encapsulated by the aphorism that we should not let the perfect be the enemy of the good. Perfection can never be achieved – ending poverty or homelessness – so let us not waste our time and energy striving for perfection when doing so prevents us from doing what is needed in the immediacy, what is good enough: providing inflatable mattresses in a carpark.

The second defence of charity illustrated by the comments draws on a nuanced understanding of charity's presence as driven by structural problems and systemic failures. Defenders of charity acknowledge that volunteers are doing their best to respond to problems not of their making. Moreover, the problems are too big, too complex, too wicked, for charity volunteers to resolve. This position sees poverty as structurally determined. Accordingly, it is only government that can reasonably be expected to solve the structural problems within which poverty is embedded and where its structural solutions lie. As the comment above pleads: "The problem is only the government has the resources to provide." The emergence of the problem is government's fault. It is government who are not only responsible, but also capable of addressing the problem. This argument works from the premise that volunteers and charities can in no way address structural problems – acts of charitable care are "all that's within their reach." They can help soothe the consequences of government failure. Indeed, acting charitably is framed as exerting agency, as opposed to passively waiting for governments to do what they are otherwise reluctant to do. Further, it is not simply the active efforts of the charitable that support this defence. The comment asserts that people accessing charity would prefer to eat what volunteers or foodbanks provide than go without altogether, or to sleep in an undercover carpark rather than out in the weather.

The third defence of charity is implicit in each of the comments, and explicit in the last: it is inadequate to criticise the efforts of the charitable, especially so when sitting (or writing) on the sideline, without offering a viable alternative. This position is encapsulated by the aphorism that the weak criticise; the strong act. This argument, that it is easy to criticise charity for its failings whilst failing to do anything practical oneself, is frequently expressed and challenging to confront. It is challenging simply because acting charitably towards people who are poor can offer genuine moments of care. We do not have to look far or think hard, on either religious or secular grounds, to understand that care, as Joan Tronto (2015, p. 38) says, is "the key to living well." Moreover, "a truly free society makes people free to care" (Tronto 2015, p. 38). Challenging acts of care is a dangerous enterprise. We go to great lengths in this book to advocate for the significance of care. In criticising charity, we need to ensure the criticism is directed at a system that renders charity both necessary and ineffective, rather than at the charitable volunteers themselves, and we need to simultaneously offer alternatives that are desirable and workable to both those on the providing and receiving end of charitable care. It is indeed, as commenter suggests, harder to achieve structural change than to roll up one's sleeves and do something practical in the here and now.

The critique of charity, and the defence of it, invigorates debate about what we ought to do as *individual* citizens when confronted with *structural* poverty. This debate forms part of a conversation about what society ought to look like. Debate about charity is, at the same time, debate about public welfare and State provision. The comments above reflect the dilemma of how we can be justified – and just – in individually acting to soothe the consequences of poverty through charity, rather than working collectively to end poverty. For John Stuart Mill (2004), it was a mistake of philanthropists "to nibble at the consequences of unjust power, instead of redressing the injustice itself." Will Kymlicka (2001) reflects on this point well. Informed by the assumption that public institutions command their authority over citizens by being just, Kymlicka (2001) argues that charity can only be the *second best* option.

As citizens, what should we do when we see people who are poor? If charity can only be the second best option, one can understand, as the comments above suggest, that the best option may seem out of hand. It is easy to empathise with volunteers who would rather provide people who are poor with food, or volunteer in charities that provide pop-up accommodation in carparks, than wait for structural change; structural change that seems beyond their capacity to enact. As the comments introducing this book make clear, people can act charitably to the poor and advocate for the continuation of charity that soothes poverty, whilst also understanding that poverty is the result of structural failure. If poverty is a product of structural systems that disadvantage some people, and we believe that it is, how can people be justified to provide voluntary care to those in poverty when they do not also attempt to disrupt the structural causes of poverty?

These questions and dilemmas animate this book. To identify a better approach than models of charity that merely soothe the consequences of poverty, we need to understand how charity sits within prevailing social and political systems. The first question this book engages with is, how can we understand and conceptualise society's willingness to continually engage in charitable acts towards the poor? In addressing this question, we seek to demonstrate that individual charitable acts cannot be understood at the individual level. Both the experience of poverty and charitable care to those experiencing poverty are deeply embedded within social and public policy institutions; and as we demonstrate throughout the following chapters, much of what is voluntarily given through charity is enabled and funded by the State and the social norms and ideals it promotes. Further, we show that the conditions that lead to the need for charity among people who are poor, and the institutions that enable charities to work with people who are poor, are driven by deliberate policy decisions. As John Weeks (2020) shows, what governments present as necessary policy decisions, for example reducing welfare entitlements to balance their budgets, are actually political decisions that reflect government's normative prescriptions for society. From this premise, the book considers how the provision of charity to people who are poor constitutes a site where the boundaries of a normative society are debated. Charity's significance lies in what its presence and function says about the organisation of society, the responsibility of the State, and the role of citizens.

We take seriously the position that the strength of critique lies in its capacity to prescribe a meaningful alternative. Erik Olin Wright (2013) explicitly engages emancipatory social science to theorise and promote *real utopias.*

He sets out a framework for imagining alternative social structures based on moral principles, but he understands that the task is not simply about identifying what is morally desirable. Emancipatory social science must explain what is viable and achievable. Without viability and achievability, prescriptions of the desirable are plainly utopian (Wright 2013). Taking heed of the necessity to offer viable and achievable alternatives, the book also addresses the question, how can charity be reimagined to contribute towards a more just society?

This is a hard question. A utopic response to this question would go something like: provide all citizens access to a living income, affordable housing, and universal services and the myriad charities that provide all manner of ameliorative resources would be superfluous. From this perspective, the question is not how to reimagine charity, but rather how to alter society to put charity out of business, so to speak. This reasoning would be generally consistent with advocacy for a Universal Basic Income. We philosophically agree with some of the Universal Basic Income (Standing 2020), and our prescription for transforming charity acknowledges the need for structural reform, so that volunteers and their charities are not in the business of mopping up the direct consequences of policies that render some citizens destitute. Setting to one side whether Universal Basic Income is desirable, and if so, viable and achievable, whether it is introduced or not, there will be people who want to provide non-professionalised care – through acting charitably – towards fellow citizens in need. Indeed, we propose that the collective action of providing charitable care, especially under conditions of reciprocity, is desirable even in the presence of more equitable access to income, housing, and other publicly funded resources. Universal resources to eliminate poverty will not just appear out of nowhere, if they ever do appear, and our ideas for transforming charity involve reframing charitable care such that it encompasses agitating for these kinds of structural transformations. Our manifesto for transforming charity aims to contribute to a more just world.

To help answer these questions, this book presents an in-depth investigation of charitable responses to poverty in Australia. The book integrates empirical evidence drawn from multiple Australian and international data sources, including government and charity administrative datasets, survey data, media analysis, policy analysis, and ethnographic data. We use this data to contribute to international empirical work and conceptual debates about how societies provide formal and informal care for their citizens living in poverty, and how they might do it differently. Before outlining our position, however, we will first sketch the complex field of perspectives on charitable responses to poverty, their prevalence, and their value to society. We then finish the chapter with a statement of the arguments we put forward in the book, and an account of how these arguments contribute to existing debates.

What is charity?

John Mohan and Beth Breeze (2016) observe that, although charity is a common feature of Western societies – in their case, the United Kingdom – we lack a clear understanding of what actually counts as charity. Writing about the United States, Rob Reich distinguishes philanthropy from charity, with the former focusing on addressing structural causes of social problems and the latter constituting a means of direct assistance. For Reich (2018, p. 20), charity is "giving away money or property for some other-regarding purpose." Jon Dean (2020) adds to this to include the provision of one's time. Similarly, Kymlicka (2001) defines charity as the giving away of property (including money). However, he restricts the definition to voluntary acts towards *anonymous others*, who will likely have no other role in the giver's life (Kymlicka 2001). This focus on the anonymous other is used to distinguish charity from the non-charitable giving – or care – that we engage in with family, friends, and others in our social circle.

Drawing on the Catholic principle of *caritas* (the Latin etymology of charity), Gregory Dees (2012) defines charity as selfless giving to help others motivated by compassion. The foregrounding of compassion draws attention to charity as an act of giving to people *in need*, especially people in poverty. Dees describes the motivation of the charitable, irrespective of what outcomes they achieve, as quintessentially charity. It is the act of compassion that animates charity that differentiates it from instrumental behaviour. He explains:

> Charity focuses on the actor's caring motivations and willingness to sacrifice his or her interests. It makes no reference to the consequences of the act, other than that the act is performed out of love or compassion. In fact, personal gain from the act dilutes its moral value.
>
> (Dees 2012, p. 322)

The importance of selflessness set out by Dees resonates with the legislative prescription from England and Wales that any benefit to the charitable can be no more than incidental (Dean 2020). This is consistent with the distinction made in the early years of the welfare state development by Lord Beveridge, who positioned philanthropy as a selfless act, which he distinguished from self-help organisations, such as friendly societies, that are designed to benefit members (Wright 2001).

There are, however, competing ideas on charity's relationship to selfless caring for others. These are important for how we think about charity in this book, especially what it takes to reimagine charity. For instance, both the act of charity and charitable organisations are historically and intrinsically embedded within the world's three large monotheistic religions: Judaism, Christianity, and Islam. Indeed, today, many people across the globe act charitably out of religious motivation. However, this motivation is not exclusively selfless. Charitable acts can also, or instead, be pursued to achieve self-perfection and salvation (Kymlicka 2001). Charity "puts out sin as water puts out fire" (Kochuyt 2009, p. 108); or as Paulinus wrote, "wealth, if diverted to the needy, might serve to extinguish the flames of the afterlife" (cited in Holland 2019, p. 134).

Faith can motivate charitable acts, and we can understand the religious motivation to help others as a process that has spiritual benefits to the giver, particularly in the afterlife. For Christians, the below passage about perfection and treasure in heaven in Matthew's testament is a strong motivator to act charitably for reasons that are not entirely selfless:

> If you want to be perfect, go, sell your possessions and give to the poor, and you will have treasure in heaven. Then come, follow me.
>
> (Matthew 19:21)

In Chapter 2 we touch on the flourishing debates about religion and secularism as a motivator for charitable giving; here, however, we note that our definition of charity does not exclude voluntary giving to a stranger that may be, at least in part, motivated by religious teachings or aspirations. As we elaborate throughout the book, we are interested in motivations to act charitably in so much as motivations are implicated in how, if at all, the recipients of charity are viewed. In Chapter 9, we argue for a reimagination of charity that requires recipients to be placed at the centre. We argue for this on the basis that the interests of the recipient are too often either insufficiently considered or simply assumed to be advanced by virtue of the charitable's compassionate motivation. When charity is motivated by the interests of the giver, even if these are spiritual interests in the afterlife, opportunities for transforming charity so that it meets the recipients' needs are not front and centre. Kymlicka (2001) provides a compelling theoretical proposition that charity motivated by achieving salvation means that the giver should not make arbitrary assessments on the deservingness or otherwise of recipients: the recipient is unimportant, so it doesn't matter whether they deserve charity. In Chapter 9, we propose that focusing squarely on the recipient is necessary to transform charity to contribute towards a more just form of care. We are thus only interested in the motivations to act charitably when they prevent the giver of charity from focusing on the recipient of their charitable care. We argue that the giver of charity needs to be motivated by the interests of the recipient if charity is to be transformed to maximise its benefit.

Taking all of these considerations on board, this book defines charity as the voluntary giving of money, resources, or time to non-kin or non-friends. The primary focus is the practice of charity, including individual acts of charitable care. We recognise, however, that the practice of charity is always larger than the individuals involved. In fact, the argument that the practice of charity towards people who are poor is a social phenomenon is a core proposition of the book. First, we have to think about an individual's need for charity at the societal level. Second, the act of providing charitable care is fostered by and encouraged as part of an idealised social order. Third, the individual resources and money that volunteers give are often societal resources. Fourth, this book is not about charitable organisations (charities), but we show that the individual practice of charity is often, although not always, provided and received through these organisations.

The growing prominence of charity

With some exceptions, we cannot know for sure the precise extent of the practice of charity within a society, much less can we clearly substantiate whether this is changing over time. There are two reasons for this. First, the informal nature of some of the practices of charity makes their extent difficult to grasp. Almost by definition, informal acts of charitable care do not leave a data trail. Notwithstanding these limitations, Chapter 5 scrutinises administrative and survey data to identify what can be systematically substantiated about the extent of charitable care to people in poverty, and in Chapters 7 and 8, we provide an in-depth analysis of the provision and experience of some contemporary charitable approaches to people in poverty.

Second, whilst we have robust data on the number of charitable organisations and the amount of money donated to charity in specific countries over time, these data provide only a limited window into the extent of charitable care. For example, the overwhelming majority of registered charities provide services and resources beyond the scope of this book. In the United Kingdom and United States, for instance, the main aims of most charities relate to education, health, research, religion, and the arts, and not to providing charitable care to people in poverty. Further, the former types of charitable organisations receive the largest share of philanthropic funding by far. Reich (2018) analysed data on the charities that receive the majority of philanthropic funding in the United States. He concluded that:

> Charity is really not much about caring for the needs of strangers, providing for the poor and disadvantaged. It is not much about almsgiving. It is not an especially significant supplement to the state's effort to establish a social safety net for citizens.
>
> (Reich 2018, p. 92)

In the United Kingdom, Mohan and Breeze (2016, p. 123) also found that "charity is always with us, but not always in the places and causes where it is most needed." Consistent with Reich's analysis from the United States, Mohan and Breeze (2016, p. 15) concluded that "despite widespread assumptions that 'charity' is synonymous with 'helping the needy', only a small percentage of charities serve those in need as a primary client group."

Data collected at the organisational and funding level provide limited insight into the prevalence of charitable care. There is, however, strong evidence that "charity is alive and well in the present era" (Mohan & Breeze 2016, p. 5). The available data on the use of food charity in particular indicates that charity is not just alive, but that the number of charities providing food to people in poverty and the use of food charity by people in poverty have increased markedly over the past two decades. This growth is particularly evident in developed countries such as the United Kingdom, parts of Europe, North America and, as we illustrate in subsequent chapters, Australia.

Drawing on a significant body of research from the United Kingdom, Hannah Lambie-Mumford (2017) reports an exponential growth in emergency food charity in the 2010s. Data reported by Trussell Trust food bank demonstrates that demand increased in the years between 2010 and 2017 (Loopstra 2018), and that the number of foodbank providers grew from 30 to 419 between 2009 and 2017 (Loopstra & Lalor 2017). Consistent with this, Elisabeth Garratt (2017) reports that repeat use of foodbanks in the United Kingdom became more prevalent between 2013 and 2015, although she argues that others have overstated the increase. Kingsley Purdam et al. (2016) observe that the number of foodbanks in the United Kingdom had grown sharply in the years prior to 2015, and that there are many independent foodbanks and informal charitable food provision models that do not appear on official statistics.

Drawing on research from several European countries, Lambie-Mumford and Tiina Silvasti (2020) show that the need for food charity to respond to poverty is growing across Europe. They trace the increasing use of foodbanks in Europe to the charity economy, which "is characterised as an alternative distribution system where surplus elementary goods are donated, or sold at minimal cost, to people with no or low purchasing power" (Lambie-Mumford & Silvasti 2020, p. 10). In Finland, Silvasti (2015) reports how social policy changes limiting access to welfare as a social right have resulted in the country being increasingly reliant on charity to address a growing problem of food insecurity. Similarly, Magnus Karlsson and Johan Vamstad (2018) show that, whilst Sweden's universal welfare state does meet the needs of citizens, there is a growing reliance amongst non-citizens on food charities (Karlsson & Vamstad 2018).

There is a long history of charitable food relief in North America (Katz 1986). Research from Canada and the United States shows that food poverty is increasing, and so is the entrenchment of charity as a poverty management strategy (Holmes et al. 2018; Tarasuk et al. 2014; Wakefield et al. 2013). In the United States, Janet Poppendieck (1999) illustrated how the number of people who rely on charity and of charitable initiatives for the poor increased exponentially in the last few decades of the twentieth century. Graham Riches (2018) maintains that, in the United States, one would need to be a "baby boomer to recall a time without foodbanks." In an in-depth analysis of the day-to-day lives of some of poorest people in the United States, Kathy Edin and Luke Shaefer (2015) found that reliance on charity is part of a survival mechanism for many Americans, some of whom are living on as little as $2 per day.

The largest survey of food charity in the United States conducted by Feeding America (2014) reported increasing numbers of Americans reliant on food charity in the four years to 2014. Approximately 46 million people, or 14.2 per cent of the American population, used food charity in 2013. The Urban Institute (2019) Well-Being and Basic Needs Survey conducted in 2018, however, estimated that more Americans are using charitable food services than what is reported in the Feeding American survey. They found that one in ten adults aged 18–64 reported a household member using charitable food in the past 30 days (Urban Institute 2019). For low income households, approximately one in five adults had used charitable food in the past 30 days (Urban Institute 2019).

The data, including foodbanks and to a lesser extent meal programs, paint a consistent picture across numerous developed countries of increasing reliance on food charity. Others, furnished with evidence of increasing use and growing numbers of food charity initiatives, argue that charity and poverty are becoming a normalised feature of social life (Booth 2004; Purdam et al. 2016). Charity is not simply an empirical reality in the lives of people who are poor, but also a phenomenon that societies accept as appropriate.

Contesting the value of charity as a response to poverty

The growing prominence of charity raises the question of how we should understand its role in both poverty relief and social life more broadly, particularly in the context of changing welfare systems. Over the next few pages, we will present a collection of perspectives that either laud or lament charity and its place in modern society. Doing this enables us to highlight the contested normative space in which our analysis and subsequent positions take place, and to sketch for the reader certain themes that will recur throughout the book.

Before we do this, however, it is worth noting that we approach these debates from the perspective that charity is an enduring feature of modern social life, and thus one that is unlikely to disappear any time soon. Indeed, predictions in the twentieth century that charity would be relegated to the past as modernisation brought about scientifically-driven and professionalised welfare states has been shown by Paul Johnson (1996) to be an exercise in Whig history. As he put it, "the neat lineage of welfare development from the poor law to Beveridge are seen to be an erroneous historical construct" (Johnson 1996, p. 246). Indeed, history seems to show that some mix of professionalised welfare and informal charity is the norm. Joanna Innes' (1996) analysis of the "mixed economy of welfare" in early modern England is telling in this respect. She shows how the growth of public provision to respond to poverty in England not only occurred alongside the persistence of voluntary charity, but also from the sixteenth century voluntary charity "in some forms and at some periods – flourished, diversified and expanded" (Innes 1996, p. 168).

Given this, the question for us is not whether or not charity should be a feature of poverty relief, but rather what form it assumes or could assume, and what function it plays in society and the lives of people experiencing poverty (and, indeed, the lives of the charitable). With this in mind, let us take a look at the arguments for and against charity's role in responses to poverty.

Charity as lauded

Why does charity remain such an enduring feature of life in developed societies? Here, we present some of the common arguments for the importance of charity, both as a response to poverty, and as a feature of society more broadly. In doing this, we show how support for charity is not only enduring, but also emanates from a variety of standpoints within modern societies, including religious, political, and academic standpoints. It also comes from across the political spectrum, revealing just how potent charity is as a signifier of the good society.

The praise for charity is frequently couched as an ideal juxtaposed to the current models of public expenditure and professionalised services. In these ways, charity is lauded as an idyllic state that we need to return to. For the globe's 1.2 billion Catholics, Pope John Paul II (1991) advocated strongly for charity. The Pontiff understood a role for State intervention in the provision of welfare, but he believed that State intervention should be a supplementary measure: he maintained that State intervention must be "as brief as possible so as to avoid removing permanently from society and business systems the functions which are properly theirs." To overcome what Pope John Paul II said was "today's widespread individualistic mentality, what is needed is a concrete commitment to solidarity and charity."

The Pontiff was assertive in his belief that charity is natural and the welfare state unnatural. Pope John II believed that the welfare state "deprived society of its responsibility." Further, the welfare state, which is funded through public provision and regulated and delivered by professionals,

> (l)eads to a loss of human energies and an inordinate increase of public agencies, which are dominated more by bureaucratic ways of thinking than by concern for serving their clients... In fact, it would appear that needs are best understood and satisfied by people who are closest to them and who act as neighbours to those in need. It should be added that certain kinds of demands often call for a response which is not simply material but which is capable of perceiving the deeper human need. One thinks of the condition of refugees, immigrants, the elderly,

> the sick, and all those in circumstances which call for assistance, such as drug abusers: all these people can be helped effectively only by those who offer them genuine fraternal support, in addition to the necessary care.
>
> (Pope John Paul II 1991)

We cite the Pontiff at length because his sentiments encapsulate many of the connected positions that advocate for charity as a dominant response to people in poverty. As we noted above, charity is never simply about an individual act, but rather a sign or aspiration for a specific model of society, especially the way that citizens ought to be *free* to provide personal care.

In evoking the centrality of local communities, rather than the distant State, as being most appropriate to provide care and address social ills, the Pontiff drew on the Catholic principle of subsidiarity. This is a principle that many align with when advocating for charity. At its core, subsidiarity signifies that issues should be decided, organised, and delivered as close as possible to the level where they have effect (Colombo 2008). Instead of the national State, subsidiarity places emphasis on smaller and local units within society. Subsidiarity prioritises autonomy and human fulfilment, and assumes that these can be achieved when people engage with other citizens with limited State control. In 1931, Pope Pius XI advocated for subsidiarity as follows:

> Just as it is gravely wrong to take from individuals what they can accomplish by their own initiative and industry and give it to the community, so also it is an injustice and at the same time a grave evil and disturbance of right order to assign to a greater and higher association what lesser and subordinate organizations can do. For every social activity ought of its very nature to furnish help to the members of the body social, and never destroy and absorb them.
>
> (Pope Pius XI 1931)

We can see from the language used by Pope Pius XI about "grave evil" and "right order" that State intervention, which is believed to subvert people's capacity for acting charitably towards their fellow citizens, is a matter of fundamental importance. However, subsidiarity is not necessarily about a complete absence of State intervention in a Libertarian way; rather it means that "the state should not intervene unless it is necessary, but equally it should intervene when it is necessary" (Colombo 2008, p. 183). From this characterisation of subsidiarity, the State plays the role of regulator, and not that of actor (Colombo 2008). The small societal units that subsidiarity emphasises are conduits to the State, with the State understood as having a legitimate role in enabling, but not undermining, the functioning of individuals and smaller scale units.

From the perspective of subsidiarity, the problem with the welfare state is that it impinges individual autonomy, on the one hand, and that it disrupts the natural connections and acts of care among small groups of citizens, on the other hand. John McKnight develops this position. In an influential book analysing social service programs in the United States, McKnight (1995) argues that professional social service providers constitute an imposition on communities by undermining their capacity to define and address their own problems. McKnight (1995, p. 169) proposes, "it is only in community that we find care."

Advocacy for charity is juxtaposed to the welfare state and formal public provision. Charity is advocated because the welfare state is not only viewed as simultaneously bad for the recipients, especially the recipients of welfare benefits, but also bad for society through preventing people from providing charitable care. Although subsidiarity has clear links to Catholicism, its core principles are advocated, and even shape charity and welfare, in secular societies governed by both conservative and progressive governments. In the United States, President Ronald Reagan (1976) believed that the "failure of welfare is due to federal interference" (Reagan 1976) where "we have let government take away those things that were once ours to do voluntarily" (Reagan cited in Giddens 2006, p. 379). President Barack Obama drew on similar ideas when advocating for faith-based charities to play a role in improving communities because,

> No matter how much money we invest or how sensibly we design our policies, the change that Americans are looking for will not come from government alone. There is a force for good greater than government. It is an expression of faith, this yearning to give back, this hungering for a purpose larger than our own, that reveals itself not simply in places of worship, but in senior centers and shelters, schools and hospitals, and any place an American decides.
>
> (White House Office Press Secretary 2009)

The advocacy by the highest political leaders that citizens should be free to enact care of their choosing, and that citizens providing charitable care achieve more than what is achieved through government, is of course not idiosyncratic to the United States. The reconfiguring of the welfare state, and the more prominent role and celebrated function of charity, has been a recurring theme in the United Kingdom. The Third Way approach advocated by Anthony Giddens (1998, 2006), amongst others, emphasised active participation of citizens in welfare provision. Giddens proposed that the traditional welfare state can be undemocratic, characterised by the top-down dispensation of benefits, and thus risks alienating welfare recipients. For these reasons, Giddens argued the traditional welfare state should be remodelled to promote local systems to foster the development of civil society.

Although not explicitly advocating for charitable care, the local systems proposed by Giddens have been extended through the ideas of Big Society and Localism. Under these political movements, subsidiarity principles have gained greater prominence, with local community groups and charities positioned as critical to both providing welfare and achieving the good society (Fitzpatrick et al. 2020; Wells & Caraher 2014). Reflecting subsidiarity principles, it was the job of government to get out of the way of local charity groups so that they could be empowered to provide welfare and support to address their local need themselves. Government provision is positioned as disempowering. Although there are fundamental differences between Third Way and Big Society politics (Lindsey et al. 2018), as prime minister, Tony Blair, David Cameron, and Theresa May each publicly linked voluntary charitable care to their notions of a successful society (Cameron 2011; Howlett & Locke 1999; May 2017).

Even more striking than these contemporary examples – all which, after all, have emerged in the wake of the neoliberal revolution and thus must respond in one way or another to its problematisation of state welfare (Rose 1999) – is the strident support for charity amongst early proponents of the welfare state. In what has colloquially become known as the *Beveridge Report*, Lord Beveridge (1942, p. 7) identified a principle that, "in establishing a national minimum, it should leave room and encouragement for voluntary action by each individual" (1942, p. 7). Beveridge emphasised making "room and a basis for additional voluntary provision" (1942, p. 122). Importantly, this principle of voluntary action sat alongside the principle that "social insurance should aim at guaranteeing the minimum income needed for subsistence" (1942, p. 14); charity was thus seen as complimentary to the welfare state, rather than an alternative to it. Indeed, the *Beveridge Report* set out a model of public provision "to make want under any circumstances unnecessary" (Beveridge 1942, p. 9).

In what Lord Beveridge (1948) described as a sequel to and completion of the 1942 *Beveridge Report*, entitled, *Voluntary Action: A Report on Methods of Social Advance,* he more explicitly laid out the role for individual and voluntary action. Beveridge believed that charity is like science, where charity "must be free to experiment and it cannot live under orders" (1948, p. 267). Once again stressing the complementarity of public provision and voluntary action, he stated that:

> Voluntary action is needed to do things which the State should not do… it is needed to do things which the State is most unlikely to do. It needs to pioneer ahead of the State and make experiments.
>
> (Beveridge 1948, pp. 301–302)

Similarly, as Labour leader and British Prime Minister in 1947 when praising the value of Toynbee House and the settlement tradition, Clement Attlee said that "our democracy does not mean that we sit down and have things done for us, but that we do things for ourselves" (Briggs & Macartney 2011, p. 136).

Perhaps we ought not to be surprised or even alarmed that our political and religious leaders advocate for and celebrate charitable care among citizens. After all, scholars lament the loss of social capital and informal reciprocal care in contemporary neoliberal societies (Edin & Kefalas 2005; Putman 2000). It would take a radical view of society and humanity to reject out of hand charitable care to people who are poor. As we noted at the beginning of this chapter, Titmuss (2019) linked the voluntary giving of blood to strangers for no immediate personal reward as a key feature of a vibrant society. Writing in the United States, Steven Smith and Michael Lipsky (1993) saw community initiatives and efforts to solve local problems as contributing the community's vitality and character, and essential to a democratic way of life.

Yet, the arguments for the worth of charitable responses to poverty require critical scrutiny. As we have argued, charitable care can assume many forms, and its desirability or otherwise is mediated by what form it assumes and the broader policy and political contexts in which it is embedded. Suzanne Fitzpatrick and colleagues' analysis of Localism in England (which includes both voluntary charitable care and state-funded resources to professionalised local third sector groups) is instructive. They found that Localism disadvantages marginalised groups; under Localism in the post-2010 decade, homelessness in England increased because it is the centralised State that has the capacity to address its structural determinants (Fitzpatrick et al. 2020).

The literature from the United Kingdom further illustrates the need to critically examine the assumption that local charitable volunteers will muster to provide care to those citizens in need because of State retrenchment. Jeremy Kendall and colleagues found that formal volunteering did not increase under Big Society in the way government intended. They suggested that some people may be demotivated because of volunteering's association with a conservative political agenda that is incongruent with their own (Kendall et al. 2018). Also in the United Kingdom, Paul Cloke and colleagues illustrate that the Conservative Government's construction of charity volunteers as the embodiment of the Big Society spirit were challenged when volunteers themselves expressed concerns about associated welfare reforms. In their words, the volunteers providing charitable care to people in need because of austerity became "unreliable political bedfellows for the government" (Cloke et al. 2017, p. 712).

Charity as lamented

Critical work about the prevalence and increase in charity is often, even if implicitly, about the failure of the State to uphold social rights (Parsell & Watts 2017). Charity is critiqued because the need for it is created by service gaps, which are themselves generated by what governments have refused to do (MacLeod et al. 2019). In this way, critiques of charity are often critiques about the social and political conditions that render charity necessary, along with the presence of charity contributing towards its reproduction.

This kind of argument is evident in critiques that link the growth of charity to the rise of neoliberalism and, more recently, austerity politics (Hackworth 2012; Jones et al. 2020; Lambie-Mumford & Silvasti 2020). We engage with these arguments in a more thorough way in Chapter 3, where we put forward our own theorisation of charity's relationship to neoliberalism. For present purposes, it is sufficient to point out that proponents of neoliberalism have long positioned voluntary action as an alternative to state welfare provision, as evidenced in the anti-statism of Thatcher's government in the United Kingdom (Lindsey et al. 2018). Recent analyses reflect this view. Lambie-Mumford (2019), for instance, argues that the growth of foodbanks in the United Kingdom intensified following the austerity programmes that began 2010, with these changes being part of a wider individualisation of poverty and risk that began in the 1970s. In addition to austerity, scholars show how broader changes under neoliberalism that include welfare conditionality and punitive policies also push people into charity by rendering them ineligible for government benefits and support (Clarke et al. 2020; Soss et al. 2011; Watts & Fitzpatrick 2018).

Taking further the critique that charity exists as a product of neoliberal reform, some argue that charity enables and even legitimises neoliberal forces that undermine public provision and drive poverty. Poppendieck (1999) analysed the emergency charitable food system in the United States. She concluded that charity allows the State to ignore its responsibility to provide everyone adequate access to food. It does so by encouraging the existence of a charitable safety net that ensures the population can get access to some food despite State retrenchment. Similarly, Lambie-Mumford (2013) warns that the rise in foodbanks in the United Kingdom may normalise both food charity and welfare retrenchment, and she thus advocates for a right to food as an alternative to charitable provision.

The concerns about what charity represents expressed by Poppendieck (1999) and Lambie-Mumford (2013) are not new. Although Attlee did not reject charity outright, his role bringing about the post-war welfare state was predicated on a belief that charity provided a means for people to ignore poverty and the inequitable structures that perpetuate it. In his own words:

> The evil of charity is that it tends to make the charitable think that he has done his duty by giving away some trifling sum, his conscience is put to sleep, and he takes no trouble to consider the social problem any further.
>
> (Attlee 1920 cited in Dickens 2018, p. 13)

At the centre of these critiques is that charity normalises poverty and constitutes a bandaid response, and a response, moreover, that enables the charitable and society at large to overlook structural injustices. Charity is lamented for not taking political action to change the conditions that give rise to it. This critique was raised by Emile Durkheim (1958, p. 58). Charity "organizes nothing; it maintains the status quo; it can attenuate the individual suffering that this [economic system's] lack of organization engenders." Durkheim's position, similar to Kymlicka's (2001) appreciation of charity being only the second best option, highlights the vexed position of providing charitable care to respond to the consequences of injustice without working to address the sources of injustice.

When assessing these kinds of critiques, we need to take account of the multiple forms that charity to the poor can assume. Not all acts of charity are the same, nor are all expressions of support for charity expressions of support for neoliberalism. Mohan and Breeze (2016) report data from the British Social Attitudes Survey on the increasing acceptance between 1991 and 2015 of charity and charitable donations. However, they concluded from the data that there is "no widespread sense that charity should rise up to replace government" (Mohan & Breeze 2016, p. 14). This contemporary public sentiment is probably not far from the ideas upheld by Lord Beveridge, who saw a valuable role for charity, but only after the State met basic need to negate want (see above).

Indeed, like the lauding of charity, critiques of charity emanate from a variety of different standpoints. Drawing on decades of charitable work as a Christian Minister in the United States, Robert Lupton (2011) laments charity for undermining the autonomy of charity recipients, and contributes to their disempowerment. He argues that charity has created:

> A permanent underclass, dismantling their family structures, and eroding their ethic of work. And our poor continue to become poorer.
>
> (Lupton 2011, p. 3)

Lupton's concern is that giving charity to people harms them, not just by subverting the recipient's autonomy, but also by undermining their capacities to do things for themselves. Further, and consistent with Peter Singer's (2015) notion of effective altruism, Lupton is concerned that the recipient of charity is harmed because scant attention is given to their needs, only the assumption that the service and good intentions of the giver are sufficient to benefit the recipient.

In a provocative and dark assessment, Friedrich Nietzsche was also concerned about the negative consequences of charity, but his concern was directed towards humanity and society, rather than the charitable or charity recipients. Nietzsche (2006, p. 43) argued that "the first principle of our charity" should be to "help... the weak and the botched [to] perish." He asked, "what is more harmful than any vice?—Practical sympathy for the botched and the weak—Christianity" (Nietzsche 2006, p. 43). For Nietzsche (2016, p. 194), compassion is "the very pinnacle of immorality." Tom Holland (2019, p. 448) believed that Nietzsche hated Christianity and its "commitment to justice by caring for the suffering." He argued that, for Nietzsche, "Christianity, by taking the side of everything ill-constituted, and weak, and feeble, had made all of humanity sick" (Holland 2019, p. 448).

Nietzsche presents an extreme view of charity with which it is difficult to see people identifying today. However, his critique and other critiques of charity, along with the multiple positions celebrating charity, all speak to contestation about ideal models of social organisation and how people's needs for care can be met – or for Nietzsche, whether they should be met at all. At their core, the positions that advocate for or reject charity are about the extent and nature of the role that the State and smaller groups should play in meeting human need. Charity, whether it should play a significant or insignificant role, therefore, is always about the structure of society and not just about individuals providing or receiving charitable care.

This book

Now that we have given a brief introduction to debates surrounding the definition, extent, and normative value of charity, we will conclude the chapter with an outline of the book, the argument and contributions that it makes, and the structure it follows. In our view, the book makes four interrelated contributions to knowledge. First, we show how the meaning and practice of charity is intimately intertwined with prevailing understandings of how social life is, or should be, organised. Charity is a deeply evocative practice that has powerful cultural and political resonances. We argue that these resonances are increasingly harnessed in efforts to recreate society in accordance with the neoliberal worldview that has come to dominate the social and political imagination of developed societies over the last 40-odd years (Harvey 2005). In doing this, however, we challenge the view popular amongst critical scholars that charity functions as a crutch for neoliberalism's "true" objectives of welfare retrenchment, fiscal constraint and expanding marketisation (Hackworth 2012; Levitas 2012; McGimpsey 2017; Peck & Tickell 2002). We argue instead that the expansion of charity is *central*, not auxiliary, to the neoliberal project. Charity is seen by proponents of neoliberalism as bringing into being forms of sociality that liberal political thought has long seen as natural and necessary to the proper functioning of society. Most especially, it is taken as evidence of the existence a dynamic and self-governing civil society, which is in turn underpinned by the moral sentiments and affective bonds that citizens feel for one another (Muehlebach 2012; Rose 1999).

Second, the book demonstrates that charitable responses to poverty are a fundamentally *cultivated* phenomenon. Charity is often celebrated as a spontaneous act driven by the selfless motivations of the giver (Dean 2020; Deas 2012). We show how, contrary to these popular conceptions, charitable responses to poverty are encouraged, facilitated, and celebrated by the State and the media. On the one hand, the State minimises and restricts access to the welfare safety net, thus exacerbating poverty and creating a need for charity amongst people who are unable to provide for themselves through paid work. On the other hand, the State supports the growth of charity by providing material (i.e. public funding), symbolic, and regulatory support to citizens and organisations engaged in providing basic assistance to the poor. The State is assisted in this process by a largely sympathetic media, who celebrate the charitable as exemplars of the ideal (neoliberal) citizen.

Third, we show how prevailing understandings and practices of charity are organised around the interests of the charitable rather than the needs of people experiencing poverty. Scholars have long questioned the ostensibly selfless motivations behind charitable giving (Kymlicka 2001; Singer 2015), and criticised charity's tendency to focus on the symptoms rather than the causes of poverty (Parsell & Watts 2017). We extend these critiques by showing how the valorisation and cultivation of charity by neoliberalising projects reduces the poor to mere fodder for the practice of charitable care. In the context of charity, the poor are not so much blamed for their poverty – as is often the case in debates over welfare dependence (Slater 2018) – but are instead positioned as vulnerable subjects who require pity and compassionate care. While less overtly hostile, this construction of people in poverty positions them as vulnerable and without agency. They are positioned as needy, but they have limited opportunity to express their needs in their own voice. There is also limited recognition of the structural circumstances in which charity recipients' needs are embedded, or of their agency in using charity to help navigate these circumstances. Reliance on charity is thus a deeply shameful and disempower experience for people experiencing poverty, one which creates barriers to the formation of solidarity and reciprocity between providers and recipients of charity.

Fourth, our analysis shows that, although the prevailing model of charity is flawed in many ways, it contains the seeds of its own transformation. Many providers of charity have a genuine desire to make a positive difference in the lives of people experiencing poverty, even if this does not always translate into practices that actually benefit those people. There are cases where charitable organisations and/or volunteers use their positions on the frontlines of poverty relief to draw attention to the impacts of neoliberal policy on the lives of charity recipients. There are also instances where volunteers defy the prevailing model and provide a space for people in poverty to give voice to their needs and experiences on their own terms. These practices point to a real utopia (Wright 2013), namely, a transformed model of charity that is built around the actual needs of people experiencing poverty, as well as recognition of the structural processes that shape their needs.

On the basis of this, we outline a manifesto for the transformation of charity. We argue that it must include advocacy to address the structural causes of poverty, as well as helping alleviate its symptoms. It must also afford people experiencing poverty with the agency to shape the care that they receive and to participate in the care of others. For without the possibility of people experiencing poverty being recognised as equals and practicing reciprocity, the opportunities for true solidarity between the providers and recipients of charity will remain few and far between. For generations, charitable responses to poverty have assumed a vexed position, with some seeing them as the mark of human kindness and others as a barrier to achieving social justice. Scholars have engaged in debate about the morality of giving something freely to those without ever since characters in Homer's Odyssey were tested with providing or refusing help to a disguised beggar. Bringing together multiple data sources, the book illustrates how – under the right structural and interpersonal circumstances – charitable care to people who are poor can contribute to a more just society.

Outline of the book

The book comprises nine chapters that are threaded together by our analysis of how charity to people who are poor constitutes a relational phenomenon that can only be understood, or changed, by considering its relations with and embeddedness within wider societal processes and structures. Next, Chapter 2 canvasses the literature on the different types of help charity is intended to realise, along with a discussion of how motivations to help through charity can structure charitable giving. In Chapter 3, and building on the above discussion on charity as lauded or lamented, we outline the theoretical framework of the book and demonstrate the value of conceptualising charity as relational, representing contested conceptions of society. In Chapter 4, we argue that charity cannot be understood as a response to people who are poor without understanding the welfare state and the cultural and political conditions in which it rests. Chapter 5 develops the analysis about the conditions that create the need for charity by examining how the State, through funding and lauding the charitable, actively enables the presence and expansion of charity to the poor. Chapter 6 extends these analyses by examining how the media represents charity, and the relationship between voluntary charitable acts and the State in particular. In Chapter 7, we present an ethnographic account of what it means, from the perspective of the charitable, to help people who are poor through charity. Chapter 8 develops the analysis, by empirically demonstrating what it means to receive charitable care from the firsthand perspectives of people living in poverty. Chapter 9 brings together the diverse data sources and analyses presented through the book to conceptualise what charity to the poor means in contemporary society, and to outline a vision of how it can be reimagined.

References

Arendt, H 2006, *On Revolution*, Penguin, New York.
Beveridge, W 1942, *Social Insurance and Allied Services*, Her Majesty's Stationery Office, London.
Beveridge, W 1948, *Voluntary Action: A Report on Methods of Social Advance*, George Allen & Unwin LTD, London.

Booth, S 2014, 'Food banks in Australia: Discouraging the right to food', in G Riches & T Silvasti (eds.), *First World Hunger Revisited: Food Charity or the Right to Food*, Palgrave Macmillan, Basingstoke, pp. 15–28.

Briggs, A & Macartney, A 2011, *Toynbee Hall: The First Hundred Years*, Routledge, Abingdon.

Bulley, D & Sokhi-Bulley, B 2014, 'Big society as big government: Cameron's governmentality agenda', *The British Journal of Politics and International Relations*, vol. 16, no. 3, pp. 452–470.

Cameron, D 2011, *PM's Speech on Big Society*, viewed 12 November 2020, https://www.gov.uk/government/speeches/pms-speech-on-big-society

Clarke, A, Watts, B & Parsell, C 2020, 'Conditionality in the context of housing-led homelessness policy: Comparing Australia's Housing First agenda to Scotland's "rights-based" approach', *Australian Journal of Social Issues*, vol. 55, no. 1, pp. 88–100.

Cloke, P, May, J & Williams, A 2017, 'The geographies of food banks in the meantime', *Progress in Human Geography*, vol. 41, no. 6, pp. 703–726.

Colombo, A 2008, 'The 'Lombardy model': Subsidiarity-informed regional governance', *Social Policy & Administration*, vol. 42, no. 2, pp. 177–196.

Dean, J 2020, *The Good Glow: Charity and the Symbolic Power of Doing Good*, Policy Press, Bristol.

Dees, G 2012, 'A tale of two cultures: Charity, problem solving, and the future of social entrepreneurship', *Journal of Business Ethics*, vol. 111, no. 3, pp. 321–334.

Dickens, J 2018, 'Clement Attlee and the social service idea: Modern messages for social work in England', *The British Journal of Social Work*, vol. 48, no. 1, pp. 5–20.

Durkheim, E 1958, *Socialism and Saint-Simon*, Antioch Press, Yellow Springs.

Edin, K & Kefalas, M 2005, *Promises I Can Keep: Why Poor Women Put Motherhood before Marriage*, University of California Press, Berkeley.

Edin, K & Shaefer, H 2015, *$2.00 A Day: Living on Almost Nothing in America*, Mariner Books, Boston.

Feeding America 2014, *Hunger in America 2014: National Report Prepared for Feeding America*, Feeding America, Chicago.

Fitzpatrick, S, Pawson, H & Watts, B 2020, 'The limits of localism: A decade of disaster on homelessness in England', *Policy & Politics*, vol. 48, no. 4, pp. 541–561.

Garratt, E 2017, 'Please sir, I want some more: An explanation of repeat foodbank use', *BMC Public Health*, vol. 828, https://doi.org/10.1186/s12889-017-4847-x

Giddens, A 1998, *The Third Way*, Polity, Cambridge.

Giddens, A 2006, 'Positive welfare', in C Pierson & F Castles (eds.), *The Welfare State Reader*, 2nd edn, Polity, Cambridge, pp. 378–388.

Hackworth, J 2012, *Faith Based: Religious Neoliberalism and the Politics of Welfare in the United States*, University of Georgia Press, Athens.

Harvey, D 2015, *A Brief History of Neoliberalism*, Oxford University Press, Oxford.

Holland, T 2019, *Dominion: The Making of the Western Mind*, Little Brown, London.

Holmes, E, Black, J, Heckelman, A, Lear, S, Seto, D, Fowokan, A & Wittman, H 2018, '"Nothing is going to change three months from now": A mixed methods characterization of food bank use in greater Vancouver', *Social Science & Medicine*, vol. 200, pp. 129–136.

Howlett, S & Locke, M 1999, 'Volunteering for Blair: The third way', *Voluntary Action*, vol. 1, no. 2, pp. 67–76.

Innes, J 1996, 'The mixed economy of welfare in early modern England: Assessments of the options from Hale to Malthus (c. 1683–1803)', in M Daunton (ed.), *Charity, Self-Interest and Welfare in the English Past*, Routledge, Abingdon, pp. 139–180.

Johnson, P 1996, 'Risk, redistribution and social welfare in Britain from the poor law to Beveridge', in M Daunton (ed.), *Charity, Self-Interest and Welfare in the English Past*, Routledge, Abingdon, pp. 225–248.

Jones D, Lowe P & West K 2020, 'Austerity in a disadvantaged West Midlands neighbourhood: Everyday experiences of families and family support professionals', *Critical Social Policy*, vol. 40, no. 3, pp. 389–409.

Karlsson, M & Vamstad, J 2018, 'New deeds for new needs: Civil society action against poverty in Sweden', *Voluntas: International Journal of Voluntary and Nonprofit Organizations*, vol. 31, pp. 1025–1036.

Katz, M 1986, *In the Shadow of the Poorhouse: A Social History of Welfare in America*, Basic Books, New York.

Kendall, J, Mohan, J, Brookes, N & Yoon, Y 2018, 'The English voluntary sector: How volunteering and policy climate perceptions matter', *Journal of Social Policy*, vol. 47, no. 4, pp. 759–782.

Kochuyt, T 2009, 'Gods, gifts and poor people: On charity in Islam', *Social Compass*, vol. 56, pp. 98–116.

Kymlicka, W 2001, 'Altruism in philosophical and ethical traditions: Two views', in J, Phillips, B Chapman & D Stevens (eds.), *Between State and Market: Essay on Charity Law and Policy in Canada*, McGill-Queen's University Press, Toronto, pp. 87–126.

Lambie-Mumford, H 2013, 'Every town should have one: Emergency food banking in the UK', *Journal of Social Policy*, vol. 42, no. 1, pp. 73–89.

Lambie-Mumford, H 2017, *Hungry Britain: The Rise of Food Charity*, Policy Press, Bristol.

Lambie-Mumford, H 2019, 'The growth of food banks in Britain and what they mean for social policy', *Critical Social Policy*, vol. 39, no. 1, pp. 3–22.

Lambie-Mumford, H & Silvasti, T 2020, 'Introduction: Exploring the growth of food charity across Europe', in H Lambie-Mumford & T Silvasto (eds.), *The Rise of Food Charity in Europe*, Policy Press, Bristol, pp. 1–18.

Levitas, R 2012, 'The just's umbrella: Austerity and the Big Society in Coalition policy and beyond', *Critical Social Policy*, vol. 32, no. 3, pp. 320–342.

Lindsey, R, Mohan, J, Bulloch, S & Metcalfe, E 2018, *Continuity and Change in Voluntary Action: Patterns, Trends and Understandings*, Policy Press, Bristol.

Loopstra, R 2018, 'Rising food bank use in the UK: Signs of a new public health emergency?,' *Nutrition Bulletin*, vol. 43, no. 1, pp. 53–60.

Loopstra, R & Lalor, D 2017, *Financial Insecurity, Food Insecurity, and Disability: The Profile of People Receiving Emergency Food Assistance from the Trussell Trust Foodbank Network in Britain*, The Trussell Trust, London.

Lupton, R 2011, *Toxic Charity: How Churches and Charities Hurt Those They Help (and How to Reverse It)*, Harper One, New York.

MacLeod, M, Curl, A & Kearns, A 2019, 'Understanding the prevalence of drivers of foodbank use: Evidence from deprived communities in Glasgow', *Social Policy & Society*, vol. 18, no. 1, pp. 67–86.

Matthew 19, *Bible Hub*, viewed 17 February 2021, https://biblehub.com/niv/matthew/19.htm

May, T 2017, 'Theresa may's shared society speech', *The Spectator*, viewed 02 February 2021, https://www.spectator.co.uk/article/full-text-theresa-may-s-shared-society-speech

McGimpsey, I 2017, 'Late neoliberalism: Delineating a policy regime', *Critical Social Policy*, vol. 37, no. 1, pp. 64–84.

McKnight, J 1995, *The Careless Society: Community and its Counterfeits*, Basic Books, New York.

Mill, JS 2004, *Principles of Political Economy: With Some of Their Applications to Social Philosophy*, Hackett Publishing Company, Indianapolis.

Mohan, J & Breeze, B 2016, *The Logic of Charity: Great Expectations in Hard Times*, Palgrave Macmillan, Basingstoke.

Muehlebach, A 2012, *The Moral Neoliberal: Welfare and Citizenship in Italy*, University of Chicago Press, Chicago.

Nietzsche, F 2006, *The Antichrist*, Translated by H. Mencken, Alfred A. Knopf, New York.

Nietzsche, F 2016, *The Will to Power*, Translated by A. Ludovici, T. N. Foulis, Edinburgh.

Parsell, C 2019, 'Beds in car parks don't solve Australia's rough sleeping problem', *The Conversation*, https://theconversation.com/beds-in-car-parks-dont-solve-australias-rough-sleeping-problem-125235

Parsell, C & Watts, B 2017, 'Charity and justice: A reflection on new forms of homelessness provision in Australia', *European Journal of Homelessness*, vol. 11, no. 2, pp. 65–76.

Peck, J & Tickell, A 2002, 'Neoliberalizing space', *Antipode*, vol. 34, no. 3, pp. 380–404.

Pope John Paul II 1991, *Centesimus Annus*, viewed 18 November 2020, http://www.vatican.va/content/john-paul-ii/en/encyclicals/documents/hf_jp-ii_enc_01051991_centesimus-annus.html

Pope Pius XI 1931, *QUADRAGESIMO ANNO*, viewed 18 November 2020, http://www.vatican.va/content/pius-xi/en/encyclicals/documents/hf_p-xi_enc_19310515_quadragesimo-anno.html

Poppendieck, J 1999, *Sweet Charity? Emergency Food and the End of Entitlement*, Penguin, New York.

Purdam, K, Garratt, E & Esmail, A 2016, 'Hungry? Food insecurity, social stigma and embarrassment in the UK', *Sociology*, vol. 50, no. 6, pp. 1072–1088.

Putman, R 2000, *Bowling Alone: The Collapse and Revival of American Community*, Simon & Schuster, New York.

Reagan, R 1976, *To Restore America, Ronald Reagan's Campaign Address*, viewed 16 October 2020, https://www.reaganlibrary.gov/sspeeches/3-31-76

Reich, R 2018, *Just Giving: Why Philanthropy is Failing Democracy and How It Can Do Better*, Princeton University Press, Princeton.

Riches, G 2018, *Food Bank Nations: Poverty, Corporate Charity and the Right to Food*, Routledge, London.

Rose, N 1999, *Powers of Freedom: Reframing Political Thought*, Cambridge University Press, Cambridge.

Silvasti, T 2015, 'Food aid – normalising the abnormal in Finland', *Social Policy & Society*, vol. 14, no. 3, pp. 471–482.

Singer, P 2015, *The Most Good You Can Do: How Effective Altruism Is Changing Ideas about Living Ethically*, Yale University Press, New Haven.

Slater, T 2018, 'The invention of the sink estate: Consequential categorisation and the UK housing crisis', *The Sociological Review Monographs*, vol. 66, no. 4, pp. 877–897.

Smith, S & Lipsky, M 1993, *Nonprofits for Hire: The Welfare State in the Age of Contracting*, Harvard University Press, Cambridge.

Soss, J, Fording, R & Schram, S 2011, *Disciplining the Poor: Neoliberal Paternalism and The Persistence of Race*, The University of Chicago Press, Chicago.

Standing, G 2020, *Battling Eight Giants: Basic Income Now*, Bloomsbury, London.

Tarasuk, V, Dachner, N, Hamelin, A, Ostry, A, Williams, P, Bosckei, E, Poland, B & Raine, K 2014, 'A survey of food bank operations in five Canadian cities', *BMC Public Health*, vol. 14, https://doi.org/10.1186/1471-2458-14-1234

Titmuss, R 2019, *The Gift Relationship: From Human Blood to Social Policy*, Policy Press, Bristol.

Tronto, J 2015, *Who Cares? How to Reshape a Democratic Politics*, Cornell University Press, Ithaca.

Urban Institute 2019, *Who Is Accessing Charitable Food in America? Results from the 2018 Well-Being and Basic Needs Survey*, viewed 04 December 2020, https://www.urban.org/sites/default/files/publication/101411/who_is_accessing_charitable_food_in_america_final_3.pdf

Wakefield, S, Fleming, J, Klassen, C & Skinner, A 2013, 'Sweet charity, revisited: Organizational responses to food insecurity in Hamilton and Toronto, Canada', *Critical Social Policy*, vol. 33, no. 3, pp. 427–450.

Watts, B & Fitzpatrick, S 2018, *Welfare Conditionality*, Routledge, Abingdon.

Weeks, J 2020, *The Debt Delusion: Living Within Our Means and Other Fallacies*, Polity Press, Cambridge.

Wells, R & Caraher, M 2014, 'UK print media coverage of the food bank phenomenon: From food welfare to food charity?', *British Food Journal*, vol. 116, no. 9, pp. 1426–1445.

White House Office Press Secretary 2009, *Obama Announces White House Office of Faith-Based and Neighbourhood Partnerships*, viewed 20 February 2021, https://obamawhitehouse.archives.gov/the-press-office/obama-announces-white-house-office-faith-based-and-neighborhood-partnerships

Wright, E 2013, 'Transforming capitalism through real utopias', *American Sociological Review*, vol. 78, no. 1, pp. 1–25.

Wright, K 2001, 'Generosity vs. altruism: Philanthropy and charity in the United States and United Kingdom', *Voluntas: International Journal of Voluntary and Nonprofit Organisations*, vol. 12, no. 4, pp. 399–416.

2 The practice of charity

Introduction

At the core of the practice of charity is the desire to help someone in need. The guiding premise of charity relies upon the self-evident assumption that its practice is beneficial to the recipient. Whether motivated by religious teachings or secular principles, charity consists of an individual – often through a charitable organisation – helping a person in need. The practice of charity requires at least two parties: a person with a need and a person who can help; the practice of charity is realised by the latter party helping the former. Charity makes no sense in the absence of the assumption that a person in need is being *helped*.

However, the idea that we can help people in need through charity, through caring for them, requires critical engagement with what charity means. Theologians and scholars have advocated and debated the meaning and value of charity for millennia. Charity has endured since time immemorial, sustaining scrutiny and provoking ongoing debate because, as we have argued in Chapter 1, its practice forms part of an ideal for how society should be organised, on the one hand, and how we should live as good citizens, on the other hand.

In this chapter, we put pressure on the concept of charity and the assumption that charity is helpful to a person in need. We pose the question, what does it mean to help someone who is poor through charity? In doing so, we demonstrate that providing charity to the poor means many things, and those meanings are rarely articulated with any precision; rather, the meaning is assumed as being self-evident. Just as the charity sector is profoundly diverse – where, "speaking of a charitable sector as if it were a homogenous entity is illusory" (Mohan & Breeze 2016, p. 114) – the meaning of helping someone who is poor is complicated. When we ask what helping someone who is poor means, we are forced to consider whether it is the meaning from the giver's or recipient's perspective that is prioritised. We must also ask, what needs should be met, by whom, and whether the practice of charity has a role to play in societies with advanced welfare states. Ultimately, any investigation into the meaning of helping someone who is poor through charity must grapple with the societal structures that generate poverty and the need for charitable care (as we do in Chapters 3–5). Similarly, any useful analysis of what it means to help someone who is poor through charity must engage the recipients of help; we take this up in Chapters 8 and 9.

To progress an initial investigation into the meaning of helping people who are poor through charity, this chapter is structured in three main parts. First, we present an analysis of the types of help charity is designed to achieve. Second, we engage with the literature on the motivations to act charitably, and consider how the motivations to help people in need are important for how "the needy" are constructed and positioned in the charity model. Third, the chapter discusses scholarship on the importance, often unrecognised, of reciprocity in helping. The analysis presented in this chapter provides insights from existing research and conceptual debates about what charity is or ought to be. We take these ideas as a springboard to jump into Chapters 7 and 8, where we develop the literature of helping people in poverty through charity with our ethnographic data on the provision and receipt of charity *in situ*.

The meanings of helping someone in need

In the same way that charity rests on the assumption that someone is helped, inherent in the meaning of charity is the charitable's volition. Charity is, by definition, a voluntary act, and this forms the basis for the social esteem in which the charitable are held: they are giving "something that [they] could rightfully keep, to people who are not rightfully entitled to it" (Kymlicka 2001, p. 95). It is the voluntary act of giving to an anonymous other that renders critique of charity problematic. Society has a low tolerance for criticism of the charitable, irrespective of what outcomes their charity achieves for recipients (Dees 2012). This is because the charitable have freely given up their time or resources to help other humans who will likely play no other role in their life. So long as the charitable are motivated to help those in need, their charity is beyond reproach, or indeed scrutiny.

Although helping people in need can be understood as a secular act to realise a virtuous life and citizenship (Bowpitt 1998), for many, the voluntary nature of helping anonymous others in need is animated by faith. The three major Western religions, Judaism, Christianity, and Islam, all position charitable giving as central to living in accordance to their faith (Eckel & Grossman 2004). In fact, nearly all of the world's religions encourage believers "to be generous with those in need" (Dees 2012, p. 322). Arthur Brooks (2004) analysis from the United States shows that, compared to secular people, religious people are far more likely to donate their time and money to charity, even to non-religious charities. Other empirical studies further show that frequent congregational attendance is associated with voluntary charitable care – potentially because of strength of religiosity, social contagion, and the ritualised act of giving (Vaidyanathan et al. 2011).

If we look to the literature, we can see that the meaning of charity features three, interrelated dimensions; charity can be about meeting a basic need for survival, a mechanism to realise a personal connection between the helper and the helped, and a means to benefit to the charitable.

Satisfying basic need

Perhaps the most common and intuitive meaning of charity is the charitable voluntarily fulfilling another individual's basic needs, such as physical sustenance, shelter, and sanctuary. There are three elements to this form of charity: (i) the unmet need of the recipient, (ii) the intention of the charitable, and (iii) a transaction whereby the charitable gives something, including their time, to the recipient. This understanding of charity can be traced back to the New Testament. As evangelist Matthew elaborates:

> For I was hungered, and ye gave me meat; I was thirsty and ye gave me drink; I was a stranger and ye took me in; Naked, and ye clothed me; I was sick, and ye visited me; I was in prison, and ye carne unto me.
>
> (Matthew 26:35–36)

This type of help, meeting a basic yet essential need, is the predominant form of charity to the poor. In most cases, the needs that charity seeks to meet are fundamental to life, such as food, shelter, and companionship. In the United States, for example, people who live in deep poverty rely on charity to access basic necessities to survive: charity is the "difference between shelter and no shelter, a meal and no meal, a new backpack for school and none at all" (Edin & Shaefer 2015, p. 102). Indeed, the increasing number of foodbanks across numerous countries with advanced welfare states provides food to people who are nutritionally deprived and going without meals (Feeding America 2014; Lambie-Mumford 2017; Lambie-Mumford & Silvasti 2020). Helping through charity is more than giving people what they do not have, it is also often about giving people what they need to survive. By providing someone in poverty with resources – be it money, food, or shelter – the meaning of helping someone is framed as the alleviation of deprivation. The St Vincent de Paul Society (2014, p. 23), one of Australia's largest faith-based providers of charitable care, state that, "the Society uses money and property to help relieve the suffering of those in need."

The association of charity with the alleviations of suffering highlights one of the paradoxes inherent in the practice of charity. On the one hand, there is a strongly felt and widely held sense of moral obligation to help people who are unable to meet their basic needs. On the other hand, responding to immediate need to address suffering emphasises "treating affected individuals rather than upon preventing problems in the first place" (Schoenfeld & Mestrovic 1989, p. 121). That is, it does little to address the *causes* of people's deprivation and the suffering it begets.

Let us elaborate on these points briefly. If people are hungry or exposed to the elements because they have no food or shelter, nearly everyone would agree that a reasonable human reaction is to respond to that visible need to alleviate suffering. If someone is hungry and has no means to access money or food, the voluntary act of giving food or money to address hunger and relieve suffering is a humane act. The alternative act, to ignore a person's suffering and to leave them to starve, is inhumane. Daniel Engster's (2015) work on the ethics of care illustrates this powerfully. He says that living in society means that we all make moral claims on others to ensure we survive, both as an infant and throughout our lives. When others make claims on us to receive care so that they survive, we must provide that care as a matter of "moral consistency." Providing charitable care to relieve suffering is critical, because if we ignore others' needs to survive, we are:

> Signalling: "I do not care about you or what happens to you." In treating others this way, we set them outside the network of human care that sustains human life and society—effectively denying their place in the human community.
>
> (Engster 2015, p. 23)

Engster's theorising probably accords with what most people would agree is eminently reasonable: as humans living in an interdependent society, we have a responsibility to meet others' needs for survival.

However, the act of meeting this need – helping the suffering person – must take account of how and why societal institutions and norms have left people without food and shelter. With an understanding of the societal drivers of poverty and its associated effects, when providing charity to meet an immediate need for food or shelter we must critically consider the unintended consequences, for example, whether charity absolves society and the State of its responsibility for the existence of poverty (Poppendieck 1999). We similarly must ask ourselves whether this type of charitable care normalises poverty and low expectations of how to respond to those impoverished (Parsell & Watts 2017): is it the case that, because the poor are in need, anything given to them is better than nothing? The humane act of helping someone in need, such as giving a hungry person food, must likewise grapple with consideration of the experience of those who are suffering. For example, we must question how people having their deprivation alleviated through anonymous others, without them being able to control their lives or reciprocate, makes them feel. We illustrate the tensions represented in this type of helping with a description of a charity that seeks to meet an immediate and fundamental human need for basic shelter (Box 2.1).

Box 2.1 Beddown

Beddown, an Australian charity established in 2019, provides inflatable mattresses in car parks to people sleeping rough. After a trial in Brisbane, Australia's third largest city, Beddown aspires to provide inflatable mattresses in 60 carparks across Australia to assist over 3,000 people per night (Silva 2019). The charity has partnered with a corporation that owns and manages central-business-district car parks. Access to the car park is provided by the corporate sponsor, and volunteers help set up the inflatable mattresses. Volunteers also conduct overnight shifts, which includes escorting homeless people from mattresses to the toilet. The charitable organisation reported a waitlist of people who want to volunteer. By enabling homeless people to sleep in a car park, Beddown (n.d.) claims that it helps to restore "health, dignity, and respect for our guests."

The Beddown example presented in Box 2.1 speaks to the tension of volunteers freely giving up their time, and corporate sponsors providing resources, to offer people something that clearly responds, albeit partially, to their need for shelter. At the same time, the Beddown model of charity raises fundamental concerns about human dignity and value: what does charity to accommodate people on mattresses in a carpark signal about what those people are worth? It similarly provokes questions about how people receiving the charitable's help, an inflatable mattress in a carpark for example, experience charity. We can assume that the waitlist of people wanting to volunteer at Beddown indicates a desire to be actively involved in alleviating the suffering of people living without shelter; but what does it mean for the recipient?

Connecting the helper and the helped

In addition to meeting a basic need, charity is also commonly understood as establishing a social connection between the helper and the helped. At times augmenting the provision of practical resources and at times as an end in and of itself, some see the true meaning of helping as the realisation of human connection. In fact, the Charity Organisation Society was established in the nineteenth century in the United States on the premise that, rather than alms, what people in poverty really needed was moral support from a true friend (a volunteer), who could help them steer their way out of pauperism (Katz 1986).

This sentiment continues to appear in contemporary discourses on charitable responses to poverty. Criticising the welfare state and charity that merely involves cash donations, Daniel Shapiro's (2007, p. 202) manifesto for charity is to "place greater emphasis on giving time rather than money."

Acknowledging that the practical act of charity consists of the provision of resources to alleviate suffering, the St Vincent de Paul Society (2014, p. 22) contends that, "giving love, talents and time is more important than giving money." This sentiment is supported by research evidence: analysis of over 400,000 records on the provision and receipt of charity during a ten-year period indicated that the duration of time given by the charitable when providing resources such as food and supermarket vouchers was the strongest predictor of people not returning for additional help (Ambrey et al. 2019).

Similarly, others have argued that charity conveys hope to recipients, "through being blessed with the provision and help received at a foodbank" (Mumford-Lambie 2017, p. 103). For Cloke et al. (2017, p. 720), the most significant role of food charity may be found through the "spaces of liminal encounter and politicization." In these ways, helping those who are poor derives its meaning from the bringing together of people with different social and economic backgrounds to create relationships and an understanding of each other's experiences.

From this perspective, the provision of a resource to meet an immediate need is necessary to facilitate empathy and commiseration between the helper and the helped (Schoenfeld & Mestrovic 1989). A recent and popular model of charity to the poor in Australia explicitly frames the provision of resources – namely clothes washing and showers – as an avenue to build personal connections between volunteers and "our homeless friends" (Box 2.2).

Box 2.2 Orange Sky

Orange Sky was established in 2014 to provide mobile clothe-washing facilities to homeless people. Orange Sky pursues this through fitting washing machines and clothes dryers to vehicles, and driving into public spaces to wash homeless people's clothes. The charity has progressively expanded the size, scope, and geographical coverage of its operations. Similar to the mobile washing machines and dryers, this involves vehicles with attached showers travelling into public spaces so that homeless people can wash themselves. In 2018, Orange Sky expanded to New Zealand, and is pursuing expansion opportunities in the United States (Orange Sky n.d.). The expansion gained momentum when the Obama Foundation visited Orange Sky in December 2019 and invited its creators to its Leaders Program.

Significantly, Orange Sky (n.d.) proclaims that the most important part of their work is not the washing and showers, but the "genuine conversation with our friends." The charity describes what it does as "a platform for every day Australians to connect." On the home page of their website, before listing how many loads of washing and showers were delivered during the week, Orange Sky reports its impact by "hours of conversation" conducted during the week.

The Orange Sky charity is an explicit version of the meaning of charity as a practice to realise connections between the helper and the helped. Like the provision of food to a hungry person, it is *prima facie* understandable that human connections and conversations are desirable, particularly given that poverty is often associated with being socially excluded from, and stigmatised by, mainstream society (Lister 2004). On the other hand, this understanding of charity raises challenging questions because there is significant money, effort, and public acclaim dedicated to an initiative that does nothing to address the causes of poverty and homelessness. Is charity that only enables conversation and fleeting relationships between the helper and helped sufficient, or indeed desirable?

As demonstrated in Chapter 5, Orange Sky and other similar charities receive significant direct State funding and indirect subsidies through tax concessions associated with donations to the charitable organisation. Although probably fostering conversations, Orange Sky does little to change the living conditions of people who wash – themselves and their clothes – in the public realm of wealthy cities. The public money received by Orange Sky means less money for social housing and related interventions that can actually help *end* people's homelessness (Parsell & Watts 2017). Moreover, the emphasis on human connections often foregrounds the benefits to the helper ("every day Australians"), not just the helped. The intuitive appeal of personal connections notwithstanding, the emphasis on genuine conversation may obscure the power differentials between the volunteers and people having their clothes washed in the streets. Might these power imbalances between the two parties subvert the capacity for people who are poor to genuinely converse with their helpers? We return to these questions in Chapter 8 where we discuss the experience of charity from the recipient's perspective.

Practicing beliefs and values

There is a third meaning of helping the poor that is manifestly different from the provision of practical resources to alleviate suffering or realisation of human connections: charity to the poor is a direct means to benefit the charitable. Helping people who are poor through charity has long been recognised as a means to benefit the helper by enabling them to live in accordance with their faith or secular values and ethics. Brooks (2004, p. 7) sums this up well noting that "real charity to support good works, be they sacred or secular – is a part of man's natural search for God." For Saint Augustine, charity is the difference between children of God and children of the devil (van de Meer 1961).

The link between providing charity to people who are poor and religion is shaped by religious interpretations of wealth. For some Christians, wealth is an affront to God: "woe to you who are rich" (Luke 6:24). Some Christians believe that the wealthy have become rich through living in an ungodly way and within a godless social order, meaning that "the possibility that riches might ever have been a blessing bestowed by God, untainted by exploitation, [is] a grotesque self-deception" (Holland 2019, p. 136). Saint Ambrose, Archbishop of Milan in the fourth century, rejected the idea that charity is the free gifting of one's possessions to those who have no rightful claim to it, arguing instead that:

> You are not making a gift of your possessions to the poor person. You are handing over to him what is his. For what has been given in common for the use of all, you have arrogated to yourself. The world is given to all, and not only to the rich.
>
> (Encyclical Letter of Pope Paul VI 1967)

Christian interpretations that contend that greed and the wealth that it breeds is ungodly provide insight into the meaning of helping people who are poor through charity. The practice of charity is an act to re-distribute resources in accordance with God's will. Richard France's (1986, p. 14) analysis of the Old and New Testaments identifies greed as "the great enemy of true discipleship." The remedy: giving to the poor. Robert Wuthnow's (1991, p. 51) research with people who provide voluntary care to strangers identified showing "thankfulness to God by helping others and seeing your life as blessed" as a motivation to help people in need.

Importantly, however, helping the poor through this theological lens is not motivated, solely at least, for the poor's sake. The wealthy giving their riches to the poor is part of "the rich man's salvation rather than the poor man's material needs" (France 1986, p. 15). This critical reading of what it means to help people who are poor as a vehicle to help the charitable is not unique to France (1986). Michael Sherwin (2012) emphasises the importance of the fact that charitable responses to poverty are both freely and knowingly undertaken. In terms of the latter, the "ultimate end of every act of charity is God himself" (Sherwin 2012, p. 228). For Timothy Jackson (2003), charity, Christian faith, and love are one and the same. To help someone who is poor is to see all people created in the image of God (*Imago Dei*); helping the poor is helping God. Charity is conceptualised as the practical manifestation of living according to the Christian teachings through ministry (Schoenfeld & Mestrovic 1989).

Helping people who are poor as seen through living in accordance with God's will prioritises the didactic between God and the charitable, rather than the interests of the recipient. We can see similar ideas in Islam. Thierry Kochuyt (2009) observes that, in Islam, the faithful are required to give because the wealth *they* possess has been provided by God. Giving charity to the poor in Islam is institutionalised through the Zakat, on the basis that resources are provided for all the faithful to share, "they give to the needy as God gave to them" (Kochuyt 2009, p. 100). The Qur'an encourages the faithful to give one's wealth to the people, not for the people, but "for the love of Allah." Quoting a passage in the Qur'an about giving charity and generous rewards, Robert Bremmer (2000, p. 16) notes that, "voluntary charity helped the donor build treasure in heaven."

The meaning of helping people in need as an endeavour to live according to faith – a life that has meaning in the relationship between God and the charitable (and the latter's afterlife) – has significant implications for the recipient: the person who we proposed at the beginning of the chapter is the *beneficiary* of the charitable act. When helping people in need through charity is motivated by a desire by the giver to improve their relationship with God, we can lose sight of the recipients' experiences and priorities – or in fact whether the recipient experiences charity as helpful at all. Thus, an understanding of charity that foregrounds the relationship between the giver and God can represent a profound barrier to reimagining charity as a mechanism that advances the recipient's interests.

Besides achieving a desired relationship with God and greater prospects in the afterlife, the scholarly literature documents a range of secular drivers and benefits that the charitable receive through giving their time and resources to the needy. As Kymlicka (2001) says, to give something to someone who is not entitled to it is a peculiar activity. Although rational choice models may question the voluntary giving of something to an anonymous other without expecting anything in return, giving to others can be so deeply ingrained in cultural and social practices that it ceases to be truly voluntary (Hanson 2015). Reflecting the reciprocal nature of giving and our interdependent society, there are benefits to the giver and society where voluntary giving is widely practiced (Dees 2012). The political rhetoric presented in Chapter 5 and the media analysis in Chapter 6 demonstrate that Australia views the existence of charity as desirable and beneficial to society. Others present charitable care as an evolutionary survival strategy (Pagel 2012), or part of people's natural instinct to look after each other (Kropotkin 2009).

Motivations to help people who are poor

The forgoing discussion raises important questions about how different understandings of charity shape our sense of its purpose and the criteria we use to assess its value. In particular, it raises the question (touched on briefly in the previous chapter) of whose perspective matters when we think about the purpose of charity: the giver or the recipient. It is often held that the meaning of charity is inextricably bound up with the motivations of the giver. Dees (2012), for instance, argues that the motivation and intention of the giver sit at the centre of the meaning of charity. What makes helping others "charity" is the fact that it is motivated by feels of compassion and sympathy, rather than any rationally calculated or instrumentally determined outcome. For some, this is a positive thing. Scott Shershow (2005), for instance, argues that charity should only be based on righteous intent, as calculation about outcomes distorts the purity of the virtues of compassion and selflessness that underpin charity. Others, however, see the centrality given to the giver's motivations as problematic. For instance, Singer's (2015) critical analysis suggests that people want to help through charity, but for many, the urge to give is to experience the warm glow they, as helper, feel from giving (irrespective of what their giving achieves).

There is thus a close connection between the meaning of charity and the motivations of the charitable. In this book, we acknowledge the benefits that the provider of charity may receive through their giving, and see no necessary problem with the helper benefiting from helping. With Kate Laffan and Paul Dolan (2020), we reject a hierarchy of giving where pure altruism is at the top. However, we also contend that the motivations to help people in need, and the individual benefits that the helper experiences, only matter in so much as they generate better outcomes for recipients (Laffan & Dolan 2020). As noted in the previous chapter, one of the key problems with the contemporary model of charity in our view is that it eschews the needs and experiences of charity recipients.

From the perspective that righteous motivation is all that is required to understand the meaning of helping people in need, we fail to appreciate what it feels like to be on the receiving end of help, for example, sleeping in a carpark or having volunteers wash one's clothes on the streets. Moreover, this model of charity only allows the poor to receive, but not to give. The recipient is thus positioned as passive and without agency. Indeed, in this view of charity, the poor are first and foremost objects of *pity*: their experience of suffering and deprivation matter only insofar as they enable the charitable's righteous motivations of compassionate concern. One effect of this is the reification of the charity recipients' problems and their status as a needy supplicant.

Arendt's work is important here. Arendt theorised about how the feeling of pity for the poor drives a form of charitable care that can be enjoyed for "its own sake" (Arendt 2006, p. 79). She argued that when the poor are pitied, it leads to a response that "has just as much vested interest in the existence of the unhappy as thirst for power has a vested interest in the existence of the weak." The privileging of the motivations of the charitable may therefore have the impact of reducing the poor to their needy status, and providing little incentive for the charitable to do what is required to address the structural processes that underpin people's problems. Building on Arendt, Andrea Muehlebach expresses this problem thus:

> Pity is not invested in the overcoming of suffering or the production of equality. It revels in the status quo and locks those who feel pity and those who are pitied into an immutable, frozen embrace.
>
> (Muehlebach 2021, p. 136)

Not all charity, of course, is motivated by pity for the poor. Our knowledge from existing academic research makes it clear that there is not a single factor or force that drives people to help others in need, be that pity or a desire to live according to sacred principles. In a systematic review of the published literature of charitable donations, Rene Bekkers and Pamala Wiepking (2011, p. 945) demonstrate that voluntary donations are generally motivated by "multiple mechanisms working at once." These include altruism, people's values, and their perceptions of the efficacy of their charitable endeavours. Analysis of the 2019 Australian General Social Survey shows that a majority of volunteers report helping others or helping the community as their motivator. However, volunteers also recurrently identify personal satisfaction and the sense of doing something worthwhile as a motivating factor (Figure 2.1).

Wuthnow (1991) offers detailed insights into the multiple forces that drive our acts of care towards people in need and the way in which our multiple motivating mechanisms can contradict one another. His work also shows that, as individuals, we struggle to find a language to describe what motivates

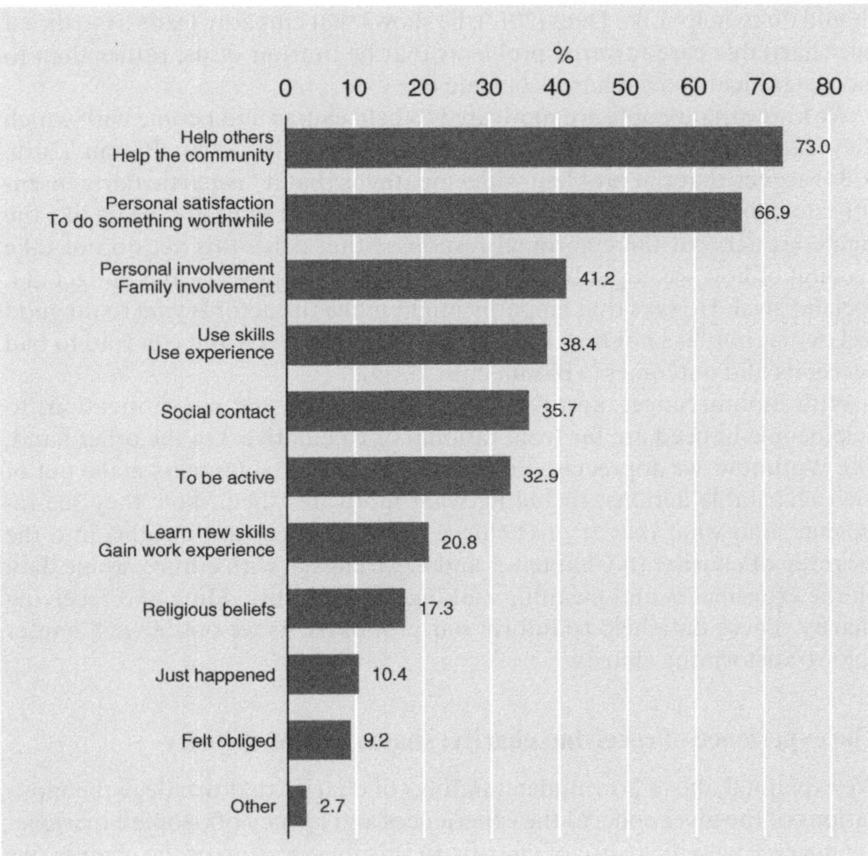

Figure 2.1 Self-reported reasons for being a volunteer.

Notes: Data from the 2019 General Social Survey obtained from the Australian Bureau of Statistics (2020).

our charitable care. People find it difficult to articulate what they want to do through providing charity. They tell stories that provide partial accounts of their motivations to care for others, but their partial accounts nevertheless "are a vitally important part of their caring" (Wuthnow 1991, p. 85).

Whilst motivations for giving are complex and multifaceted, it is clear that our charity is rarely based on a comprehensive understanding of what people's needs are, or how our actions can achieve the greatest impact for them. As noted, Singer (2015) has argued that people are motivated to help others because of the warm glow they feel from helping. He similarly critiques the irrationality of helping – giving to charity, for example. He does so on the grounds that people give based on emotional rather than rational calculations about the consequences of their charity to human life. In his book entitled *Against Empathy*, Paul Bloom (2016) makes similar arguments about the way in which empathy, or what Arendt might perhaps call pity, is a problematic motivator for what constitutes moral behaviour and what we should do to help. Like Dees (2012), he shows that empathy leads us to direct our charitable care towards problems that lie in front of us, rather than to more significant social harms outside our view.

We know that people are motivated to help causes and people with which they can personally identify (Beyerlein & Sikkink 2008). Bloom (2016, p. 34) argues that the problem with empathy is that it "is particularly insensitive to consequences." Feeding the hungry in front of us may seem like the righteous act, but the emotional responses that drive this act do not take account of how we might be involved in preventing poverty and hunger at a societal level. He says that empathy might make the actor trying to do good feel better, but "it's not how to improve things [poverty] and can lead to bad decisions and outcomes" (Bloom 2016, p. 39).

With Bloom, Singer, and Dees, we acknowledge that our motivations to help people in need are far from rational or calculative. On the other hand, like Wuthnow, we appreciate that the meaning that volunteers make out of their charitable actions, including what motivates them, how they see recipients, and what they try to achieve, provide important insights into the meaning of charity. In Chapters 7 and 8, we engage with ethnographic data on the experiences and meaning making of people providing and receiving charity. These data help to inform our proposals, as we outline in Chapter 9, for transforming charity.

The experience of receiving charity: shame and reciprocity

We explained above how understandings of charity that privilege the motivations of the giver conceal the experiences and agency of people experiencing poverty who make use of charity. In this final section of the chapter, we discuss scholarly accounts of the meaning of charity that take account of the recipients' perspective, highlighting the central themes of shame and its basis in the reciprocal nature of social relations.

Mary Douglas (1990, p. ix) famously wrote, "though we laud charity as a Christian virtue we know that it wounds." The idea that charity wounds, despite the positive position it assumes in society, draws on a vast body of literature. This literature makes it clear that the act of asking for charity is not simple, but rather a daunting and embarrassing experience (Frederick & Goddard 2008). A quote from a person in Australia who accessed food charity presented by Rebecca Lindberg and colleagues captured this embarrassment well, noting that when you present to ask for food, "you're leaving your pride and your dignity at the front door" (Lindberg et al. 2017, p. 35). The shame of charity is so grave that when Australian soldiers returned from WWI and could not find employment, they drew on their warrior status to argue that they should not be left to rely on charity, and should instead be protected by the State as a matter of right (O'Brien 2015).

People who rely on charity feel shame because their reliance signals a failure to provide for themselves and their families (Purdam et al. 2016). Charity serves to illustrate one's subordinate position in the social hierarchy (Aptekar 2016); receiving charity underscores the receiver's lower status than the giver's (Guinea-Martin 2014). Even when not overtly shamed, people accessing charity feel that they must take what they are given and have limited capacity to "express their needs, outlooks, and feelings related to the assistance" (Salonen et al. 2018). As opposed to the ideal of universal public provision based on citizenship, charity is lamented for the capacity of the charitable to withhold care and resources based on moral judgements of people's deservingness (Piven & Cloward 1972).

Richard Sennett (2003) proposed that a person who is poor receiving charity from a person who is not poor may experience the act of compassion and care as condescending. Daniel Guinea-Martin (2014) even found that recipients of charity can hold a grudge against volunteers, who they believe are only offering charity to gain public acclaim for their virtuous acts. People who were homeless and receiving charity were affronted by the sympathy the volunteers showed towards them (Guinea-Martin 2014).

Henry Thoreau illustrates, with some irony, the shame of being helped by a caring stranger. He remarked:

> If I knew for a certainty that a man was coming to my house with the conscious design of doing me good, I should run for my life.
>
> (Thoreau 1852 cited in Dees 2012, p. 328)

We have to think about the shameful experience of receiving someone's charity as not necessarily an indictment on the charitable or even a nod to the critique that nothing is as cold as charity. The shame that people feel accessing charity is rather a reflection on societal norms that construct normality as self-sufficiency and value reciprocity: people are expected to be able to look after themselves, and if they receive something from others, they ought to be able to give something back. One hundred years ago, Attlee (1920) recognised that charity could not be dignified if it occurred between unequal groups. The inequality between the two furthermore, where the giver assumes power over the receiver, means that the giver can exploit their powerful position to help only those who they deem of good character (Attlee 1920).

The wounds that Douglas (1990) referred to are driven by receiving charity but not being able to reciprocate. Her work draws on and responds to Marcel Mauss' seminal book *The Gift*. For Mauss (2011, p. 72), accepting a gift without reciprocating is "to face subordination, to become a client and subservient." This idea rests on the proposition that giving an unreciprocated gift means that the giver holds power over the recipient. The "gift not yet repaid debases the man who accepted it" (Mauss 2011, p. 63). Failure to reciprocate is damaging because reciprocity – giving, receiving, and giving back – contributes to social solidarity. The act of giving, which Mauss calls "the gift," is important for the mutually beneficial and perpetuating exchanges that it fosters: the gift is an individual act that achieves social ends. It is precisely the social nature of the gift – being part of a reciprocal exchange that ties people together – that helps illustrate the shame that people feel when they rely on the gift of charity but are unable to give back. Or indeed, accessing charity in a model that excludes them from giving back. As Sennett (2003, p. 219) observes, "reciprocity is the foundation of mutual respect."

Providing help to others and receiving help back represent core interpersonal dynamics that constitute our interdependent society. Receiving charity where people cannot give is seen as shameful because it positions the passive recipient of charitable care outside of societal norms. Reciprocity is critical in charitable giving because the recipient is receiving the care from someone who is voluntarily offering their help. They do not receive the care as a right, but rather as a gift. In Chapters 7 and 8 we return to the types of help volunteers try to deliver, including their motivations to help, and link these to the visceral experiences that people in poverty feel when accessing charity. This ethnographic account provides a useful lens to drive a reimaged model of charitable care, including what it means to care for people in poverty, which we outline in Chapter 9.

This chapter has provided an overview of the key themes and debates surrounding the meaning of efforts to help people experiencing poverty through charitable care. We have demonstrated how charity has multiple, overlapping, and sometimes contested meanings, which include meeting basic needs, fostering human connection, and practicing particular sets of beliefs and values. We also demonstrated how the meaning of charity varies depending upon whether the perspectives of providers or recipients are foregrounded; and we highlighted some of the dangers of a model of charity that reduces the poor to objects of pity. In the next chapter, we shift our focus to the contemporary social and political contexts in which charitable responses to poverty are practiced today. In doing this, we provide a theoretical framework for understanding the resurgence of charity and its connection to the rise of neoliberalism and related political projects.

References

Ambrey, C, Parsell, C, Spallek, M & Robinson, R 2019, 'An investigation into repeat requests for charity: Evidence from the St Vincent de Paul Society Queensland, Australia', *Nonprofit and Voluntary Sector Quarterly*, vol. 48, no. 1, pp. 91–107.

Aptekar, S 2016, 'Gifts among strangers: The social organization of freecycle giving', *Social Problems*, vol. 63, no, 2, pp. 266–283.

Arendt, H 2006, *On Revolution*, Penguin, New York.

Attlee, C 1920, *The Social Worker*, G. Bell and Sons LTD, London.

Australian Bureau of Statistics 2020, *General Social Survey: Summary Results, Australia*, viewed 26 February 2021, https://www.abs.gov.au/statistics/people/people-and-communities/general-social-survey-summary-results-australia/latest-release#data-download

Beddown n.d., viewed 26 February 2021, https://beddown.org.au/

Bekkers, R & Wiepking, P 2011, 'A literature review of empirical studies of philanthropy: Eight mechanisms that drive charitable giving', *Nonprofit and Voluntary Sector Quarterly*, vol. 40, no. 5, pp. 924–973.

Beyerlein, K & Sikkink, D 2008, 'Sorrow and solidarity: Why Americans volunteered for 9/11 relief efforts', *Social Problems*, vol. 55, no. 2, pp. 190–215.

Bloom, P 2016, *Against Empathy: The Case for Rational Compassion*, The Bodley Head, London.

Bowpitt, G 1998, 'Evangelical Christianity, secular humanism, and the genesis of British social work', *The British Journal of Social Work*, vol. 28, no. 5, pp. 675–693.

Bremner, R 2000, *Giving: Charity and Philanthropy in History*, Transaction Publishers, Somerset.

Brooks, A 2004, 'Faith, secularism, and charity', *Faith & Economics*, vol. 43, pp. 1–8.

Cloke, P, May, J & Williams, A 2017, 'The geographies of food banks in the meantime', *Progress in Human Geography*, vol. 41, no. 6, pp. 703–726.

Dees, G 2012, 'A tale of two cultures: Charity, problem solving, and the future of social entrepreneurship', *Journal of Business Ethics*, vol. 111, no. 3, pp. 321–334.

Douglas, M 1990, 'Forward: No free gifts', in M Maus (ed.), *The Gift*, Routledge, London, pp. ix--xxiii.

Eckel, C & Grossman, P 2004, 'Giving to secular causes by the religious and nonreligious: An experimental test of the responsiveness of giving to subsidies', *Nonprofit and Voluntary Sector Quarterly*, vol. 33, no. 2, pp. 271–289.

Edin, K & Shaefer, H 2015, *$2.00 A Day: Living on Almost Nothing in America*, Mariner Books, Boston.

Encyclical Letter of Pope Paul VI 1967, *Populorum Progressio on the Development of Peoples*, viewed 23 February 2021, https://www.cctwincities.org/wp-content/uploads/2015/10/Populorum-Progressio.pdf

Engster, D 2015, *Justice, Care, and the Welfare State*, Oxford University Press, New York.

Feeding America 2014, *Hunger in America 2014: National Report Prepared for Feeding America*, Feeding America, Chicago.

France, R 1986, 'Liberation in the New Testament', *The Evangelical Quarterly*, vol. 58, no. 1, pp. 3–23.

Frederick, J & Goddard, C 2008, 'Sweet and sour charity: Experiences of receiving emergency relief in Australia', *Australian Social Work*, vol. 61, no. 3, pp. 269–284.

Guinea-Martin, D 2014, 'Compassionate and egalitarian: The charity paradox in two voluntary associations', *Ethnography*, vol. 15, no. 4, pp. 540–563.

Hanson, J 2015, 'The anthropology of giving: Toward a cultural logic of charity', *Journal of Cultural Economy*, vol. 8, no. 4, pp. 501–520.

Holland, T 2019, *Dominion: The Making of the Western Mind*, Little Brown, London.

Jackson, T 2003, *The Priority of Love: Christian Charity and Social Justice*, Princeton University Press, Princeton.

Katz, M 1986, *In the Shadow of the Poorhouse: A Social History of Welfare in America*, Basic Books, New York.

Kochuyt, T 2009, 'Gods, gifts and poor people: On charity in Islam', *Social Compass*, vol. 56, no. 1, pp. 98–116.

Kropotkin, P 2009, *Mutual Aid*, Cosmo, New York.

Kymlicka, W 2001, 'Altruism in philosophical and ethical traditions: Two views', in J Phillips, B Chapman & D Stevens (eds.), *Between State and Market: Essay on Charity Law and Policy in Canada*, McGill-Queen's University Press, Toronto, pp. 87–126.

Laffan, K & Dolan, P 2020, 'In defence of charity which both giver and receiver', *Nature Human Behaviour*, vol. 4, pp. 670–672.

Lambie-Mumford, H 2017, *Hungry Britain: The Rise of Food Charity*, Policy Press, Bristol.

Lambie-Mumford, H & Silvasti, T 2020, 'Introduction: Exploring the growth of food charity across Europe', in H Lambie-Mumford & T Silvasto (eds.), *The Rise of Food Charity in Europe*, Policy Press, Bristol, pp. 1–18.

Lindberg, R, Lawrence, M & Caraher, M 2017, 'Kitchens and pantries—helping or hindering? The perspectives of emergency food users in Victoria, Australia', *Journal of Hunger & Environmental Nutrition*, vol. 12, no. 1, pp. 26–45.

Lister, R 2004, *Poverty*, Polity, Cambridge.

Luke 6:24, *Bible Hub*, viewed 26 February 2021, https://biblehub.com/luke/6-24.htm

Matthew 19, *Bible Hub*, viewed 17 February 2021, https://biblehub.com/niv/matthew/19.htm

Mauss, M 2011, *The Gift: Forms and Functions of Exchange in Archaic Societies*, Martino Publishing, Connecticut.

Mohan, J & Breeze, B 2016, *The Logic of Charity: Great Expectations in Hard Times*, Palgrave Macmillan, Basingstoke.

Muehlebach, A 2012, *The Moral Neoliberal: Welfare and Citizenship in Italy*, University of Chicago Press, Chicago.

O'Brien, A 2015, *Philanthropy and Settler Colonialism*, Palgrave Macmillan, Basingstoke.

Orange Sky n.d., viewed 23 February 2021, https://orangesky.org.au/

Pagel, M 2012, *Wired for Culture: Origins of the Human Social Mind*, W. W. Norton & Company, New York.

Parsell, C & Watts, B 2017, 'Charity and justice: A reflection on new forms of homelessness provision in Australia', *European Journal of Homelessness*, vol. 11, no. 2, pp. 65–76.

Piven, R & Cloward, F 1972, *Regulating the Poor: The Functions of Public Welfare*, Vantage Books, New York.
Poppendieck, J 1999, *Sweet Charity? Emergency Food and the End of Entitlement*, Penguin, New York.
Purdam, K, Garratt, E & Esmail, A 2016, 'Hungry? Food insecurity, social stigma and embarrassment in the UK', *Sociology*, vol. 50, no. 6, pp. 1072–1088.
Salonen, A, Ohisalo, M & Laihiala, T 2018, 'Undeserving, disadvantaged, disregarded: Three viewpoints of charity food aid recipients in Finland', *International Journal of Environmental Research and Public Health*, vol. 15, no. 12, pp. 2896
Schoenfeld, E & Mestrovic, S 1989, 'Durkheim's concept of justice and its relationship to social solidarity', *Sociological Analysis*, vol. 50, no. 2, pp. 111–127.
Sennett, R 2003, *Respect in a World of Inequality*, W. W. Norton & Company, New York.
Shapiro, D 2007, *Is the Welfare State Justified?*, Cambridge University Press, New York.
Shershow, S 2005, *The Work & The Gift*, University of Chicago Press, Chicago.
Sherwin, M 2012, *By Knowledge & By Love: Charity and Knowledge in the Moral Theology of St. Thomas Aquinas*, The Catholic University of America Press, Washington.
Silvasti, T 2015, 'Food aid – normalising the abnormal in Finland', *Social Policy & Society*, vol. 14, no. 3, pp. 471–482.
Singer, P 2015, *The Most Good You Can Do: How Effective Altruism Is Changing Ideas about Living Ethically*, Yale University Press, New Haven.
St Vincent de Paul Society 2014, *The Rule: 7th Edition 2012, Australia*, viewed 23 February 2021, https://www.vinnies.org.au/icms_docs/168122_The_Rule.pdf
Vaidyanathan, B, Smith, C & Hill, J 2011, 'Religion and charitable financial giving to religious and secular causes: Does political ideology matter?', *Journal for the Scientific Study of Religion*, vol. 50, no. 3, pp. 450–469.
van der Meer, F 1961, *Augustine the Bishop: The Life and Work of a Father of the Church*, Translated by B Battershaw & G Lamb, Sheed & Ward, London.
Wuthnow, R 1991, *Acts of Compassion: Caring for Others and Helping Ourselves*, Princeton University Press, Princeton.

3 Neoliberalising charity

Introduction

When we think of charity, we tend to imagine a heroic individual or organisation stepping up to tackle a vexing social problem. The citizen providing charitable care is one who is intrinsically motivated to address an injustice or to help people in need, whether this is on the basis of moral/religious conviction, humanistic compassion, or a desire to perform a virtuous self. They are their own prime mover, taking matters into their own hands in order to mould the world (or indeed themselves) to their ideals. Insofar as they relate to broader social and political processes, it is as independent agents of amelioration or change; that is, as sovereign subjects, who stand over and against a set of objective social problems, such as poverty or disadvantage, and who have decided to do something about it. Yet, despite the banal ubiquity and seductive power of this image, charity is far from the discrete and self-generating phenomenon we imagine it to be. Indeed, if existing scholarship on charity teaches us anything, it is that charity is a fundamentally *relational* phenomenon (DeVerteuil et al. 2019) that is shaped by, and itself helps to shape, the changing social, political, and institutional worlds in which it is embedded.

The relations through which charity is constituted are manifold. At the micro level, charity is comprised of relations between those who act charitably and their ostensible beneficiaries, namely people experiencing poverty. This relationship is a fundamentally unequal one, as it presupposes the deprivation, and subsequent dependence, of one party (the charity recipient) relative to the other (the charitable). This point, in turn, highlights the fact that charity operates within, and on the basis of, a broader set of unequal social relationships that cut across society, and which are mediated in various ways by the State and its welfare apparatus. The relationship between charity, poverty, and the welfare state is in fact a longstanding concern of scholarship on poverty governance (Katz 1986), as both the necessity of charity, and the form that it takes, are shaped by the level and type of State intervention to address poverty.

This chapter lays out the theoretical approach that we employ to make sense of charity in the context of this complex set of relations. As we noted in

Chapter 1, much contemporary scholarship approaches the question of charity through the prism of neoliberalism, and the vast changes to welfare and poverty governance that it has wrought in recent decades. As we discuss below, there is a tendency in this literature to view charity, along with associated processes such as volunteering and the professionalization of the third sector, as a kind of crutch for neoliberal reform. That is, charity is seen as enabling the withdrawal of the State from direct welfare provisioning in accordance with the core neoliberal goals of fiscal constraint and reducing public spending, and the promotion of individual self-reliance through expansion of market relations throughout society (including to the domain of welfare provision itself).

Whilst recognising the insights produced by this literature, in this chapter we seek to reframe the connections between neoliberalism and charity. We argue that the resurgence of charity in contemporary poverty governance is more than a mere crutch for welfare state retrenchment. Although we recognise that charity can and often does play this role, we contend that it is also mobilised *for its own sake*, as it is seen as enacting a mode of sociality that has long been at the heart of liberal conceptions of how society is, and should be, organised. Both classical and contemporary variants of liberal political reason valorise forms of sociality that exist beyond the state (Miller & Rose 2008), and which symbolise natural and self-regulating domains of human conduct and relationality. These include not only the market but also civil society and, more recently, the community, all of which are conceived as spaces of spontaneous human sociality, affective connection, and the coming together of free individuals to respond to the problems that they confront in their day-to-day lives (including poverty).

Drawing on the work of Bruno Latour (2005), we argue that both the mobilisation of charity and the reconfiguring of traditional State welfare functions are part of a broader project to reassemble the social in accordance with these (neo)liberal conceptions. For Latour, society is always in the making, and struggles over how to define its natural or ideal state are an endogenous feature of this process. Practices, such as charity, and the people and things they implicate, are enrolled in this process to the extent that they help perform and make real the forms of the social world advanced by particular projects; yet, they retain a relative autonomy from those projects, and have the capacity to divert their energies to incommensurable ends. What is at stake in the debates over charity and its role in poverty governance is thus much more than welfare budgets and expanding markets. Rather, such debates speak to how society is assembled in a neoliberalising world.

Charity, neoliberalism, and the withdrawal of the welfare state

Charity has a long and tangled history with the welfare state when it comes to poverty governance. As described in Chapter 1, there has been contestation over the growth and demise of both publically funded welfare and charity.

Yet it is a mistake to assume that charity was discarded by the welfare state through a process of societal modernisation (Johnson 1996). Charities proliferated in the nineteenth century in response to the poverty and disorder wrought by rapid industrialisation and urbanisation, and it evolved and persisted throughout the twentieth century in line with the establishment and expansion of post-war welfare states, albeit on a reduced scale. In countries like the United Kingdom and the United States, State welfare provision was justified on the basis of the failure of charity to adequately address poverty and its associated social pathologies (Marshall 1950). Advocates of public provision saw charity as too patchy and piecemeal, too exclusionary and preoccupied with questions of deservingness, and too stigmatising of recipients to be able to adequately address poverty.

Although charity to aid people in poverty has never ceased, from the 1980s, the restructuring and retrenchment of the welfare state have coincided with a resurgence in charitable responses to poverty. This shift is typically understood as part of the broader, yet somewhat fuzzy, set of processes that contemporary scholarship refers to as neoliberalism. Neoliberalism is conceptualised variously as a policy regime, a process of political-economic restructuring, an ideology, and a way of rationalising the exercise of political power (a governmentality) (Brady 2016; Flew 2014; Larner 2000). However, its conceptualisation is almost always associated with a thorough-going problematisation of the forms of top-down State welfare provisioning that came to prominence in the post-war period. This problematisation was derived from a convergence of welfare state critiques emanating from across the political spectrum (Clarke & Newman 1997; Miller & Rose 2008). These critiques represented the welfare state as stifling the self-governing capacities of individuals and communities by shielding them from the discipline of the market, and by creating a culture of dependence wherein people rely on external authorities (society, the State, etc.) to secure their well-being. As we saw in Chapter 1, the welfare state was also criticised for producing a class of unresponsive welfare experts and professionals, who were insensible to the diverse and changing needs of citizens, and who engaged in self-interested empire building under the pretence of public service and specialised, esoteric knowledge of welfare needs (McKnight 1995).

It is in the context of these problematisations that charity has re-emerged as a prominent response to poverty. Indeed, a central feature of neoliberalism has been the transfer of responsibility for welfare provisioning from State organs to a diverse range of civil society actors, including non-profits, non-governmental organisations (NGOs), and grassroots charity initiatives. Referred to variously as the community sector, third sector, or voluntary sector, these actors are now a major provider of frontline welfare assistance to people experiencing poverty (Milligan & Conradson 2006; Wolch 1990). This transfer of responsibility has both enabled and been driven by the withdrawal of the State from direct welfare provisioning, and by efforts to marketise the provision of welfare: many welfare state functions have been retrenched, whilst others have been privatised or contracted out to non-state actors through competitive tendering processes.

These shifts have been accompanied by efforts to revalorise civil society generally and charity in particular. In contrast to the abstract and impersonal welfare state, civil society initiatives are presented as being naturally more responsive to local circumstances and needs (Smith & Lipsky 1993). In line with subsidiarity reasoning, they have a perceived proximity to the people they serve, both in terms of their being more grassroots and by being driven by ordinary people, rather than out of touch bureaucrats and experts (Newman & Clarke 2009). Civil society is also presented as a source of untapped entrepreneurial and compassionate energy that can and should be harnessed to address social problems like poverty. Bottom-up charity and community initiatives are portrayed as having being crowded out by the welfare state; hence, welfare state retrenchment is positioned as providing the space for these initiatives to play a greater role in poverty governance (Hackworth 2012).

For many scholars, the promotion of charity and other civil society responses to poverty is about facilitating, legitimising, and sustaining the core neoliberal reforms of welfare state retrenchment and the extension of market relations. From this perspective, the valorisation of civil society is something of an ideological ruse, a tactic deployed to distract from the core political and economic changes brought on by neoliberalisation (Hackworth 2012; Levitas 2012; Wolch 1989). For instance, in his analysis of the nexus between neoliberalism and the religious right in the United States, Jason Hackworth argues that the turn to (particularly faith-based) charity provides an ideological cushion,

> to soften the hard-edged language of neoliberal social policy. Demolishing public housing, cutting social security, eliminating food stamps, and cutting Aid to Families with Dependent Children (AFDC) all sound harsher than relying on the compassion of churches to serve the poor. It is a sentimentality that moderates neoliberalism and fuels anti-statist, anti-welfare antipathy.
>
> (Hackworth 2012, p. 3)

In addition to this ideological/legitimising function, scholars also highlight how the mobilisation of charity/civil society provides necessary political-economic support for welfare state withdrawal. It is often argued that civil society functions as a source of unpaid (voluntary) or cheap (contractual) labour for governments intent on reducing welfare spending (Dowling & Harvie 2014; Levitas 2012; Macmillan & Townsend 2006). Ruth Levitas puts this particularly starkly in her critique of the Coalition Government's (2010–2015) Big Society agenda in the United Kingdom, which sought to replace big State responses to social needs with bottom-up volunteerism and charity.

> Talk of the 'Big Society' is... little more than an attempt to get necessary social labour done for nothing, disproportionately by women, by pushing work back across the market/non-market boundary. We'll sack your librarians, but if you want you can keep your libraries open using volunteers. We'll cut your care services, so if you don't look after your relatives and neighbours they will be abandoned, or left unfed and untended even in hospitals. We'll axe the programme for intensive social work with families with multiple problems, and replace it with untrained volunteers in the Working Families Everywhere programme.
> (Levitas 2012, p. 322)

Such a perspective draws on a tradition of scholarship that highlights capitalism's reliance on unpaid labour – particular that of women – to ensure social reproduction (e.g. Engels 2010; Oakley 1974). Neoliberalism, then, is seen as seeking to augment and harness this aspect of the capitalist division of labour in order to facilitate State withdrawal from direct welfare provisioning.

There is also a related view that the mobilisation of civil society constitutes an effort to manage the contradictions and consequences of neoliberal reform, and the stage of late capitalism that it corresponds to. In a seminal piece, Jamie Peck and Adam Tickell (2002) list the mobilisation of charities and voluntary initiatives amongst a set of regulatory practices that they argue constitute a second, rollout phase of neoliberalism. The earlier rollback phase of the Thatcher/Reagan era, with its focus on economic deregulation and welfare retrenchment, produced new forms of social and economic marginalisation and insecurity that threatened the legitimacy of the neoliberal project. Rollout neoliberalism focused on managing these emerging problems by moving to a more interventionist approach involving various institutional and policy innovations of the Third Way variety. Amongst these was "the mobilization of the little platoons in the shape of (local) voluntary and faith-based associations in the service of neoliberal goals" (Peck & Tickell 2002, p. 390). Recent work from the United Kingdom follows a similar logic, highlighting the way in which civil society is mobilised to ameliorate the social insecurity caused by the 2008 financial crisis and the austerity program that followed it (Dowling & Harvie 2014; McGimpsey 2017).

As the preceding discussion illustrates, there is a strong sense amongst scholars that charity/civil society is a kind of crutch that political authorities mobilise to facilitate and buttress neoliberal reforms. In Rob Macmillan and Alan Townsend's (2006, p. 15) words, the "voluntary and community sector" functions as a "new institutional fix" that offers "a putative solution to a number of governing dilemmas" in the context of political-economic crisis and fiscal constraint. Whilst we agree that charity can and often does play this role, we see this framing as too narrow to adequately account for either its relationship to neoliberalism, or for its role in contemporary poverty governance. For us, charity also plays a more central and *productive* role in the neoliberal reimaging and reshaping of poverty governance. We use the term productive here in the Foucauldian sense (e.g. Foucault 1995), to refer to how the mobilisation of charity gives rise to new forms of citizenship, power, and social solidarity that are central – not auxiliary – to efforts to reconfigure society in accordance with neoliberal ideals. It is to these productive functions that we now turn.

(Neo)liberal definitions of the social

In this book, we adopt an alternative perspective on charity's relationship to neoliberalism and changing welfare states to the literature reviewed above and in Chapter 1. Drawing on the work of Latour (2005), we view both welfare state restructuring and the resurgence of charity as part of a broader project of reassembling the social along primarily (but not exclusively) neoliberal lines. For Latour, the social is not a pre-given or fixed entity, but rather a mobile set of relationships or associations that are constantly being reassembled, that is, made and remade. At the core of this process is an ongoing struggle to define what society is, and how it should be organised, with different actors and projects seeking to reassemble the social in accordance with their preferred definitions, and to enrol others' support to make these definitions a reality (Latour 1986). Thus, to understand the resurgence and contemporary function of charity, we must take account of the broader definition or theory of the social that it is being mobilised to help produce.

Whilst neoliberalisation does not involve the smooth implementation of a coherent theory or plan (Theodore et al. 2011), it does entail the reanimation and renewal of key elements of what Foucauldian scholars call the political ontology of classical liberal thought (Collier 2011; Gordon 1991); that is, the ways in which liberalism defined and sought to reassemble the social. For classical liberalism, society is composed of distinct spheres that exist prior to, and independent of, political power and the State. These spheres include not only the touchstone of all liberal thought, the market but also an active and dynamic civil society (Dean 2002; Miller & Rose 2008; Muehlebach 2012). Civil society was imagined as a space of voluntary associations formed between free citizens on the basis of mutually identified interests or concerns, be they political, social, or philanthropic. Like the market, it was seen as comprising its own dynamics and regularities, and thus as possessing certain self-governing capacities. It was hence positioned by liberal thinkers as imposing natural limits on State intervention in the everyday lives of citizens, as the State can never understand or respond to citizens' needs as well as they can themselves (Miller & Rose 2008). At the same time, and for much the same reasons, civil society was also positioned as an invaluable resource for the efficient and effective exercise of political power, in that its self-regulating capacities can be augmented and harnessed to advance the State's political objectives (Foucault 2008).

Whilst this characterisation and positioning of civil society is similar to how classical liberalism conceptualised the market, civil society was seen as distinct from the market in important ways. Namely, civil society was seen as grounded in the spontaneous compassion and fellow feeling of free individuals, rather than in the pursuit of rational self-interest (Muehlebach 2012). It is therefore a highly moralised domain, wherein people come together to pursue shared objectives and address social problems out of a sense of moral obligation and ethical duty. As Muehlebach (2012) argues, civil society offers something of a counter-balance to the amoral and atomised domain of the market in liberal thought, in that it provides a space for actions that are both affective and other-oriented (rather than rational and self-interested), and which are epitomised by spontaneous acts of charity. These actions correspond to that other side of human nature that was seen as existing alongside rational autonomy: the spontaneous compassion we feel for one another, particularly those experiencing suffering, and the desire for connection, belonging, and community. Thus, as well as being a limit on and resource for the State, civil society is for liberal thought an essential domain for the cultivation of ethical virtue in capitalist societies that are otherwise at risk of descending into nihilistic and amoral individualism.

These classical understandings of the composition and functioning of society have been taken up and reworked by neoliberal thinkers in response to the emergence, expansion, and crisis of welfare and the social State in the late twentieth and early twenty-first centuries (Collier 2011). A renewed belief in the primacy and value of civil society is clearly at play in critiques of the welfare state, particularly the ideas that welfare stifles society's self-regulating capacities and creates dependency, and concerns about the capacity of detached bureaucrats and professionals to understand and address citizens' problems as well as they can themselves (Miller & Rose 2008). What is perhaps most striking, though, is the way in which neoliberalism has mobilised the political ontology of civil society to reconfigure the forms of power, citizenship, and social solidarity built during the golden age of the welfare state.

As Nikolas Rose (1999, 2000) argues, one of the key shifts associated with what he calls advanced liberalism (a concept intended to have broader reference than the supposedly market-centric term neoliberalism) is the rescaling of political ontology from a focus on national, State-centred and politically-mediated societies to autonomous individuals situated within pre-political communities. During the heyday of welfare, citizens were governed through mechanisms that aimed at creating national solidarity and mutual interdependence. Initiatives like social security and universal public services meant that citizens were tied to one another through the abstract political institutions of the welfare state, creating a situation where risk was socialised and the economic and social security of each was guaranteed by all. Poverty was seen as a structural problem associated with the vagaries of labour markets and the capitalist business cycle, and thus as the responsibility of the State acting as the proxy of society more broadly. It was these great political technologies of social welfare that gave meaning to the idea of social citizenship and the belief that citizens have social rights that flow from their membership of an integrated and interdependent national society (Marshall 1950).

In light of the thorough-going problematisation of these State-centred modes of governing, neoliberalism (or advanced liberalism) entails a new set of strategies and mechanisms for configuring social relations that relies heavily on a revised version of the political ontology of civil society. Neoliberalism not only entails a renewed focus on cultivating autonomous and self-reliant citizens capable of securing their own well-being through the market, rather than relying on the State (Miller & Rose 2008), but it also entails the cultivation of "ethical citizens" who are active and responsible members of specific local-moral communities (Rose 1999, 2000). Community is here conceived as a spontaneous and pre-political space where autonomous citizens experience obligations to others, and engage in collective actions, without the pacifying mediation of the State. Like the civil society of classical liberal thought, community is treated as an ethical domain, where social bonds are the product of quasi-natural effects and investments that implicate otherwise autonomous individuals with binding moral obligations (to neighbours, to faith groups, to ethnic, sexual or other communities of identity, and so on).

However, unlike classical liberalism, where both civil society and the market are conceived as naturally occurring domains that are independent of, and impose limits upon, State power, neoliberalism promotes an active role for the State in securing the conditions that allow competitive markets and strong communities to flourish (Foucault 2008). This entails the State both directly investing in the cultivation of community, including the development of programs aimed at instilling communities with the capacity for responsible self-governance (Rose 1999). It also entails the State securing and enforcing conformity with community norms, values, and expectations, positioning those who fail to meet these standards as irresponsible subjects, and subjecting them to coercive, paternalistic, or other seemingly illiberal interventions (Dean 2002).

Like civil society for classical liberalism, community is also seen as a key resource for neoliberal government, in that it provides a way of mobilising social interdependencies and collective action that does not rely on the apparently artificial and stifling relations of State-mediated solidarity and welfare (Rose 1999). As Rose (1999, 2000) argues, political authorities increasingly seek to govern *through* community by eliciting and harnessing the spontaneous ethical commitments and obligations that are believed to comprise it, as well as its bottom-up capacities and modes of self-regulation. This allows them to address social problems and pursue collective ends whilst appearing to maintain the autonomy and self-reliance of political subjects, and their independence from the State.

Insofar as ethics are at the heart of governing through community, Rose (2000) argues that it signals the emergence of a new field of ethopower, where power "works through the values, beliefs, and sentiments thought to underpin the techniques of responsible self-government and the management of one's obligations to others" (Rose 2000, p. 1400). Corresponding to this is the emergence of an ethopolitics that replaces the welfarist emphasis on social citizenship with a new model of *ethical* citizenship, where the emphasis is on the ethical duties, rather than the social rights, that flow from collective life. These duties manifest in various ways. However, they tend to centre on the expectation that people will take responsibility for themselves, their families, and their communities, and avoid placing an undue burden on others. For Rose, the focus is thus no longer on the production of solidarity through the socialisation of risk and security, but rather on the production of resilient, responsible and self-governing citizens and communities that have the initiative and capacity to address their own problems with only indirect support from the State.

This shift towards ethical citizenship does not amount to an abandonment of social solidarity as a governmental objective, however. As Muehlebach (2012) shows, solidarity remains a core concern of the neoliberal project and is a central target of efforts to mobilise civil society in general and charity in particular. The basis of solidarity is dramatically changed, however, as neoliberalism eschews the State-mediated forms of solidarity associated with social citizenship, and instead outsources solidarity to civil society and the community. Here, solidarity is achieved, not through the abstract and artificial mechanisms of social security and publicly funded services, but rather through the proximate relations of care, compassion, fellowship, and reciprocity that result from bottom-up charity and other community initiatives. It is thus an *ethical*, rather than political, form of solidarity, one that the State must help foster, but from which it must be, at least symbolically, excluded.

(Neo)liberal understandings of social life as spontaneous, ethical, and pre-political are thus central to the processes of reassembling the social that we examine in this book. Following Muehlebach (2012) and Rose (1999, 2000), we are particularly interested in the way that charity is mobilised to generate new forms of social solidarity and citizenship, and how these coincide with broader process of welfare state restructuring and the neoliberalisation of poverty governance. We are also concerned with the implications of this process of reassembling for how charity is enacted and experienced, and the implications it has for the concrete social relations in which people experiencing poverty are embedded. In the next section, we outline in greater detail our approach to theorising charity and the forms of solidarity it produces.

Assembling the neoliberal social

Whilst linking neoliberalism to social solidarity is at odds with the received wisdom of contemporary social theory (Harvey 2005), there is a sense in which all attempts at reassembling the social can be seen as having some form of solidarity as their ultimate aim. As Latour (1986, 2005) argues, projects to reassemble the social are characterised by efforts to not only forge but also to *stabilise* associations, and thus institute a particular understanding of the social as a taken-for-granted and enduring reality. To stabilise associations means to *solidify* them, to give them a durable form that persists through time. It is precisely this solidity and durability of relations that classical social theorists like Durkheim (1933) had in mind when they talked about social solidarity. However, whilst Durkheim saw solidarity as a spontaneous and functionally adapted feature of normal or healthy societies, following Latour, we see the stabilisation of associations as something that must be actively *produced.*

How, then, are neoliberal forms of solidarity and ethical citizenship produced, and how is charity implicated in this process? To analysis these processes, we employ Latour's concept of translation (Latour 1986, 2005). Translation is the key process through which the reassembling of associations is achieved. Put simply, it involves enrolling the support of people (and things) into, and through, the enactment of a particular definition of the social. Latour (1986) makes it clear that reassembling the social is not something that can be achieved by fiat: it is not because particular actors possess power that they are able to make their ideals a reality. Rather, they become powerful by harnessing the energies and capacities of others. They do this by *aligning the interests* of those others to their projects and worldviews. Translation refers to this process of alignment. Translation is the arrangement of things such that, in order to pursue their own projects, people must (or at least believe they must) contribute to the projects of the translating party.

This process of aligning is both discursive and material. As the term translation implies, aligning interests entails their conversion from one set of terms into another. A reframing takes place, where it becomes possible to rearticulate an actor's projects and concerns in ways that align with the definition of the social advanced by the party doing the translating. However, translation in the Latourian sense is more than a linguistic or discursive process, for it also typically entails material or more-than-human alignments, where the affordances and constraints inherent to non-human actors are used to align the interests of one party with those of another. Thus, translation often entails one party coming to rely on resources, technologies, infrastructure, etc. controlled by another to realise their goals (Latour 1987).

The concept of translation enables us to analyse how the charitable have their interests or goals – to make a difference, give back to the community, do God's work, etc. – aligned or filtered through the neoliberalising projects of governments and other authorities. In the chapters that follow, we document a variety of translation strategies employed by the State to achieve this alignment. This includes the (partial) withdrawal of the State from the field of direct poverty alleviation, creating increased material need for bottom-up charitable responses to address, as well as increasing material and symbolic support by the State for particular charitable initiatives in the form of funding, awards, accolades, and legislative reform. It also includes the perpetuation and dissemination of political discourses that foreground citizens' ethical obligations to their communities, national-cultural traditions of community self-reliance and mutual support, and visions of the State as an enabler of self-governing communities.

Importantly, the concept of translation also highlights the active role played by charitable actors and charity recipients in engaging with, advancing, transforming, and/or resisting these more top-down efforts by political authorities to enrol their support for neoliberalising projects. As Latour (1987) argues, enrolled actors are not mere dupes or functionaries who will automatically carry out the will of those enrolling them. Rather, once enrolled, they become active mediators of the broader project, adding to it capacities and energies that the enrolling party cannot deliver on their own. Indeed, harnessing these capacities and energies is precisely the point of translation, for no actor, no matter how prominent their position, can reassemble the social without the contributions of others (Latour 1986). It is hard to imagine, for instance, how a government would enact a dynamic civil society without enrolling charities, volunteers, NGOs, and other non-state actors in this process.

However, the active, mediating role played by these other actors means that translation is an inherently risky enterprise (Latour 1987). There is always the chance that those enrolled will eschew the roles imagined for them, and redirect the relationships, policies, and/or resources through which they were enrolled towards alternative and incommensurable ends. For instance, as illustrated by Cloke et al. (2017), charity organisations may use the public prominence and proximity to poverty granted to them by neoliberal reforms as a basis from which to highlight and critique the consequences of those reforms, and/or as a platform to campaign for the necessity of direct State involvement in addressing poverty – a point we return to in Chapter 9. Translation is thus a dynamic and open-ended process, wherein attempts at enrolment and the alignment of interests is a mutual – if often unequal – enterprise.

In light of this, it is important to recognise that the production of neoliberalised forms of solidarity and ethical citizenship is a messy and incomplete process that is open to challenge and redirection. Moreover, whilst charity is mobilised to help reassemble the social according to neoliberal ideals, neither charity itself, the values it enacts, nor the relations it entails are themselves *inherently* neoliberal. They are rather complex and multivalent social processes that have diverse historical and cultural resonances and articulations. Indeed, it is precisely these resonances and articulations that make charity attractive to, and useful for, neoliberal projects of reassembling. Not only does charity often bring with it ready-made networks of motivated volunteers, organisational infrastructures, and community resources that can be harnessed for governing poverty, it also brings certain forms of symbolic power (Dean 2020) that assist in enrolling actors who might otherwise eschew or co-opt neoliberalising initiatives.

This symbolic power includes what Dean (2020) calls the good glow of charity: the aura of selfless, relational virtue that charity confers on those engaged in it. However, insofar as charity is seen as representing spontaneous community and civil society, it also derives symbolic power from its resonance with that deep longing for communal forms of social connection and solidarity that are persistent features of the culture of modernity. Indeed, modern societies have long been haunted by the image of a lost *gemeinschaft*: that form of communal sociality that classical social theory associated with the pre-modern village, and where social relations were based on personal familiarity, emotional attachment, and shared sentiments and experiences (Durkheim 1933; Tönnies 1957). This longing is grounded in a diffuse and enduring sense that there is something inauthentic about, or missing from, contemporary social relations; relations which have been rendered overly rationalised and transactional due to the mediating role played by capitalist markets and the modern nation State. The longing for a lost gemeinschaft therefore manifests itself in an often unspoken belief that the rehabilitation of at least some aspects of communal life is necessary to address social problems like poverty.

The (neo)liberal conceptions of the social discussed above have a number of continuities and connections with this image of the lost *gemeinschaft*. The most central of these is perhaps the shared understanding of the basis of solidarity as being the spontaneous bonds that arise from shared ethical sentiments. Durkheim (1933) called this phenomenon the collective conscience: a kind of group psyche that aligns individuals' modes of perception and moral judgement, creating a sense of connectedness, identity, and cohesion. Like the ethical connections that constitute liberalism's civil society and neoliberalism's community, the form of solidarity produced by the collective conscience is spontaneous, or "mechanical" (Durkheim 1933), in nature, and thus exists prior to any forms of institutional mediation, such as those of the state. Indeed, for Durkheim (1933), the State, at least in its pre-modern forms, emerges *from* the collective conscience in order to secure and protect the shared sentiments on which it is based. Again, there are strong resonances here with the neoliberal idea that the State's role is to facilitate and bolster community (Rose 1999), and to enforce conformity with community norms and expectations (Dean 2002).

Our point here is not that Durkheim was some kind of proto-neoliberal, nor is it that neoliberalism is essentially Durkheimian. Rather, it is that neoliberal efforts to reassemble the social have multiple cultural and theoretical resonances – some of them unexpected – and that accounting for this is necessary if we are to understand how the mobilisation and valorisation of charity works as a translational strategy. Additionally, it allows us to use insights regarding the cultivation of pre-modern/*gemeinschaft* forms of solidarity to help us understand how the translational functions of charity beyond the narrow view of it as neoliberalism's crutch discussed above. Specifically, we have found it productive to think about how charity is mobilised to produce something like a collective conscience for the neoliberal age.

Durkheim argued that the collective conscience is reinforced through ritualised social practices, particularly the punishment of crime. Crime, for Durkheim, is nothing more than actions that offend the moral sentiments that a given group of people hold in common, and which bind them in solidary relations. Punishment functions to restore and reinforce these offended sentiments, and thus the solidary relations they sustain. This is accomplished not only by deterring future breaches but also by signalling to members of the group their continued collective investment in these sentiments and, in turn, in their bond to one another. Punishment is thus about much more than instrumental concerns like deterrence; it is a means of securing the collective conscience and solidarity that flows from it.

The valorisation of charity can be seen as performing a similar function for neoliberal efforts to reassemble the social. Political and popular representations of charitable acts, as we demonstrate in subsequent chapters, reinforce an (ostensibly) shared belief in the value of spontaneous and unmediated compassion – key values and motivations underpinning the responsible practice of ethical citizenship (Rose 2000). Like Durkheim's example of punishment, the (intended) social function of charity thus exceeds its immediate instrumental purpose – relieving the suffering of the poor – to cultivate and reinforce social solidarity through the theatrical staging of shared moral sentiments. This perspective helps explain why charity, again like punishment, persists regardless of its ineffectiveness in achieving its ostensible aim: addressing poverty. It also helps us understand the kinds of social relations produced by charity as a response to poverty. In the next section, we discuss these relations.

Theorising the consequences of neoliberalised solidarity

Beyond nuancing theories of neoliberalism and the relationship of charity to it, understanding how charity is mobilised to reassemble the social matters for identifying and responding to its consequences. If the function of charity exceeds its ostensive purpose of addressing poverty, what does this mean for relations between the charitable and charity recipients? We suggest it means that, like the criminal who is punished to reinforce the collective conscience, the recipient of charity is positioned as a *resource* for the production of neoliberal solidarity and ethical citizenship. That is, the poor are taken as a necessary object for ethical citizens to practice compassionate care, and for governments to cultivate spontaneous and dynamic moral community. This is not to say that there is an explicit desire for the poor to remain poor (although neither can we rule this out). Rather the relations of charity are configured to enable the enactment of ethical virtues and to cultivate ethical solidarity, more so than to understand the true needs of the poor or to address the causes of poverty.

The consequences of this model are numerous. First, there is a risk that it places the poor outside of the relations of solidarity forged through charity. As noted in the previous chapter and demonstrated more fully in Chapter 8, the relationship between the charitable and the poor is one in which the latter lack the capacity to practice reciprocity. In the charity encounter, the charitable exchange their time and resources for what we call ethical capital: symbolic recognition of their performance of the virtues of ethical citizenship. Whilst the poor receive (often meagre) material and emotional support, and sometimes companionship and moral support, they are denied the opportunity to reciprocate the act of giving and thus to accrue the ethical capital that comes with it. Insofar as neoliberalised citizenship and solidarity is premised on the performance of ethical acts of spontaneous compassion and care, those without ethical capital are at risk of being seen as less than full citizens.

Second, the mobilisation of charity for the production of ethical citizenship and solidarity can also contribute to the depoliticisation of poverty. Poverty is taken for granted in the (neo)liberal conceptions of civil society as something which motivates charitable giving and makes possible solidarity built on shared sentiments of pity and compassion. The focus of charity is thus on responding to the immediate manifestations of poverty, and on the value of these responses for the broader community. This focus diverts attention from the actual needs of people experiencing poverty, as well as from the structural processes that produce those needs. At the same time, and somewhat paradoxically, there is an increased focus on the *experience* of poverty, as pathos-laden images and accounts of the lives of the poor both motivate acts of ethical citizenship and contribute to the symbolic power of those acts as addressing an urgent need (Muehlebach 2012).

These depoliticising tendencies contribute to what we call, following Fraser (2013), the *misrecognition* of people experiencing poverty. Rather than recognising the poor as full and complex subjects with the agency to define and articulate their own needs, they are constituted as objects of pity, and thus as passive and one-dimensional subjects who are a mere symbolic and material resource for others' reassembling projects. There is thus a limiting of properly *political* relations with people experiencing poverty; relations wherein they are afforded the capacity to define their own needs and interests, and to enrol others – namely the charitable and the State – in the pursuit of these. Put differently, misrecognition precludes what we might call the *democratisation of translation*, where the poor are included as co-participants in reassembling the social.

In addition to the depoliticisation of poverty, the harnessing of charity to the neoliberal project contributes to the depoliticisation of civil society itself. Whilst civil society is often imagined as a space for rational deliberation on collective political concerns (Habermas 1989), the focus on charity as a source of ethically-charged responses to problems like poverty positions civil society more in terms of apolitical and pragmatic solutions than as a one of the political debate and the critical questioning of the *status quo*. Moreover, the forms of community that charity is believed to enact are valued by neoliberalism precisely because they are pre-political and pure (Rose 1999). Indeed, community is celebrated as an *alternative* to politics, as it is imagined to be comprised of ordinary people who are both *above* the venal self-interest and grubby power plays of institutional politics, and *below* the artificial and abstract calculations of welfare bureaucracies that are out of touch with the realities of everyday life (Clarke 2010).

What is lost (or at least limited) through these processes of depoliticisation and exclusion is the potential for charity to act as a conduit or champion for the interests of people experiencing poverty, and as a means for enabling structural change. As elaborated in Chapter 9, we argue for the transformation of charity such that it centres on the needs of the recipient, rather than those of the charitable giver and the neoliberalising forms of community that they are taken to represent. Such a transformation aims at making the democratisation of translation a reality, thus enabling people experiencing poverty, and the charitable individuals who volunteer alongside them, to contribute to defining and reassembling the social on the basis of their needs and perspectives. Given the relationality of charity, this project will necessary entail transforming the systems of poverty governance in which charity is implicated, particularly the operations of the welfare state. It also entails the production of forms of citizenship and solidarity that are inclusive of people experiencing poverty, and which enable them to engage in relations of reciprocity and connectedness across existing social divides.

We now turn in the following three chapters to our analysis of the translation strategies used by the State to enrol charity in the production of the neoliberal social, and how they are supported in this process by the media, using our Australian data as a case study. We begin in the next chapter by showing how the State creates a need for charity by limiting and restricting access to social protections by people experiencing poverty. We then turn to the strategies used by the State to cultivate charitable responses to poverty, and how the neoliberalising discourses promoted by the state are amplified by the media.

References

Brady, M 2016, ‘Neoliberalism, governmental assemblages, and the ethnographic imaginary’, in M Brady & R Lippert (eds.), *Governing Practices: Neoliberalism, Governmentality and the Ethnographic Imaginary*, University of Toronto Press, Toronto, pp. 3–31.

Clarke, J 2010, ‘Enrolling ordinary people: Governmental strategies and the avoidance of politics?’, *Citizenship Studies*, vol. 14, no. 6, pp. 637–650.

Clarke, J & Newman, J 1997, *The Managerial State: Power, Politics and Ideology in the Remaking of Social Welfare*, Sage, Thousand Oaks.

Cloke, P, May, J & Williams, A 2017, 'The geographies of food banks in the meantime', *Progress in Human Geography*, vol. 41, no. 6, pp. 703–726.

Collier, S 2011, *Post-Soviet Social: Neoliberalism, Social Modernity, Biopolitics*, Princeton University Press, Princeton.

Dean, J 2020, *The Good Glow: Charity and the Symbolic Power of Doing Good*, Policy Press, Bristol.

Dean, M 2002, 'Liberal government and authoritarianism', *Economy and Society*, vol. 31, no. 1, pp. 37–61.

DeVerteuil, G, Power, A & Trudeau, D 2019, 'The relational geographies of the voluntary sector: Disentangling the ballast of strangers', *Progress in Human Geography*, vol. 44, no. 5, pp. 919–937.

Dowling, E & Harvie, D 2014, 'Harnessing the social: State, crisis and (big) society', *Sociology*, vol. 48, no. 5, pp. 869–886.

Durkheim, E 1933, *The Division of Labor in Society*, Translated by G Simpson, The Free Press of Glencoe, Glencoe.

Engels, F 2010, *The Origin of the Family, Private Property and the State*, Penguin, London.

Flew, T 2014, 'Six theories of neoliberalism', *Thesis Eleven*, vol. 122, no. 1, pp. 49–71.

Foucault, M 1995, *Discipline and Punish: The Birth of the Prison*, 2nd edn, Vintage, New York.

Foucault, M 2008, *The Birth of Biopolitics: Lectures at the Collège de France, 1978–79*, Palgrave Macmillan, London.

Fraser, N 2013, *The Fortunes of Feminism: From State-Managed Capitalism to Neoliberal Crisis*, Verso, London.

Gordon, C 1991, 'Governmental rationality: An introduction', in G Burchell, C, Gordon, & P Miller (eds.), *The Foucault Effect: Studies in Governmentality*, University of Chicago Press, Chicago, pp. 1–52.

Habermas, J 1989, *The Structural Transformation of the Public Sphere: An Inquiry Into a Category of Bourgeois Society*, MIT Press, Cambridge.

Hackworth, J 2012, *Faith Based: Religious Neoliberalism and the Politics of Welfare in the United States*, University of Georgia Press, Athens.

Harvey, D 2007, *A Brief History of Neoliberalism*, Oxford University Press, Oxford.

Johnson, P 1996, 'Risk, redistribution and social welfare in Britain from the poor law to Beveridge', in M Daunton (ed.), *Charity, Self-Interest and Welfare in the English Past*, Routledge, Abingdon, pp. 225–248.

Katz, M 1986, *In the Shadow of the Poorhouse: A Social History of Welfare in America*, Basic Books, New York.

Larner, W 2000, 'Neo-liberalism: Policy, ideology, governmentality', *Studies in Political Economy*, vol. 63, no. 1, pp. 5–25.

Latour, B 1986, 'The powers of association', in J Law (ed.), *Power, Action and Belief*, Routledge & Kegan Paul, London, pp. 264–280.

Latour, B 1987, *Science in Action: How to Follow Scientists and Engineers through Society*, Harvard University Press, Cambridge.

Latour, B 2005, *Reassembling the Social: An Introduction to Actor-Network-Theory*, Oxford University Press, Oxford.

Levitas, R 2012, 'The just's umbrella: Austerity and the Big Society in Coalition policy and beyond', *Critical Social Policy*, vol. 32, no. 3, pp. 320–342.

Macmillan, R & Townsend, A 2006, 'A 'new institutional fix'? The 'community turn' and the changing role of the voluntary sector', in C Milligan & D Conradson (eds.), *Landscapes of Voluntarism: New Spaces of Health, Welfare and Governance*, Bristol University Press, Bristol, pp. 15–32.

Marshall, T 1950, *Citizenship and Social Class*, Cambridge University Press, Cambridge.

McGimpsey, I 2017, 'Late neoliberalism: Delineating a policy regime', *Critical Social Policy*, vol. 37, no. 1, pp. 64–84.

Miller, P & Rose, N 2008, *Governing the Present: Administering Economic, Social and Personal Life*, Polity, Cambridge.

Milligan, C & Conradson, D 2006, 'Contemporary landscapes of welfare: The 'voluntary turn'?', in C Milligan & D Conradson (eds.), *Landscapes of Voluntarism: New Spaces of Health, Welfare and Governance*, Policy Press, Bristol, pp. 1–14.

Muehlebach, A 2012, *The Moral Neoliberal: Welfare and Citizenship in Italy*, University of Chicago Press, Chicago.

Newman, J & Clarke, J 2009, *Publics, Politics and Power: Remaking the Public in Public Services*, Sage, London.

Oakley, A 1974, *Woman's Work: The Housewife, Past and Present*, Vintage Books, New York.

Peck, J & Tickell, A 2002, 'Neoliberalizing space', *Antipode*, vol. 34, no. 3, pp. 380–404.

Rose, N 1999, *Powers of Freedom: Reframing Political Thought*, Cambridge University Press, Cambridge.

Rose, N 2000, 'Community, citizenship, and the third way', *American Behavioral Scientist*, vol. 43, no. 9, pp. 1395–1411.

Theodore, N, Peck, J & Brenner, N 2011, 'Neoliberal urbanism: Cities and the rule of markets', in G Bridge & S Watson (eds.), *The New Blackwell Companion to the City*, Blackwell Publishing Ltd., Hoboken, pp. 15–25.

Tönnies, F 1957, *Community and Society. [Gemeinschaft und Gesellschaft]*, Michigan State University Press, East Lansing.

Wolch, J 1989, 'The shadow state: Transformations in the voluntary sector', in J Wolch & M Dear (eds.), *The Power of Geography: How Territory Shapes Social Life*, Routledge, Abingdon, pp. 197–221.

Wolch, J 1990, *The Shadow State: Government and Voluntary Sector in Transition*, Foundation Center, New York.

4 Creating conditions for charity

Introduction

The role of charity in responding to poverty in modern societies is inextricably linked to the structure, policies, and operations of the welfare state. We can therefore only understand, and subsequently change, the practice of charity to people in poverty by first understanding the welfare system, and the normative ideals and conceptions of the social world that inform that system. It follows that, to conceptualise the practice of charity to the poor, we must scrutinise public welfare provision. This is the aim of this chapter.

Although the relationship between charity and the welfare state cannot be reduced to a simple zero-sum game (where more welfare state means less charity and vice versa), the withdrawal of direct State support for people experiencing material hardship is central to understanding charity's contemporary forms and functions. Taking Australia as a case study, we show here how poverty is driven by changes to welfare policy that limit or restrict access to public resources that many people rely upon to meet their basic needs. We argue that these changes contribute to the cultivation of charitable responses to poverty, and their enrolment in broader projects of social transformation.

As we demonstrated in Chapter 3, the mobilisation of charity is an important feature of efforts to reassemble the social in accordance with a neoliberal worldview that has come to prominence in recent decades. In this worldview, the State exists to cultivate and facilitate the self-governing spheres of civil society, community, and the market (Foucault 2008; Rose 1999). Generous State welfare provision is seen as contrary to this facilitative role, in that it is believed to stifle communities' self-governing capacities, and instead encourages dependency, laziness, and worklessness (Rose 1999). It is also seen as antithetical to the neoliberal goal of promoting new forms of ethical citizenship which emphasise the ethical duties, rather than social rights, that flow from social life (Muehlebach 2012; Rose 2000). As we show below, receipt of welfare is construed as a failure to fulfil the obligations of ethical citizenship, and thus thoroughly stigmatised.

Yet, while the problematisation and reorientation of the welfare state is central to the neoliberal project, it is not an end in itself, as is often supposed (cf.

Hackworth 2012; Levitas 2012). Rather, as we argued in Chapter 3, it is part of a broader struggle to create a society wherein the ethical commitments of, and affective bonds between, self-reliant citizens drive responses to social problems. Charitable responses to poverty have a strong resonance with this conception of the social, and they are therefore cultivated as an alternative to direct top-down intervention by the State. Given this, we contend that State withdrawal from direct welfare provision is central to what we are calling the *translation* (Latour 2005) of charity: attempts by government and other political actors to align the interests of the charitable with the objective of neoliberalising the social.

It is well documented that neoliberal discourse promotes State withdrawal on the basis that it creates spaces for community groups and charities to engage in poverty relief, by ensuring that State agencies do not crowd them out (Shapiro 2007; Wolch 1989). However, we argue that welfare reform also contributes to the translation of charity in a more direct and productive way. Namely, it creates the manifest poverty and social need that stimulates and motivates charitable giving. As explained in Chapters 1 and 2, charity is underpinned by feelings of compassion, sympathy, and a sense of moral obligation: it is people's affective response to the manifest suffering or unmet needs of others. We illustrate below that policies withdrawing or limiting access to State welfare support increase the levels of visible suffering in society, thus providing charitable responses to poverty with their *raison d'etre*.

This interpretation of the link between State withdrawal and rising charity is strengthened by research that shows that, contrary to the arguments put forward by proponents of neoliberalism, welfare reform does not stem from a lack of money or resources in the economy. Weeks (2020) has demonstrated that many policy decisions justified on the basis of economic necessities (e.g. cutting welfare spending to balance government budgets) are more appropriately understood as political decisions to pursue specific normative ends. Governments, especially those that control Central Banks, have significant capacity to fund generous welfare systems to ensure citizens avoid poverty. Thus, the existence of poverty is the product of deliberate policy decisions. This point is further reinforced by David Brady's (2019) demonstration that countries that choose to use social policy to advance the welfare state exhibit lower levels of poverty, and that the effects of behaviour as a cause of poverty are weakened by progressive social policy. Similarly, in the Australian context, Peter Saunders (2011) shows that Australian governments have the capacity to end poverty; yet, they do not do so because of a lack of commitment and failed policy responses.

Drawing on literature that proposes that poverty is a political and policy problem rather than an economic one, this chapter starts from the assumption that the need for charity amongst people who are poor is not a product of the State's inability to provide resources, such as adequate income and affordable housing. Rather, it is a deliberate strategy to directly foster the forms of ethical citizenship and affective solidarity that are at the heart of neoliberal conceptions of the social. The chapter proceeds by first demonstrating the role of welfare policy in generating and deepening poverty in Australia. We then discuss the discursive and ideological processes that underpin these changes. In doing so, we illustrate how they are underpinned by neoliberal critiques of State-induced welfare dependency and concerns about the stigmatisation of people on welfare as failing to live up to the obligations of ethical citizenship. The chapter concludes with a discussion of welfare responses to the COVID-19 pandemic, which we argue demonstrate the capacity of Australian Governments to address poverty when they want to.

Unemployment benefits below the poverty line

A key driver of the manifest poverty that motivates charitable giving in Australia is the low level of cash transfers provided by the State to unemployed citizens. In 2017–2018, a single person receiving Youth Allowance was entitled to AUD$289 per week, which is AUD$168 per week below the poverty line. Youth Allowance is paid to citizens between the ages of 16 and 21 who are unemployed; the rate of AUD$289 per week includes a government-funded Rent Assistance and Energy Supplement. Citizens aged between 22 and 65 who are unemployed receive AUD$340 per week, and this too includes the Rent Assistance and Energy Supplement. This unemployment benefit, formerly referred to as Newstart and now as Jobseeker, is AUD$117 per week below the poverty line (ACOSS 2020). Therefore, depending on their age, unemployed Australians without dependent children receive welfare that is 37 per cent (Youth Allowance) and 26 per cent (adult unemployment benefits) below the poverty line.

The Australian Council of Social Services (ACOSS) calculates the Australian poverty line at 50 per cent or below of the median income, after accounting for housing costs (ACOSS 2020). In 2017–2018, 13.1 per cent of the Australian population, or ~3.2 million people, were estimated to be living below the poverty line (ACOSS 2020). This is the same rate of relative poverty than 18 years before, in 2000, despite strong and sustained overall economic growth (ACOSS 2020). Yet, whilst the rate of poverty is relatively stable, the depth of poverty is steadily increasing. The gap between the poverty line and people's average income was 34.3 per cent (approx. AUD$165) in 1999, but had risen to 44.2 per cent (approx. AUD$280) by 2017 (ACOSS 2020, p. 29) (Figure 4.1).

The vast majority of those living below the poverty line rely on unemployment benefits as their main or sole source of income. The rate at which unemployment benefits are paid in Australia is well below what is required for people to meet their basic needs. The Australian 2010 unemployment benefit was so low that the OECD recommended:

> The [then] Newstart Allowance should be raised (subject to fiscal constraints and in line with community expectations that payments are affordable, sustainable and fair) to provide a more adequate level of income support.
>
> (OECD 2010, p. 131)

Despite recognition that unemployment benefits are paid at an inadequate level, adult unemployment benefits have been progressively lowered in the

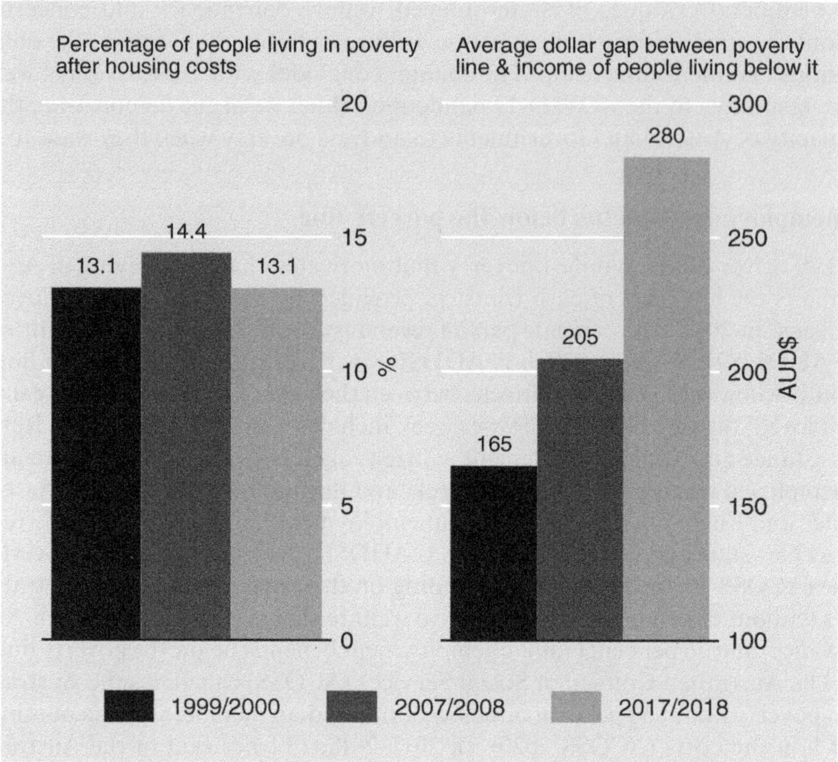

Figure 4.1 Trends in and depth of poverty within Australia, 1999–2017.

Notes: Adapted from ACOSS (2020). Data come from the ABS Survey of Income and Housing, 2017–18.

period following this OECD recommendation, at least up to 2017–2018, as can be seen from Figure 4.2. In 1994–1995, for example, the unemployment benefit for a single person was 3.5 percentage points below the poverty line. Some 20 years later, by 2015–2016, it sat at 19.3 percentage points below the poverty line.

The increasing depth of poverty experienced by people receiving unemployment benefits is the product of a policy decision to not index such benefits with wage growth and the cost of living. Since 1994, the unemployment payment has been benchmarked to the consumer price index. This meant that, although "the buying power of the median household disposable income has climbed 55%, the buying power of Newstart has barely budged" (Whiteford et al. 2018). In the 21 years between 1994–1995 and 2015–2016, a single person receiving the unemployment benefit in Australia went from receiving AUD$24 per week less than a low-earning household at the top of the bottom decile of the income distribution, to AUD$175 per week less (Whiteford et al.

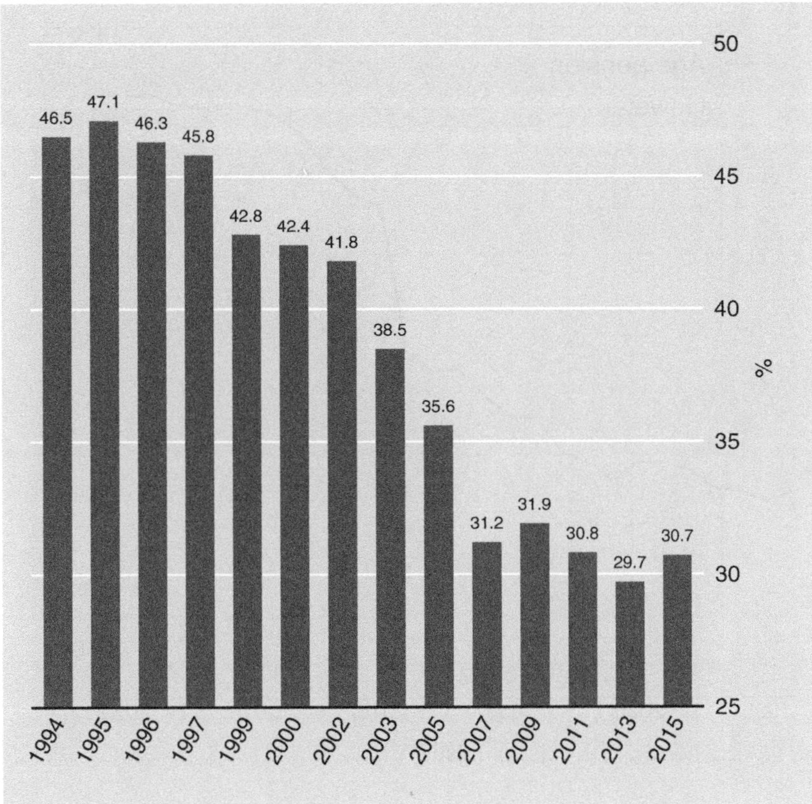

Figure 4.2 Single adult rate of unemployment benefit payments (Newstart), as a percentage of median equivalised household income.

Notes: Adapted from Whiteford et al. (2019). Benefit rates are for a single person without children. Unemployment benefit data obtained from the Australian Government (2021). Household income data obtained from the Australian Bureau of Statistics (2019).

2018). By benchmarking the level of unemployment benefit in line with the consumer price index, people who are unemployed do not benefit from the increasing incomes driven by society's economic growth (Saunders 2018).

We describe the stagnation of the unemployment payment as *deliberate policy* because the Australian Government has significant capacity to act otherwise. A clear example of this capacity is the Government's approach to structuring and revising the Aged Pension. Since 1997, the Australian Government benchmarked the Aged Pension to average weekly earnings. As Figure 4.3 shows, the differences in weekly income between Australians receiving the Aged Pension and Australians receiving the unemployment benefit (Newstart) in 2020 are stark (around AUD$150 per fortnight), whereas the two payments were almost identical in 1995.

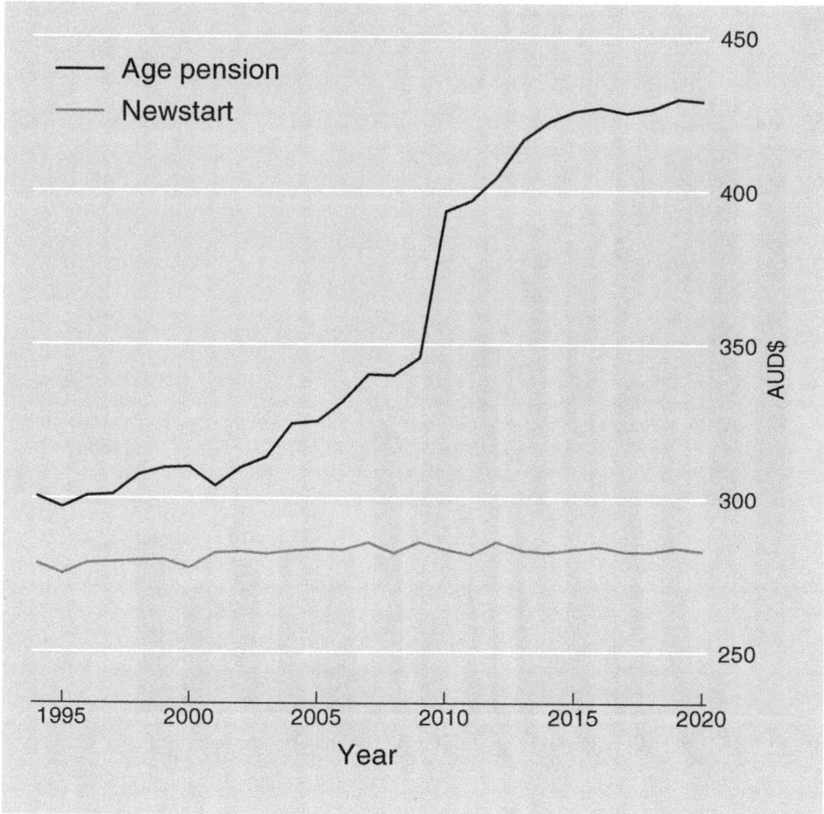

Figure 4.3 Single adult rates of Age Pension and unemployment benefits (Newstart), in 2020 dollars.

Notes: Data obtained from Australian Government (2021). All amounts are inflation-adjusted to 2020 prices based on the Consumer Price Index.

Australia's unemployment benefit compared with the OECD

How does Australia's unemployment benefit rate compare internationally? There are three immediate answers to this question. First, Australia's unemployment benefit level is far lower than that in most OECD nations. Second, comparing levels across countries with different taxation and welfare systems requires careful analysis. Third, when key nuances and differences across countries are accounted for, Australia's unemployment benefit is only slightly lower than the OECD average. In this section, we present data to develop these three points. We follow Peter Whiteford (2006) in comparing Australia with OECD nations on cash benefits to people who are unemployed. We therefore exclude other significant components of the welfare state such as healthcare, childcare, and education, as the available data make the comparisons difficult and inconsistent.

A common measure used to compare the generosity of unemployment benefits across OECD countries is the replacement rate. The replacement rate refers to the proportion of previous in-work income maintained after a certain period of unemployment. Figure 4.4 presents unemployment replacement rates across OECD countries after two months of unemployment, including both unemployment benefits and housing benefits. On this measure, Australia provides the *lowest* unemployment replacement rate in the OECD.

The two-month replacement rate is a commonly used measure, but the OECD provides data that enables cross-national comparisons of the replacement rate over longer time horizons. Although Australia's two-month replacement rate is the lowest in the OECD – or, as Whiteford et al. (2019) note, "stingy" – Australia's comparative generosity varies considerably over a longer period. After five years, Australia's replacement rate (including unemployment and housing benefits) is closer to, but still less than, the OECD average (Figure 4.5).

The significant change in Australia's relative performance depending on whether two-month or five-year replacement rates are analysed highlights the complexities inherent to undertaking cross-national comparisons in the

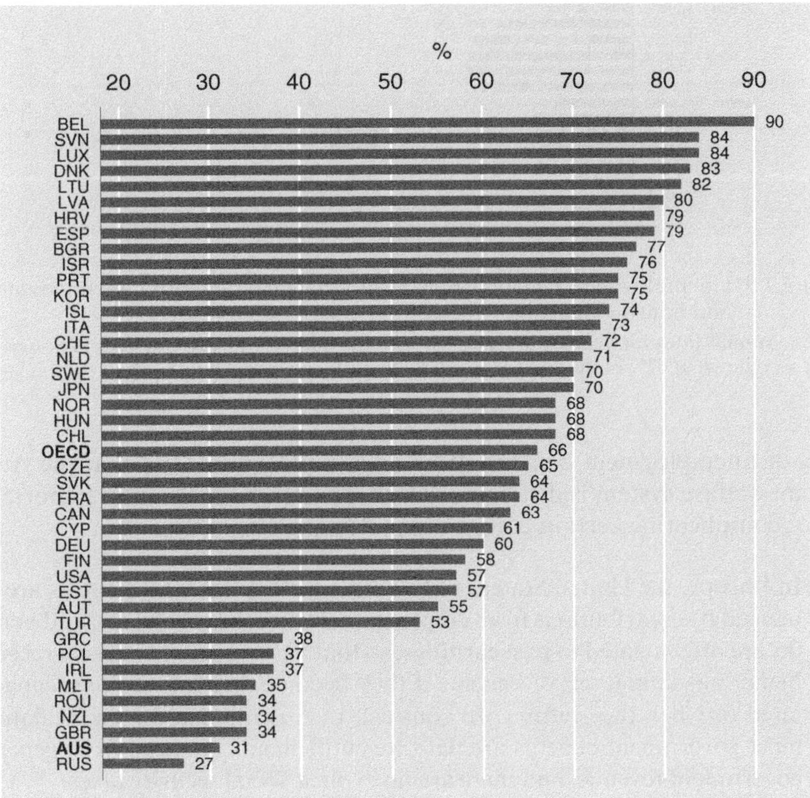

Figure 4.4 Unemployment benefits after two months, as a percentage of previous in-work income.

Notes: Annual rates for year 2019 or latest available over the 2016–2019 period.

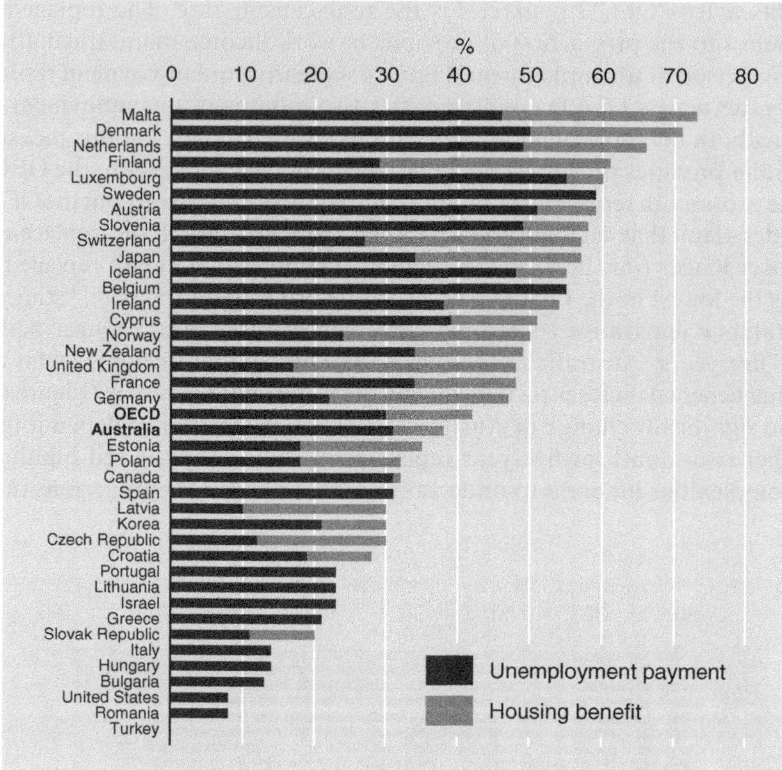

Figure 4.5 Unemployment benefits after 60 months, including both unemployment and housing benefits.

Notes: Annual rates for year 2019. Rates for a single person without children. Previous in-work income set at 67% of the average wage. Data obtained from OECD (2021).

level of unemployment benefits. Whiteford (2017) points out that the Australian welfare system is different from that in other countries in important ways, complicating certain comparisons. He explains:

> In Europe, the United States, and Japan, most government benefits are financed by contributions from employers and insured employees, and benefits are often related to past earnings, so that higher income workers receive higher absolute levels of benefits if they become unemployed or incapacitated or when they retire… In contrast, in Australia (and New Zealand), most government benefits are flat-rate entitlements financed from general government revenue, and there are no explicit social security taxes.
>
> (Whiteford 2017, p. 20)

In Australia, in contrast to many OECD countries, the unemployment subsidy has no relationship with past earnings. People are provided with a nationally set rate of unemployment benefit, and they receive the benefit for as long as they are eligible. Unlike in many OECD countries, there is no time limit for receiving unemployment benefits in Australia. As Australia's two-month and five-year replacement rate comparisons with OECD countries make clear, in some countries other than Australia the unemployment benefit is high for an initial short period, and then reduces progressively with time since job loss.

In addition, comparisons between the unemployment benefit in Australia and other OECD countries must take account of who receives the benefit. This comparison is significant because Australia's unemployment benefit is financed through general government revenue rather than an insurance scheme. As Whiteford (2017, p. 29) notes,

> Australia's reliance on income-testing [means] cash benefits are more targeted to the poorest 20% of the population than in any other OECD country, and correspondingly, the richest 20% of the population receive a lower share of benefits than in any other high-income country.

This is reflected starkly in Figure 4.6.

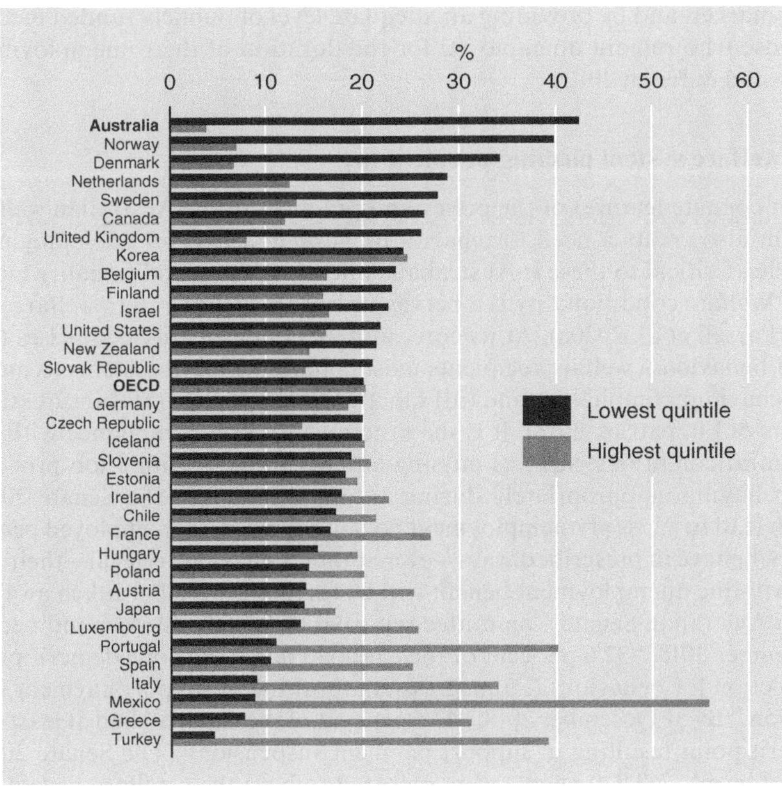

Figure 4.6 Share of social benefits going to the lowest income (bottom quintile) and highest income (top quintile) households.

Notes: Annual rates for year 2011. The lowest (highest) income quintile is defined as the 20% of the population with the lowest (highest) equivalised disposable income. Data obtained from OECD (2016).

Based on analyses of which citizens receive unemployment benefits, Klein (2014) argues that – despite appearing ungenerous – Australia provides cash benefits to those people who are actually poor. This is confirmed in Figure 4.6, which shows that Australia is the OECD country that provides the highest share of public social benefits to individuals in the lowest quintile of the income distribution (42.4 per cent), and the country that provides the smallest share to individuals in the highest quintile (3.8 per cent). This is in contrast to countries such as France, Italy, Austria, Portugal, and Spain, where more welfare spending is directed to the top fifth of the income distribution.

Altogether, this and the preceding section have shown that, although simple cross-country comparisons are problematic due to different tax, insurance, and entitlement conditions, Australia's welfare system creates the need for charity by compensating unemployed people with benefits that fall well below the poverty line. This is in contrast to many OECD countries where, although the amount provided reduces over time and citizens receive an amount based on their prior income, the initial unemployment benefit is above the poverty line. In Sweden, for example, the welfare state is designed to negate the need for charity by swiftly moving the unemployed into the labour market, and by providing an adequate level of publicly funded income to those who remain unemployed for the duration of their unemployment (Vamstad & Essen 2012).

The welfare system pushing people away

Other cognate features of the policy and practices of the Australian welfare system also create a need for charity by *pushing people off* unemployment benefits. Critical to these is Australia's suite of welfare conditionality measures. Welfare conditionality is a pervasive feature of Australia's welfare system (Parsell et al. 2020a). At its core, welfare conditionality comprises (i) a set of behaviours welfare recipients must comply with, (ii) systems to monitor behaviour compliance, and (iii) sanctions for behavioural transgressions (Watts & Fitzpatrick 2018). It is the sanctions for non-compliance with behavioural conditions, such as missing an appointment with a job provider or "behaving inappropriately during an appointment" (The Senate 2019), which lead to a loss of unemployment benefits. That is, if unemployed people do not behave in prescribed ways – even if their behaviour is legal – their sub poverty-line unemployment benefit will be further lowered or taken away.

An Australian Senate Committee reported that in the three months to 30 September 2018, "32.6 per cent of the caseload has a least one demerit point [a sanction for behavioural transgression] resulting in support payment suspension." By 31 December 2018, "42.5 per cent of the caseload had at least one demerit point resulting in support payment suspension" (The Senate 2019). In real terms, 763,920 people were reported to have their welfare benefit entitlements suspended between 1 June 2017 and 30 June 2018 (Department of Social Services 2018). A suspension of payment for people already living on an income that is 26 per cent below the poverty line not only creates a need for charity, but can also have devastating effects on their mental health, ability to sustain housing, and capacity to access employment (The Senate 2019).

Mounting evidence suggests that conditional welfare is not simply about creating opportunities for employment (Parsell et al. 2020a; Taylor et al. 2016), as the formal policy states (Australian Government 2019a), but rather an element of the welfare system that is designed to punish recipients and dissuade them from government support. For example, people are sanctioned – resulting in a loss of unemployment benefits – yet many of these sanctions are due to Commonwealth mistakes. In fact, it has been reported that 50 per cent of the sanctions imposed throughout 2015–2016 were government errors (The Senate 2019).

The impacts of welfare policy and the functioning of the welfare system are not distributed evenly across the population. Aboriginal and Torres Strait Islander people, and people who are homeless, are sanctioned at disproportionate rates (The Senate 2019). Indeed, a conditional welfare program designed explicitly for parents with dependent children – that sits alongside the conditional unemployment benefit for single people – stopped providing benefits to vulnerable parents because their poverty created barriers to compliance. For example, these parents had insufficient money for transport to attend appointments or to pay for internet data/telephone to meet government reporting requirements (Goldblatt 2019). There is further evidence to suggest that these breaches and ensuing loss of unemployment benefits are not entirely accidental, but consistent with a broader mandate to penalise and indeed push people off public welfare.

The Australian Government introduced what is popularly referred to as the Robodebt scheme in 2016 – so called due to its use of automated data-matching techniques to detect welfare overpayments – with the stated purpose of cutting red tape, more efficiently allowing recipients to meet their obligations, and preventing fraud (Morrison & Porter 2016). In practice, Robodebt was a scheme that forced welfare recipients to pay back to the Australian Government overpayments amounting to a total of AUD$721 million. The scheme, however, relied on incorrect methods to calculate debt levels, and many of the welfare debts – most of which were initially paid back – were not in fact overpayments. Moreover, the High Court of Australia ruled that the Robodebt system was illegal (Henriques-Gomes 2020). Documents submitted to court show that the Australian Government was warned 76 times by a tribunal that Robodebt was illegal; government officials were also reportedly advised that welfare recipients subject to the illegal scheme disclosed the risk of self-harm (Henriques-Gomes 2020). Despite advice about the scheme's illegality and harms, the Australian Government continued to use Robodebt to pursue welfare recipients to repay debts that in many cases did not exist. Terry Carney (2020) referred to Robodebt as an illegal and immoral injustice.

Robodebt is indicative of a broader Australian welfare system that goes to great lengths, even illegal and knowingly harmful practices, to coerce citizens who are unemployed to avoid drawing financial support from the State. By doing so, it creates the need for charity. This end is also achieved by a sustained campaign by the State to stigmatise welfare and institutionalise mechanisms within the system that make accessing welfare demeaning for recipients. Australia's infamous compulsory income management system is a primary example of institutionalised practices that stigmatise the recipient of unemployment benefits, on the one hand, and make drawing on welfare difficult to sustain, on the other hand. Through compulsory income management, some recipients of unemployment benefits have 20 per cent of their income in cash to use freely, with the remaining 80 per cent being restricted to government prescribed purchases (Australian Government 2019b).

The income management system is premised on the rationale that unemployed people do not, of their own volition, know what their best interests are, nor do they know how to pursue them (Parsell et al. 2020a). Compulsory income management is framed as a necessary measure to address the dysfunction and addiction that the government claims underpins unemployment (Bielefeld 2018). Although welfare conditionality has been a feature of Australia's welfare system since the end of WWII, its scope and severity has increased in recent years (Carney 2019). Phillip Mendes and colleagues argue that Australia's use of income management "took conditionality further than other countries" (Mendes et al. 2016, p. 393).

Compulsory income management, like the parenting program for vulnerable parents (Goldblatt 2019), is highly racialised (Bray 2016). When initiated in 2007, it was almost exclusively targeted towards Aboriginal and Torres Strait Islander people: the Australian Government suspended the *Racial Discrimination Act 1975*, so that Indigenous people could not access legal redress (Bielefeld 2018). Compulsory income management has been extended to broader areas of Australia, so that it is now less explicitly targeted at Aboriginal and Torres Strait Islander people. Research shows that compulsory income management is ineffective in achieving its intended objectives, such as reducing alcohol and tobacco consumption or increasing school attendance (Bray 2016). Instead, compulsory income management makes mobility for employment difficult (Marston et al. 2019), and the stigma and shame recipients experience constitute significant hidden harms (Mendes et al. 2020).

In addition to disincentivising welfare through a humiliating process that restricts what citizens can purchase, Australia's welfare system does what it can to make access to it unpleasant through mandatory drug testing. Since 2016, the Australian Government has tabled to parliament three pieces of legislation that sought to drug test welfare recipients (Lee 2019). In 2017 and 2018 respectively, the two proposals did not pass the Australian Senate (Lee 2019). However, despite serious objections raised by the Royal Australasian College of Physicians (2019), in 2019 the Senate passed the third piece of legislation, which led to a drug testing trial of welfare recipients in three Australian locations (Australian Government 2020a). If unemployment benefit recipients test positive to illicit substances, they are deemed to have an addiction, and will undergo 24 months of compulsory income management with 80 per cent of their unemployment benefit quarantined to certain purchases (Ruston 2019). These cognate measures sit within a broader field where public welfare is positioned as an affront to the Australian identity.

Underinvestment in social housing

Alongside the limiting of unemployment benefits to below-the-poverty-line levels, and the use of punitive and conditionality mechanisms to discourage people from accessing welfare, Australian social policy also contributes to poverty through restricting the supply of social and affordable housing. In Australia, "social housing" is an umbrella category that includes both public housing, which is owned and managed by government, and community housing, which is managed by community organisations who either own the housing stock or lease it from government. The Australian social housing system was established between 1945 and 1956 in what is commonly referred to as the golden age of public housing, which saw large-scale government investment and broad commitment and coordination across different levels of government to the sector (Heyward 1996). Whilst social housing in Australia never reached the levels it did in Europe, it did provide an affordable and secure housing option for low-income families and, from the 1980s onwards, people experiencing poverty and other interrelated vulnerabilities.

The 1980s and 1990s saw major shifts in Australian housing policy, including a diversion of funding from public housing towards private rental subsidies, the increased targeting of social housing to the most disadvantaged, and the ongoing transfer of public housing stock and tenancy management responsibilities to the community sector (Groenhart & Burke 2014). Declining government investment in particular has led to the supply of social housing shrinking relative to population growth (Figure 4.7). The research of Hal Pawson and colleagues has demonstrated that Australian Government spending on social housing has drastically declined since 1996/1997, falling by 24 per cent in that year alone (Pawson et al. 2020a). Since this time, government funding for social housing has declined a further 7 per cent, from $1.42 billion in 2011 to $1.32 billion in 2016 (Pawson et al. 2018). The number of social housing dwellings per 100 households has subsequently fallen from 6.2 in 1991 to 4.2 in 2018 (Pawson et al. 2018, 2020b).

These changes in the social housing sector have coincided with declining affordability in the private market, as house prices have soared and more and more people have turned to the increasingly competitive private rental market to meet their housing needs. Recent research by Pawson and colleagues shows that people falling in the bottom two quintiles of the income distribution (the standard definition of low income in Australia for the purpose of determining housing affordability) have seen their housing costs increase from 23 per cent of their income in 2011 to 29 per cent in 2018 (Pawson et al. 2020a). The proportion of people on low incomes experiencing rental stress (defined as paying more than 30 per cent of one's income in rent) has increased from 40 to 45 per cent over roughly the same period and is 48 per cent in capital cities. Housing unaffordability is a

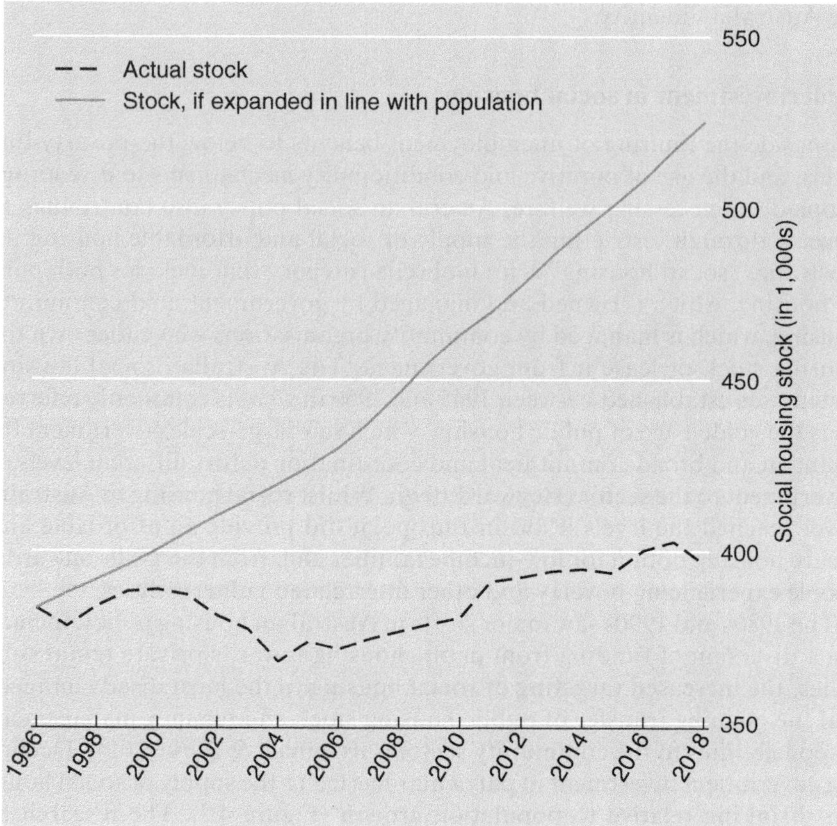

Figure 4.7 Social housing provision in Australia, relative to population.
Notes: Adapted from Pawson, Parsell, Lui, Hartley & Thompson (2020). Data obtained from the Productivity Commission Report on Government Services (various editions).

particularly pronounced issue for people receiving government income support. Using data from Anglicare's annual rental affordability snapshot, Pawson et al. (2020a) show that, in 2020, only 0.1 per cent of advertised rental properties are affordable for a single adult with a child relying on unemployment benefits, dropping from 0.2 per cent in 2016. A couple on the age pension – which is indexed to average wages and has therefore increased well above unemployment benefits – fair slightly better in this analysis, being able to afford 2.7 per cent of properties in 2020, down from 4.3 per cent in 2016.

In conjunction with these market conditions, the declining government investment in social housing in Australia has contributed to increasingly housing insecurity and homelessness. The rate of homelessness in Australia increased by 29.8 per cent between 2006 and 2016 (Pawson et al. 2018). The 2016 Australian Census estimated that 116,000 people were experiencing homelessness in Australia on census night (Australian Bureau of Statistics 2018). This includes around 8,200 people who were sleeping rough, or as the

Australian Bureau of Statistics defines them, people living in improvised dwellings, tents, or sleeping out. Many of these people are on the waitlist for social housing, which, as of June 2018, had ballooned to 140,600 people (Australian Institute of Health and Welfare 2019). The undersupply of social housing means that many homeless people remain on these waitlists for extended periods, sometimes indefinitely (Clarke & Parsell 2020), and many rely on charity to survive in the interim (Parsell 2018).

Homelessness is, in the words of the OECD (2020, p. 3), "the most extreme form of housing and social exclusion" experienced by people in the developed world. It is also one of the most visible manifestations of poverty, one that evocates a visceral response in the wider community (Gerrard & Farrugia 2015). It is thus unsurprising that homelessness is the target of a plethora of charitable initiatives, such as the Beddown and Orange Sky Laundry examples that are discussed elsewhere in this book. The production of a large and vulnerable homeless population through underinvestment in social and other forms of affordable housing is thus another way in which the State creates a need for charity, and stimulates people to provide it.

Problematising State welfare

We contend that the poverty-inducing welfare policies discussed so far in the chapter are best understood as part of a broader attempt to reconfigure the social along neoliberal lines. As explained in Chapter 3 and at the beginning of this chapter, neoliberalism views the State's role as being one of cultivating and facilitating the self-governing capacities of individuals and communities. It therefore problematises direct State welfare provision on the basis that it creates dependency, and thus undermines the very capacities that the State is meant to cultivate. This problematisation of welfare permeates Australian political debates regarding State welfare provision. This is nowhere more apparent than in the debate over whether the government should raise the rate of unemployment benefits.

To raise or to not raise

On recognition that the level of cash transfer forces people to live in poverty, there has been a long-term and widely supported campaign to increase the magnitude of the unemployment benefit (Raise the Rate 2019). The Raise the Rate campaign argues for a AUD$95 per week increase in unemployment benefit payments. Their advocacy is premised on moving people out of poverty, increasing opportunities to gain employment, and stimulating economic growth (Raise the Rate 2020).

The call to raise the rate has received support from various sectors of Australian society, including the charity sector. The St Vincent de Paul Society, for instance, advocates raising the rate of unemployment benefits, as the income provided does not enable people to pay for essentials of life. They describe "the *brutality* of struggling to survive" on unemployment benefits in Australia (St Vincent de Paul Society 2020). Support has also come from traditionally conservative actors, such as the Australian Business Council, who assert that raising the level of unemployment benefit will improve people's chances of finding work (Business Council of Australia 2019). Even some prominent conservative politicians have called for unemployment benefit payments to be raised. Former Deputy Prime Minister, Barnaby Joyce, broke ranks with his government colleagues to argue that raising the unemployment benefit was necessary to ensure that recipients are not so poor that they are "forced to sell drugs" to survive (Bolger 2019). Most surprisingly, the politician who oversaw the decision that the rate of benefit payments would not increase with the cost of living, former conservative Prime Minister John Howard, has also come out in support of raising the rate. In 2018, he stated that "I was in favour of freezing that [the rate of unemployment benefits] when it happened, but I think the freeze has probably gone on too long" (Bagshaw 2018).

Despite the broad support for the Raise the Rate Campaign, successive Australian Governments have rejected calls to increase unemployment benefit payments. The rationale given for these rejections has drawn heavily on neoliberal arguments about the dependency inducing impacts of welfare. A favourite response of current Prime Minister Scott Morrison to the campaign is to assert that "the best form of welfare is a job" (see, for example, Hansard 2019, p. 4892). Morrison began deploying this phrase during his time as the Minister for Social Services, including in a speech to the National Press Club titled "The best form of welfare" (Morrison 2015). In the speech, Morrison argued that the Australian welfare system should be oriented to preventing welfare dependency by assisting and encouraging people to find work. For Morrison, the core question regarding welfare payments is not whether or not they are adequate to meet people's basic needs, but rather, "is it helping people develop self-reliance and independency? Is it being leveraged to help people get into jobs or is it stifling opportunity and at worst creating an underclass of intergenerational welfare dependents?"

Subsequent Social Services Ministers have repeated Morrison's arguments. In 2017, Alan Tudge repeated the maxim that the best form of welfare is a job and claimed that welfare dependency was the biggest problem that Australia's welfare system faced.

> Too many people are led into lives of dependence and passivity, with insufficient incentive to make the most of their innate potential... While welfare, for a short period, can be a blessing for a capable person temporarily out of work, long-term welfare dependence can become a poison. Over time, welfare dependence sucks the life out of people and can diminish their capability.
>
> (Tudge quoted in Knaus 2017)

In 2019, the Minister for Social Services, Anne Ruston, rejected calls for unemployment benefits to be raised on the basis that the money would be used to feed people's substance addictions (a problematic assumption in and of itself), and thus perpetuate their dependence on State support (Henriques-Gomes 2019).

Other political leaders have used similar arguments to reject calls to raise unemployment benefits. Invoking the idea of "less eligibility" that emerged with the English Poor Laws (Pantazis 2016), former Prime Minister Malcolm Turnbull trod a path well worn by conservatives in arguing that a low unemployment benefit was necessary to incentivise people "to get a job or to stay in the workforce" (Bagshaw 2018). The assumption here is, of course, that welfare payments that enable people to meet basic needs would create dependency upon public assistance, as people would have no incentive to find employment.

Rejecting calls to increase social housing

A similar dynamic can be observed in the struggles over the supply of social housing in Australia. A partnership of homelessness and housing organisations launched the Everybody's Home Campaign in 2018. The campaign calls on the Federal Government to "develop a National Housing Strategy to meet Australia's identified shortfall of 500,000 social and affordable rental homes" (Everybody's Home 2018). A key plank of the Housing Strategy sketched out by the campaign is "new capital investment to generate 300,000 new social and Aboriginal housing properties." The demands of the campaign are echoed by housing academics (e.g. Lawson et al. 2018; Pawson et al. 2020a) and large charity organisations (e.g. Anglicare 2019, 2020), who argue that large-scale investment in social housing is required to arrest rising rates of homelessness and rental stress in Australia.

As with the Raise the Rate campaign, the Everybody's Home campaign has for the most part fallen on deaf ears amongst those in Government. The Federal Government has attempted to sidestep the issue by claiming that social housing is a State/Territory responsibility, despite the core role played by the Federal Government in the establishment and coordination of the social housing system (Hayward 1996) and recent historical examples of large-scale Federal investment during the Global Financial Crisis (Parsell & Jones 2014). Some Government Members of Parliament have taken the campaign head on, arguing that social housing is a failed policy approach that perpetuates rather than alleviates poverty. For instance, in an opinion piece on housing affordability, Member of Parliament Jason Falinksi stated that,

> What Australians need is root and branch reform, not more of the same lavish social housing projects. This is a trigger warning for those who think the answer to any problem is more government: the answer lies not in more government help but less. At some point we must accept that the orthodox solutions are making the problem worse.
>
> (Falinksi 2020)

Falinksi's description of social housing projects as lavish and his rejection of more government intervention as a solution to housing unaffordability reflect longstanding neoliberal critiques of social housing as producing welfare dependency (Clarke et al. 2020; Jacobs et al. 2010). The low rents and tenure security offered by social housing is portrayed as a kind of luxury that discourages people from securing their needs independently in private housing markets. It is this dominant framing of social housing as a problem, consistent with the depiction of unemployment benefits, that helps understand Australia's sustained disinvestment in social housing, on the one hand, and an increasing homeless population requiring charitable care, on the other.

Welfare dependency and (un)ethical citizenship

As we stated in Chapter 3, a key feature of neoliberal efforts to reassemble the social is the promotion of new forms of citizenship that foreground people's ethical attachments and obligations to their communities over their rights to social protection (Muehlebach 2012; Rose 2000). In Australia, as in many other liberal democratic nations, these obligations include taking responsibility for the wellbeing of oneself, one's family, and one's community. This includes not letting oneself become a burden on others, and instead making sure that one makes a contribution to the meeting of community needs. Welfare dependency is thus construed as a failure of citizens to fulfil the obligations of ethical citizenship, leading to widespread denigration and stigmatisation of the unemployed, and justifying the kinds of paternalistic and poverty-generating policies outlined earlier in the chapter.

Australians have long been told by their political leaders that working, rather than sitting by and benefiting from others' work, is core to the Australian identity. Australia's longest serving Prime Minister (1939–1941 and 1949–1966) and founder of the Liberal Party, Sir Robert Menzies, famously proclaimed that being a "lifter," not a "leaner," was an act of nobility (Menzies 1942). Menzies said that "leaners grow flabby; lifters grow muscles." Working was the path of becoming responsible and free citizens, whereas a person who relies on others, who receives welfare, "ceases to be a human being and becomes a cipher" (Menzies 1942).

Menzies' conception of the dependent unemployed as outside the norms of Australian citizenship has been resurrected in recently times by proponents of neoliberal welfare state reform. When justifying the Federal Budget in 2014 that included a proposal to force people applying for unemployment benefits to wait six months for government assistance, the Australian Treasurer Joe Hockey said that, "we are a nation of lifters, not leaners" (Hockey 2014). In a statement that perfectly encapsulates the shift from social to ethical citizenship, Hockey went on to proclaim that the welfare reforms proposed by his government were intended to signify that "the age of entitlement is over;" the leaners needed to become lifters: "it is time for everyone to contribute now" (Hockey 2014). Acceptance of the poor as full citizens is thus rendered conditional upon their fulfilment of certain ethical obligations – in this case, self-sufficiency – and those that fail to do so are assigned a stigmatised social position.

Of course, this positioning of the unemployed receiving welfare as a stigmatised *other* is not uniquely Australian. In the United Kingdom, Elaine Chase and Robert Walker (2013) show how people living in poverty and accessing public welfare experience visceral shame because of the stereotypes society ascribes to them. Even prior to the current United Kingdom austerity policies, welfare recipients had long been constructed as shirkers or scroungers (Romano 2015). In the United States, Kathy Edin and Luke Shaefer (2015) remark that, as long as welfare is seen as outside of employment and thus outside of deeply held American values, recipients will always hold a stigmatised position. They advocate for welfare reforms that normalise public support for unemployment benefits by embedding it within employment and tax credits.

In Australia, the stigmatisation that comes with failing to live up to the obligations of ethical citizenship is encapsulated by the derogatory reference to the unemployed as "dole bludgers," which became part of popular language in the 1970s, at the dawn of the neoliberal era. Verity Archer (2009, p. 177) contends that the term "dole bludger" deliberately constructs the "welfare recipients as parasites upon ordinary Australian taxpayers." As Social Services Minister, Scott Morrison (2015) explained, "every single benefit paid is *paid* by a taxpayer." Emphasising this point, he said that there are two parties: "the people we're trying to help and the people who *have* to pay for it." Similarly, Hockey (2014) stated that "we must always remember that when one person receives an entitlement from the government it comes out of the pocket of another Australian." People receiving welfare are thus positioned as placing an unfair burden on those citizens who meet their ethical obligations to contribute to society and provide resources that help others in their communities.

The rhetoric surrounding welfare retrenchment in Australia thus makes a clear distinction between ethical citizens who fulfil their moral obligation to look after themselves and others, and unethical citizens – dole bludgers – who are not only lazy, but also exploitative (Archer 2009). From this positioning, we can see why governments, both right-of-centre and left-of-centre, refuse to increase unemployment benefits. Moreover, it also provides insight into public attitudes towards welfare in Australia. Although we noted above that the Raise the Rate campaign enjoys support amongst a wide variety of influential stakeholders, the reality is that most Australians do not support governments increasing the level of unemployment subsidy. Figure 4.8 shows that only 16 per cent of Australians believed that the government should spend more on unemployment benefits, a far smaller proportion than most of OECD countries (for which the mean was 42 per cent).

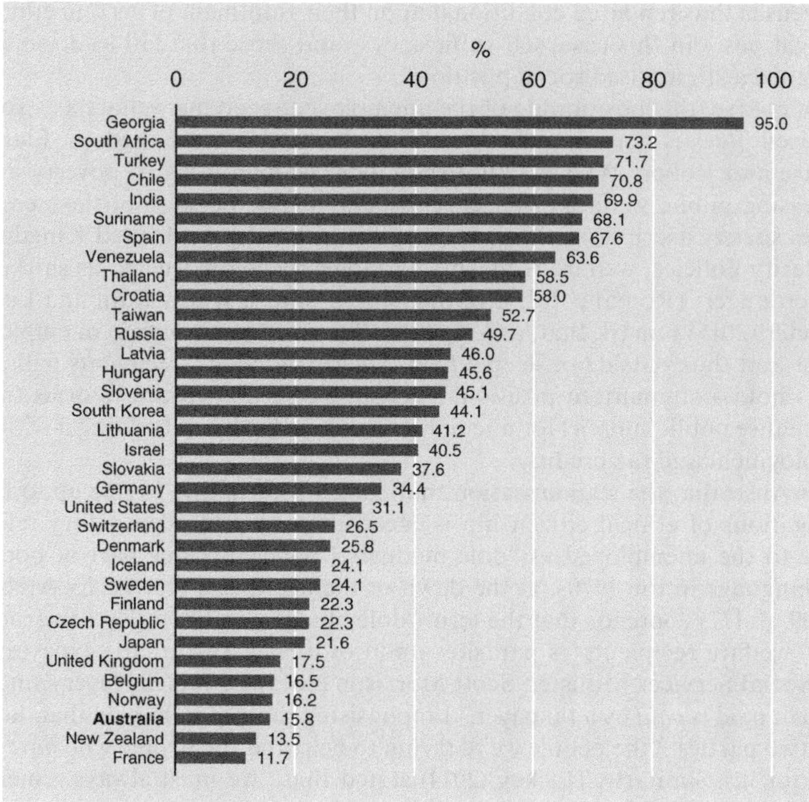

Figure 4.8 Percentage of the population who believe that government should spend more in unemployment benefits.

Notes: Authors' calculations based on data from the International Social Survey Programme (2015–2018). Respondents were asked the following statement: *Listed below are various areas of government spending. Please show whether you would like to see more or less government spending in each area … Unemployment benefits.* Agreement was inferred from the response options Spend much more and Spend more, whereas disagreement was inferred from the response answers Spend the same as now, Spend less and Spend much less.

Alternatives to poverty-inducing welfare policy

We have argued that poverty in Australia is the product of deliberate policy decisions. We demonstrated this proposition by illustrating the meagre level of unemployment benefit, underinvestment in social housing, and features of the welfare system that stigmatise and push people off welfare. In addition, through the example of the government's progressive increase of the Aged Pension payment, we argued that the government showed that it can act differently to provide people outside of the labour market a living income. It is within the Australian Government's means to provide people who are unemployed with a benefit that enables them to live above the poverty line, as it is to provide adequate levels of social housing to address housing insecurity and homelessness. We proposed that the below-the-poverty-line unemployment benefits, together with underfunding of social housing, create both poverty and people's need for charitable care.

When we began writing this book, our assertion that the Australian Government could provide people experiencing poverty with a level of benefit that enabled them to live decently was only theoretical. To further support our proposition, we had planned to cite economic data that shows the immense wealth held by average Australians: "Australia's wealth per adult is fourth highest in the world in US dollars… [I]n terms of median wealth, it [Australia] ranks second after Switzerland" (Credit Suisse 2019, p. 59). We had similarly intended to support our proposition by citing the Australian Government boasting that the country holds a record among all developed nations for the longest uninterrupted period of recession-free growth, 28 years between 1991 and 2019 (Australian Trade and Investment Commission 2019). There are thus macro-economic indicators to show precisely what Weeks (2020) proposed: that governments can afford to pay a living wage and their decision not to do so is political rather than economic.

As 2020 unfolded, it became apparent that we did not need to rely on theoretical arguments to substantiate our proposition. The human, social, and economic devastation that COVID-19 has caused (or, indeed, is causing) provided us with a real-life counterfactual to illustrate precisely what we had theorised. We no longer need to speculate. COVID-19 provides a natural experiment to test whether people in Australia experience poverty by design.

In the stroke of a metaphorical pen, the Australian Government effectively doubled the level of welfare benefit that unemployed people received during COVID-19 by providing a Coronavirus Supplement. People did not even need to apply for this; the additional fortnightly money was automatically transferred to eligible recipients, and the administering State authority fast-tracked assessment and processing (Whiteford & Bradbury 2020). Between April and the end of September 2020, people who were unemployed received a government unemployment benefit of approximately AUD$1,115 per fortnight, well above the poverty line of AUD$816 per fortnight (Phillips et al. 2020).

This impact has been significant. Ben Phillips and collaborators (2020) found that, for the section of the population most reliant on the unemployment benefit prior to the doubling of the unemployment benefit during COVID-19, the rate of poverty fell from 67 per cent to a mere 6.8 per cent. Further, their modelling shows that "the rate of single-parent poverty has fallen dramatically, too, from 20.2 to 7.6 per cent and could have been as high as 27.9 per cent in the absence of policy change" (Phillips et al. 2020, p. 24). Figure 4.9 presents the level of unemployment benefit vis-à-vis the poverty line.

In what is almost tautological, when people who are unemployed are provided with an unemployment benefit that is above the poverty line, they no longer experience poverty. Figure 4.9 makes it clear that the level of welfare provision, whether it is above or below the poverty line, determines the existence and extent of poverty.

The Australian Government providing a Coronavirus Supplement that effectively doubled the unemployment benefit and demonstrably reduced the number of citizens who lived in poverty is incongruent with the historical narrative outlined in this chapter. The Australian Government's engagement

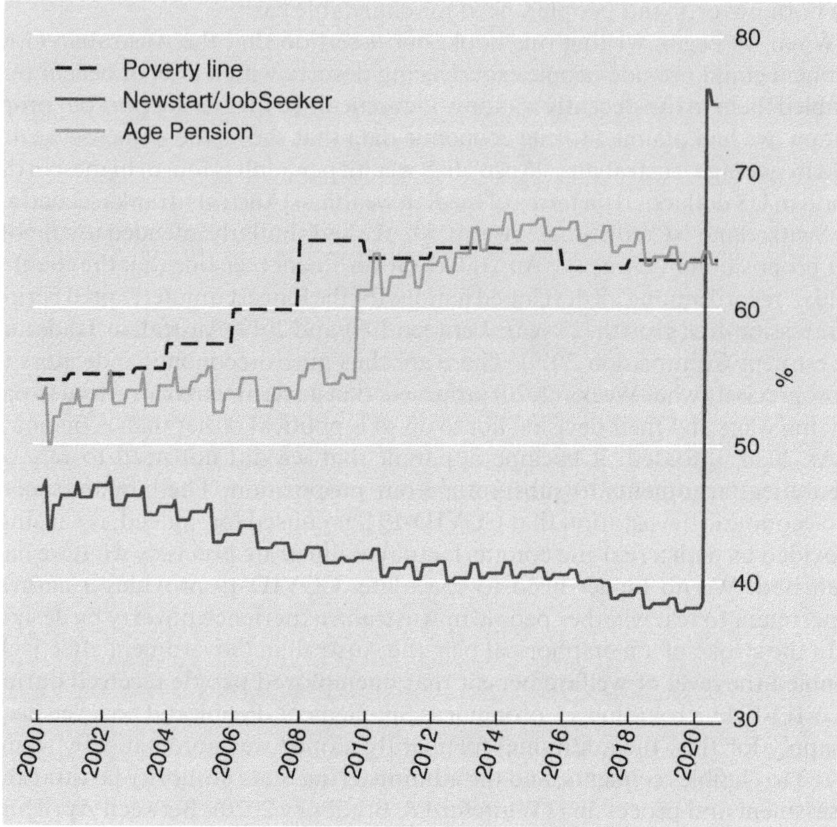

Figure 4.9 Unemployment benefits (Newstart/Jobseeker) and Age Pension rates as a percentage of the minimum wage.

Notes: Adapted from Bradbury and Whiteford (2020), who kindly provided the underlying data. Unemployment payments and Age Pension rates are for a single adult. Unemployment payments and Age Pension rates are relative to net income from a full-time minimum wage (deducting tax and Medicare levy, and adding employer superannuation contributions). The poverty line is calculated at half of median equivalised household income for individuals in paid employment (excluding the self-employed).

with people who are unemployed during the pandemic is part of "some of the most significant changes to social security payments Australia has ever seen, even if only on a temporary basis" (Whiteford & Bradbury 2020). Less than four months prior to the pandemic, Prime Minister Scott Morrison ridiculed the proposal to increase Newstart, telling parliament that his government would not engage in "unfunded empathy" (Hansard 2019). Similar radical and beneficial changes happened with homelessness policy during the pandemic, including coordinated efforts by the State and community sector to accommodate people sleeping rough in empty hotels and student accommodation facilities (Parsell et al. 2020b). These efforts were accompanied by promises that those temporarily accommodated would be transitioned into permanent housing, and not returned to the street.

Why, during April and September 2020, did the Prime Minister, with full support of the Australian Government, double the unemployment benefit, when the government had consistently justified not increasing the income to unemployed people because… "the best form of welfare is a job?" Why did we decide we could now fund our empathy? The Australian Government has not yet provided a detailed and clear explanation for why it so drastically increased the income of unemployed people. The increased unemployment benefit was part of a suite of government cash transfers, for example to support industry to keep their staff. The Australian Government simply explained that increasing the unemployment benefit was "decisively in the national interest to support households," or to "set the foundation for a strong economic recovery" (Australian Government 2020b). There is scant mention of the unemployed people themselves. In fact, the only time they are mentioned is when it was announced that the increased unemployment benefit would be reduced and removed so, as Prime Minister Morrison said, the above-the-poverty-line unemployment benefit was not "an impediment to people going out and doing work" (Bradbury & Whiteford 2020).

Concluding remarks

The Australian Government's response to people who were unemployed during the first five months post-COVID-19 offers insights that can help us understand how the State creates the need for charity. As proposed in the introduction to this chapter, people experience poverty by design. In wealthy countries such as Australia, governments can end poverty on a mass scale through changed policy. Australia reduced poverty overnight by increasing cash transfers to people out of work.

Government measures to increase the unemployment benefit relied upon a vastly different problematisation of unemployment than they did pre-pandemic. For many years prior to COVID-19, the unemployed who experienced poverty were cast as unethical, irresponsible dole bludgers. They were constructed as a group of people leaching from ordinary Australian workers. From this position, on the one hand, they are provided an inadequate income, and on the other hand, responded to with a welfare system that is designed to disincentivise them from using it. Public policy does not respond to objective social facts. Rather, policy is predicated on a specific problematisation (Bacchi 1999). Successive governments have refused to pay people an unemployment benefit on which they can survive on the basis that they should simply get a job – "the best form of welfare."

For a brief time in 2020 during the COVID-19 pandemic, however, people without jobs were no longer seen as dole bludgers. Unemployment was immediately understood to be a public issue, a concern that affects the masses, not just people who were apparently lazy drug addicts. The Australian Government understood that unemployment, and the needs of the unemployed in particular, was evidently a product of the "economic and political institutions of the society," no longer "the personal situation and character" of the unemployed (Mills 2000, p. 9).

From a structural understanding of unemployment as a problem affecting the mainstream, the unemployed were normalised during the pandemic and provided an unemployment benefit that ensured they could live with dignity. As Treasurer Josh Frydenberg (2020) explained when justifying this policy, "we are very conscious that people still need to meet the costs of their groceries and other bills." As normal people are subjected to structural employment out of their control – they "might be stood down or they might have lost their job" – the government provided them an income so they could live. As Marshall (1950) might have put it, people were supported to live in accordance with society's prevailing norms. Pre-COVID-19, however, the unemployed were dole bludgers, and the government felt minimal responsibility to ensure they could live with dignity and participate as full members of society. In the absence of doubling of the unemployment benefit following the COVID-19 pandemic, how do people who are poor survive?

They may, for example, as the former Deputy Prime Minister Barnaby Joyce speculated, engage in illegal activity to derive an income. Indeed, research from the United States shows that petty crime is a part of the survival strategy of Americans who live on US$2 per day (Edin & Shaefer 2015). The research literature has similarly shown that people survive poverty through sharing resources among family, friends, and neighbours (Dominguez & Watkins 2003). The grind of poverty and broader neoliberal forces do, however, subvert the informal networks that people who are poor have traditionally drawn upon (Desmond 2012). In addition to, or instead of, these survival strategies, people who experience poverty rely on the practice of charity to survive. In the next chapter, we continue our analysis of the translation strategies employed by the State to enrol charity in the production of the neoliberal social. Building on the observations in this chapter about how the State creates a need for charity through poverty, we show how it also deploys a range of strategies to encourage and facilitate the charitable to respond to that poverty.

References

ACOSS 2020, *Poverty in Australia 2020*, viewed 18 February 2021, http://povertyandinequality.acoss.org.au/wp-content/uploads/2020/02/Poverty-in-Australia-2020_Part-1_Overview.pdf

Anglicare 2019, *Anglicare Rental Affordability Snapshot: National Report, 2019*, Anglicare Australia, Canberra.

Anglicare 2020, *Anglicare Rental Affordability Snapshot: National Report, 2020*, Anglicare Australia, Canberra.

Archer, V 2009, 'Dole bludgers, tax payers and the new right: Constructing discourses of welfare in 1970s Australia', *Labour History*, vol. 96, pp. 177–190.

Australian Bureau of Statistics 2018, *Census of Population and Housing: Estimating Homelessness, 2016*, Australian Government, Canberra.

Australian Bureau of Statistics 2019, *Household Income and Wealth, Australia*, viewed 22 February 2021, https://www.abs.gov.au/statistics/economy/finance/household-income-and-wealth-australia/latest-release#data-download

Australian Government 2019a, *Program Fact Sheet for Jobactive*, viewed 04 February 2021, https://docs.employment.gov.au/documents/program-fact-sheet-jobactive

Australian Government 2019b, *Cashless Debit Card*, viewed 20 February 2021, https://www.dss.gov.au/families-and-children/programmes-services/welfare-conditionality/cashless-debit-card-overview

Australian Government 2020a, *Drug Testing Trial*, viewed 03 December 2020, https://www.dss.gov.au/benefits-payments/drug-testing-trial

Australian Government 2020b, *Economic Response to the Coronavirus*, viewed 22 February 2021, https://treasury.gov.au/coronavirus

Australian Government 2021, *Social Security Guide*, viewed 22 February 2021, https://guides.dss.gov.au/guide-social-security-law/5/2/1/20

Australian Institute for Health and Welfare 2019, *Housing Assistance in Australia 2019*, viewed 15 July 2020, https://www.aihw.gov.au/reports/housing-assistance/housing-assistance-in-australia-2019/contents/priority-groups-and-wait-lists#pg4

Australian Trade and Investment Commission 2019, *Investor Updates*, viewed 15 January 2021, https://www.austrade.gov.au/international/invest/investor-updates/2019/2019-benchmark-report-positions-australia-as-ideal-investment-destination

Bacchi, C 1999, *Women, Policy and Politics: The Construction of Policy Problems*, Sage, London.

Bagshaw, E 2018, "Freeze has gone on too long': John Howard calls for dole increase', *Sydney Morning Herald*, https://www.smh.com.au/politics/federal/freeze-has-gone-on-too-long-john-howard-calls-for-a-dole-increase-20180509-p4ze83.html

Bielefeld, S 2018, 'Government mythology on income management, alcohol, addiction and Indigenous communities', *Critical Social Policy*, vol. 38, no. 4, pp. 749–770.

Bolger, R 2019, 'Barnaby Joyce says Newstart is so low recipients may need to sell drugs to survive', *SBS News*, https://www.sbs.com.au/news/barnaby-joyce-says-newstart-is-so-low-recipients-may-need-to-sell-drugs-to-survive

Bradbury, B & Whiteford, P 2020, 'Unemployment support will be slashed by $300 this week. This won't help people find work', *The Conversation*, https://theconversation.com/unemployment-support-will-be-slashed-by-300-this-week-this-wont-help-people-find-work-146289

Brady, D 2019, 'Theories of the causes of poverty', *Annual Review of Sociology*, vol. 45, pp. 155–175.

Bray, J 2016, 'Seven years of evaluating income management – what have we learnt? Placing the findings of the New Income Management in the Northern Territory evaluation in context', *Australian Journal of Social Issues*, vol. 51, no. 4, pp. 449–468.

Business Council of Australia 2019, *Business Council Releases a Plan for a Stronger Australia*, viewed 17 December 2020, https://www.bca.com.au/business_council_releases_a_plan_for_a_stronger_australia

Carney, T 2019, 'Conditional welfare: New wine, old wine or just the same old bottle?', in P Saunders (ed.), *Revisiting Henderson: Poverty, Social Security and Basic Income*, Melbourne University Press, Melbourne.

Carney, T 2020, 'Government to repay 470,000 unlawful robodebts in what might be Australia's biggest-ever financial backdown', *The Conversation*, https://theconversation.com/government-to-repay-470-000-unlawful-robodebts-in-what-might-be-australias-biggest-ever-financial-backdown-139668

Chase, E & Walker, R 2013, 'The co-construction of shame in the context of poverty: Beyond a threat to the social bond', *Sociology*, vol. 47, no. 4, pp. 739–754.

Clarke, A, Cheshire, L & Parsell, C 2020, 'Bureaucratic encounters 'after neoliberalism': Examining the supportive turn in social housing governance', *The British Journal of Sociology*, vol. 71, no. 2, pp. 253–268.

Clarke, A & Parsell, C 2020, 'The ambiguities of homelessness governance: Disentangling care and revanchism in the neoliberalising city', *Antipode*, vol. 52, no. 6, pp. 1624–1646.

Department of Social Services 2018, *Jobseeker Compliance Data – June Quarter 2018*, viewed 22 February 2021, https://docs.employment.gov.au/system/files/doc/other/job_seeker_compliance_public_data_-_june_quarter_2018.pdf

Desmond, M 2012, 'Disposable ties and the urban poor', *American Journal of Sociology*, vol. 117, no. 5, pp. 1295–1335.

Dominguez, S & Watkins, C 2003, 'Creating networks of survival and mobility: Social capital among African-American and Latin-American low-income mothers', *Social Problems*, vol. 50, no. 1, pp. 111–135.

Edin, K & Shaefer, H 2015, *$2.00 A Day: Living on Almost Nothing in America*, Mariner Books, Boston.

Everybody's Home 2018, viewed 22 February 2021, https://everybodyshome.com.au/our-campaign/more-social-and-affordable-homes/

Falinski, J 2020, 'Australia's housing insanity', *Financial Review*, https://www.afr.com/policy/economy/australia-s-housing-insanity-20201207-p56ldd

Foucault, M 2008, *The Birth of Biopolitics: Lectures at the Collège de France, 1978–79*, Palgrave Macmillan, London.

Frydenberg, J 2020, 'Interview with Karl Stefanovic and Allison Langdon', *The Today Show*, Channel9. https://ministers.treasury.gov.au/ministers/josh-frydenberg-2018/transcripts/interview-karl-stefanovic-and-allison-langdon-today-5

Gerrard, J & Farrugia, D 2015, 'The 'lamentable sight' of homelessness and the society of the spectacle', *Urban Studies*, vol. 52, no. 12, pp. 2219–2233.

Glodblatt, B 2019, 'More than unpopular. How ParentsNext intrudes on single parents' human rights', *The Conversation*, https://theconversation.com/more-than-unpopular-how-parentsnext-intrudes-on-single-parents-human-rights-108754

Groenhart, L & Burke, T 2014, 'What has happened to Australia's public housing? Thirty years of policy and outcomes, 1981 to 2011', *Australian Journal of Social Issues*, vol. 49, no. 2, pp. 127–149.

Hackworth, J 2012, *Faith Based: Religious Neoliberalism and the Politics of Welfare in the United States*, University of Georgia Press, Athens.

Hansard 2019, *Senate Official Hansard, Australian Government*, viewed 22 February 2021, https://parlinfo.aph.gov.au/parlInfo/download/chamber/hansards/1cdc3522-fc63-47ec-93f8-0af82f6bf492/toc_pdf/Senate_2019_12_03_7415_Official.pdf;fileType=application%2Fpdf

Hayward, D 1996, 'The reluctant landlords? A history of public housing in Australia', *Urban Policy and Research*, vol. 14, no. 1, pp. 5–35.

Henriques-Gomes, L 2019, 'Raising Newstart would 'give drug dealers more money', social services ministers says', *The Guardian*, https://www.theguardian.com/australia-news/2019/oct/02/raising-newstart-would-give-drug-dealers-more-money-social-services-minister-says

Henriques-Gomes, L 2020, 'Robodebt court documents show government was warned 76 times debts were not legally enforceable', *The Guardian*, https://www.

theguardian.com/australia-news/2020/sep/19/robodebt-court-documents-show-government-was-warned-76-times-debts-were-not-legally-enforceable

Hockey, J 2014, 'Federal budget 2014 – Full speech', *The Sydney Morning Herald*, https://www.smh.com.au/national/federal-budget-2014--full-speech-20140513-3887i.html

Jacobs, K, Atkinson, R, Spinney, A, Colic Peisker, V, Berry, M & Dalton, T 2010, *What Future for Public Housing? A Critical Analysis*, Australian Housing and Urban Research Institute, Melbourne.

Klein, M 2014, 'Welfare Spending across the OECD', *Financial Times*, https://ftalphaville.ft.com/2014/11/27/2053392/welfare-spending-across-the-oecd/

Knaus, C 2017, 'Welfare dependency 'poison' for jobless, human services minister says', *The Guardian*, https://www.theguardian.com/australia-news/2017/may/26/welfare-dependency-poison-for-jobless-human-services-minister-says

Latour, B 2005, *Reassembling the Social: An Introduction to Actor-Network-Theory*, Oxford University Press, Oxford.

Lawson, J, Pawson, H, Troy, L, van den Nouwelant, R & Hamilton, C 2018, *Social Housing as Infrastructure: An Investment Pathway*, Australian Housing and Urban Research Institute, Melbourne.

Lee, N 2019, 'Drugs don't affect job seeking, so let's offer users help rather than take away their payments', *The Conversation*, https://theconversation.com/drugs-dont-affect-job-seeking-so-lets-offer-users-help-rather-than-take-away-their-payments-123096

Marshall, T 1950, *Citizenship and Social Class*, Cambridge University Press, Cambridge.

Marston, G, Zhang, J, Peterie, M, Ramia, G, Patulny, R & Cook, E 2019, 'To move or not to move: Mobility decision-making in the context of welfare conditionality and paid employment', *Mobilities*, vol. 14, no. 5, pp. 596–611.

Mendes, P, Marston, G & Katz, I 2016, 'Introduction for special issue on income management', *Australian Journal of Social Issues*, vol. 51, no. 4, pp. 393–397.

Mendes, P, Roche, S, Marston, G, Peterie, M, Staines, Z & Humpage, L 2020, 'The social harms outweigh the benefits: A study of compulsory income management in greater Shepparton and Playford', *Australian Social Work*, https://doi.org/10.1080/0312407X.2020.1820536

Menzies, R 1942, *The Forgotten People*, viewed 22 February 2021, http://www.liberals.net/theforgottenpeople.htm

Mills, C 2000, *The Sociological Imagination*, 40th Anniversary edn., Oxford University Press, New York.

Morrison, S 2015, *Address to the National Press Club: "The Best Form of Welfare"*, viewed 22 February 2021, https://formerministers.dss.gov.au/15959/address-to-the-national-press-club-the-best-form-of-welfare/

Morrison, S & Porter, C 2016, *The Coalition's Plan for Better Management of the Social Welfare System*, viewed 22 February 2021, https://cdn.theconversation.com/static_files/files/1050/turn1.pdf?1590734108

Muehlebach, A 2012, *The Moral Neoliberal: Welfare and Citizenship in Italy*, University of Chicago Press, Chicago.

OECD 2010, *OECD Economic Surveys: Australia*, viewed 22 February 2021, https://www.oecd-ilibrary.org/docserver/eco_surveys-aus-2010-en.pdf?expires=1600302843&id=id&accname=ocid177546&checksum=6C5AA67DDE8DCB0093E619C9AACE1926

OECD 2016, *Net Social Expenditure Indicator*, viewed 23 February 2021, http://www.oecd.org/els/soc/OECD2014-Social-Expenditure-Update-Nov2014-NetSocx-Data-2011-Fig7.xlsx

OECD 2021, *Net Replacement Rate in Unemployment*, viewed 23 February 2021, https://stats.oecd.org/Index.aspx?DataSetCode=NRR

OECD n.d., *Benefits in Unemployment, Share of Previous Income*, viewed 23 February 2021, https://data.oecd.org/benwage/benefits-in-unemployment-share-of-previous-income.htm

Pantazis, C 2016, 'Policies and discourses of poverty during a time of recession and austerity', *Critical Social Policy*, vol. 36, no. 1, pp. 3–20.

Parsell, C 2018, *The Homeless Person in Contemporary Society*, Routledge, Abingdon.

Parsell, C & Jones, A 2014, 'Bold reform or policy overreach? Australia's attack on homelessness: 2008–2013', *International Journal of Housing Policy*, vol. 14, no. 4, pp. 427–443.

Parsell, C, Vincent, E, Klein, E, Clarke, A & Walsh, T 2020a, 'Introduction to the special issue on welfare conditionality', *Australian Journal of Social Issues*, vol. 55, no. 1, pp. 4–12.

Parsell, C, Clarke, A & Kuskoff, E 2020b, 'Understanding responses to homelessness during COVID-19: An examination of Australia', Housing Studies, https://doi.org/10.1080/02673037.2020.1829564

Pawson, H, Parsell, C, Lui, E, Hartley, C & Thompson, S 2020a, *Australian Homelessness Monitor, 2020*, Launch Housing, Melbourne.

Pawson, H, Milligan, V & Yates, J 2020b, *Housing Policy in Australia: A Case for System Reform*, Palgrave Macmillan, Singapore.

Pawson, H, Parsell, C, Saunders, P, Hill, T & Liu, E 2018, *Australian Homelessness Monitor, 2018*, Launch Housing, Melbourne.

Phillips, B, Gray, M & Biddle, N 2020, *COVID-19 JobKeeper and JobSeeker Impacts on Poverty and Housing Stress Under Current and Alternative Economic and Policy Scenarios*, viewed 22 February 2021, https://csrm.cass.anu.edu.au/sites/default/files/docs/2020/8/Impact_of_Covid19_JobKeeper_and_Jobeeker_measures_on_Poverty_and_Financial_Stress_FINAL.pdf

Raise the Rate 2020, *Raise the Rate of Newstart Fact Check – January 2020*, viewed 22 February 2021, https://raisetherate.org.au/wp-content/uploads/2020/01/RTR-Fact-Check-2020-1-scaled.jpg

Romano, S 2015, 'Idle paupers, scroungers and skirkers: Past and new social stereotypes of the undeserving welfare claimant in the UK', in L Foster, A Brunton, C Deeming & T Haux (eds.), *In Defence of Welfare*, Policy Press, Bristol, pp. 65–67.

Rose, N 1999, *Powers of Freedom: Reframing Political Thought*, Cambridge University Press, Cambridge.

Rose, N 2000, 'Community, citizenship, and the third way', *American Behavioral Scientist*, vol. 43, no. 9, pp. 1395–1411.

Royal Australasian College of Physicians 2019, *Drug Testing Welfare Recipients Doesn't Work: Physicians Disappointed in Senate Report that Flies in the Face of Evidence*, viewed 22 February 2021, https://www.racp.edu.au/news-and-events/media-releases/drug-testing-welfare-recipients-doesn-t-work-physicians-disappointed-in-senate-report-that-flies-in-the-face-of-evidence/

Ruston, A 2019, *Media Release: Drug Testing Trials to Help Welfare Recipients Become Job Ready*, viewed 22 February 2021, https://www.anneruston.com.au/media_release_drug_testing_trials_to_help_welfare_recipients_become_job_ready

Saunders, P 2011, *Down and Out: Poverty and Exclusion in Australia*, Policy Press, Bristol.

Saunders, P 2018, 'Using a budget standards approach to assess the adequacy of Newstart allowance', *Australian Journal of Social Issues*, vol. 53, no. 1, pp. 4–17.

Shapiro, D 2007, *Is the Welfare State Justified?* Cambridge University Press, New York.

St Vincent de Paul Society 2020, *Briefing: Raising the Rate of Newstart*, viewed 22 February 2021, https://www.vinnies.org.au/page/Publications/National/Factsheets_and_policy_briefings/Briefing_Raising_the_Rate_of_Newstart/

Taylor, D, Gray, M & Stanton, D 2016, 'New conditionality in Australian social security policy', *Australian Journal of Social Issues*, vol. 51, no. 1, pp. 3–26.

The Senate 2019, *Jobactive: Failing Those It Is Intended to Serve*, Commonwealth of Australia, Canberra.

Thomas, M 2015, *Waiting Period for Young People to Access Income Support*, Parliament of Australia, viewed 22 February 2021, https://www.aph.gov.au/About_Parliament/Parliamentary_Departments/Parliamentary_Library/pubs/rp/BudgetReview201516/IncomeSup#_ftn1

Vamstad, J & Essen, J 2012, 'Charitable giving in a universal welfare state – charity and social rights in Sweden', *Nonprofit and Voluntary Sector Quarterly*, vol. 42, no. 2, pp. 285–301.

Watts, B & Fitzpatrick, S 2018, *Welfare Conditionality*, Routledge, Abingdon.

Weeks, J 2020, *The Debt Delusion: Living Within Our Means and Other Fallacies*, Polity, Cambridge.

Whiteford, P 2006, 'The welfare expenditure debate: 'Economic myths of the left and the right' revisited', *The Economic and Labour Relations Review*, vol. 17, no. 1, pp. 33–77.

Whiteford, P 2017, *Social Security and Welfare Spending in Australia: Assessing Long-Term Trends*, viewed 22 February 2021, https://taxpolicy.crawford.anu.edu.au/sites/default/files/publication/taxstudies_crawford_anu_edu_au/2018-05/combined_pdf_whiteford_trends_in_soc_sec_spending_2017.pdf

Whiteford, P & Bradbury, B 2020, 'Coronavirus supplement: Your guide to the Australian payments that will go to the extra million on welfare', *The Conversation*, https://theconversation.com/coronavirus-supplement-your-guide-to-the-australian-payments-that-will-go-to-the-extra-million-on-welfare-134358

Whiteford, P, Innis, S, Bradbury, B & Stanton, D 2019, *Adequacy of Newstart and Related Payments and Alternative Mechanisms to Determine the Level of Income Support Payments in Australia Submission 71*, Submission to Senate Standing Committees on Community Affairs Inquiry into the Adequacy of Newstart and related payments and alternative mechanisms to determine the level of income support payments in Australia, viewed 22 February 2021, https://www.aph.gov.au/Parliamentary_Business/Committees/Senate/Community_Affairs/Newstartrelatedpayments/Submissions

Whiteford, P, Phillips, B, Bradbury, B, Stanton, D, Gray, M & Stewart, M 2018, 'It's not just Newstart. Single parents are $271 per fortnight worse off. Labor needs an overarching welfare review', *The Conversation*, https://theconversation.com/its-not-just-newstart-single-parents-are-271-per-fortnight-worse-off-labor-needs-an-overarching-welfare-review-107521

Wolch, J 1989, 'The shadow state: Transformations in the voluntary sector', in J Wolch & M Dear (eds.), *The Power of Geography: How Territory Shapes Social Life*, Routledge, Abingdon, pp. 197–221.

5 Cultivating charity

Introduction

There is recognition amongst contemporary scholars that welfare state retrenchment is increasingly driving reliance upon charity (Lambie-Mumford 2019; Levitas 2012). State withdrawal from direct welfare provisioning exacerbates poverty, and creates demand for bottom-up charitable initiatives that help to meet people's basic needs. This analysis largely holds for the Australian case. In the previous chapter, we showed how the erosion of welfare support in Australia has produced growing and deepening poverty; and this chapter will extend this analysis by demonstrating that reliance on charity is growing alongside this. However, the focus on welfare state withdrawal means that the literature often overlooks the more direct methods that the State uses to cultivate charitable responses to poverty. This chapter will bring these methods to the fore.

The analysis presented in this chapter illustrates how the State cultivates and mobilises charity to bring prevailing neoliberal understandings of what constitutes a good society to fruition. Key to the appeal of charity is the idea that it is a bottom-up, spontaneous response to manifest social and material need, a response that is grounded in the selfless concern and compassion that the charitable feel for people less fortunate than themselves (Dean 2020; Dees 2012). This image resonates strongly with neoliberal conceptions of the ideal society, which foreground the self-governing capacities of civil society and the community, and lament the stifling impact that top-down welfare provision has on these capacities. However, despite charity being valued for its spontaneity, creating poverty and material need for the charitable to address through welfare state retrenchment is not the sole means through which charity is cultivated. Rather, the State employs a number of productive strategies to induce, facilitate, and bolster charitable responses to poverty, and to explicitly link it to prevailing conceptions of citizenship and social solidarity.

In the chapter, we identify three key translations strategies used by the State to cultivate charitable responses to poverty. These include: (i) the provision of material support to facilitate and supplement charity; (ii) the valorisation and symbolic recognition of the charitable; and (iii) the development of governance infrastructures that help coordinate and enable charitable activities at a national scale. We also examine how some of Australia's largest charitable organisations respond to these efforts to enrol them. As also noted in Chapter 3, translation is never a *fait accompli* (Latour 1987); actors like the charitable play an active role in the shaping of the projects they are enrolled in, and they therefore have the capacity to respond in ways that contradict the aims of the enrolling party.

We begin the chapter by documenting the growing reliance on charity by people in poverty. We then seek to explain this growing reliance, building on the analysis presented in earlier chapters, by demonstrating the ways in which the State actively cultivates charitable responses to poverty. After describing how neoliberal definitions of the social are perpetuated by Australian political leaders, we outline the three key strategies used by the State to realise this vision through the cultivation of charity just mentioned. We then explore how large charitable organisations in Australia respond to efforts to enrol them in the enactment of the neoliberal social, documenting both their partial acquiescence to neoliberal conceptions of a good society and their potential to redirect the State's neoliberalising strategies to pursue the alternative goal of advancing social justice.

Growing reliance on charity by people in poverty

Reflecting trends observed in other developed countries (Lambie-Mumford 2019; Mohan & Breeze 2016), there is a growing reliance on charity amongst people experiencing poverty in Australia. This is evident in the increasing use of foodbanks over the last few years. Foodbank Australia reported assisting 815,000 people per month in 2019, and that the number of people seeking food relief increased by 22 per cent from that in the previous year (Foodbank Australia n.d.). Similarly, a recent analysis of the amount of food delivered by charity organisations in Australia between 2008 and 2016 shows a significant upward trend (see Figure 5.1 below). In 2008, food charities delivered around 20,000 tons of food in total; by 2018 this figure had risen to over 50,000 tons.

The growing reliance on charity in Australia is also evident in data on the use of emergency relief. Emergency relief is instigated by the Australian Government (2020a), which allocates public funds to charities to enable them to "provide immediate financial and/or material support" in order to "help people address immediate basic needs in times of crisis." The resources provided vary, but they typically include food, transport or chemist vouchers; part-payment of utility account/s; food parcels or clothing; budgeting assistance; and/or referrals to other services that help address the underlying causes of financial crisis. Emergency relief is administered

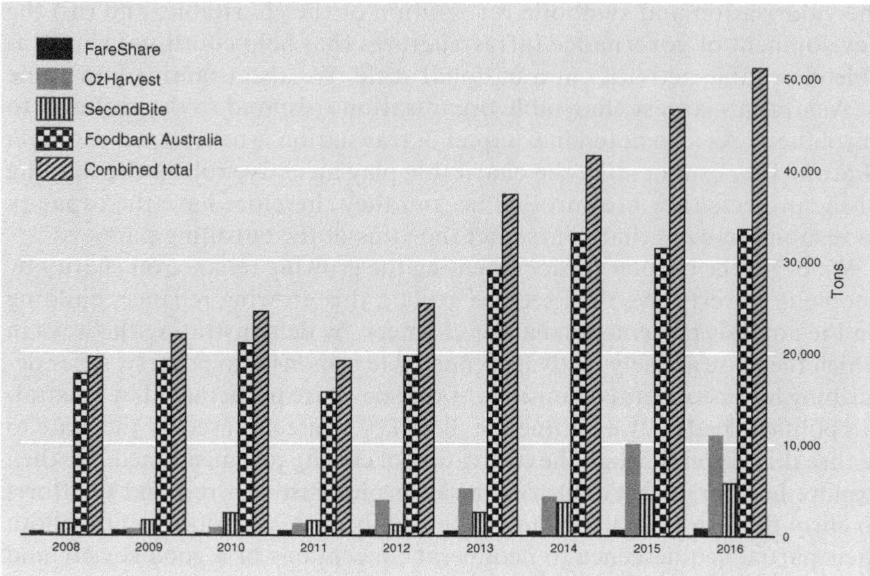

Figure 5.1 Amount of food delivered by charity organisations in Australia, 2008–2016.

Notes: Adapted from McKay and Lindberg (2019), who sourced the statistics from the annual reports of the respective charities.

by charities, such as The Salvation Army or the St Vincent de Paul Society, who draw on their reservoir of voluntary labour to deliver State-funded resources to people in need, often supplementing the resources available with financial and in-kind donations they have received from the general public.

While the rationale (and indeed the name) for emergency relief implies addressing a temporary crisis, government data shows that it is in fact an enduring feature in the lives of many people who are poor. Seventeen per cent of emergency relief recipients accessed it "five or more times in a 6 month period"; and almost half of those who accessed emergency relief had accessed it three or more times in six months (Department of Social Services 2017, p. 14). As we show in Chapter 8, people in poverty use charity, which is partly funded through Emergency Relief, to survive.

The analysis of the inadequate levels of State welfare support presented in Chapter 4 goes some way to explaining this growing reliance on charity. The freezing on employment benefits at levels well below the poverty line, coupled with declining investment in social housing, create the conditions where more and more people are unable to meet their basic needs, resulting in people turning to charity to bridge the gap. However, this is only part of the story. The State not only creates demand for charity by retrenching its welfare functions, it also redeploys public resources to support the growth of charitable responses to poverty. Charity is thus not an automatic response to rising need; it is instead a *cultivated* response.

Defining the ideal social

To understand the cultivation and mobilisation of charity in contemporary responses to poverty, we must take account of the conception of the social that it is believed to represent and enact. As we argued in Chapter 3, contemporary mobilisations of charity are linked to the prominence of neoliberal conceptions of the social, particularly amongst political authorities. Australia has experimented with various manifestations of neoliberal thinking over the past four decades. In a seminal study, Michael Pusey (1991) described how, through the 1980s, policymaking in Australia came to be dominated by economic rationalist perspectives that promoted the self-regulating capacity of markets, and critiqued the distorting impact of State intervention in social and economic life. This economic rationalist perspective displaced an earlier focus on State-led national building projects and the (modest) redistribution of the benefits of economic growth. For Pusey (1991, p. 10), these changes were underpinned by new projections of reality, wherein the economy and the market came to be seen as the fundamental basis of social life, and as essential to its coordination and proper functioning.

The variant of neoliberalism described by Pusey (1991) is a fundamentally economistic one, which appears to leave little room for the relational domains of civil society and community that are typically associated with charity. However, these domains were later brought to the fore in the late 1990s and early 2000s, where the economic rationalist focus on markets began to be supplemented with a concern for the relational contexts of individual action. This was a time when Third Way discourse was ascendant in liberal democracies across the world; and whilst those discourses did not take hold as strongly in Australia as in the United Kingdom or the United States, they nevertheless ushered in a new emphasis on community-based solutions to social problems (Reddel 2004).

The most overt champion of Third Way principles in Australia was former Opposition Leader and leader of the Australian Labor Party (ALP), Mark Latham. Latham (1998) advanced the typical Third Way view that liberalised markets could – indeed *must* – coexist with a strong and fair society; and that the welfare state needed to be reformed, rather than withdrawn, as the neoliberals of the 1980s would have it (Scanlon 2001). A key feature of the reforms that Latham had in mind was a greater role for communities in the governance of social problems such as poverty. He advocated for, as he put it, "a public sector arising as much from civil society as central government" (Latham 1998, p. 386). This was to be coupled with a renewed emphasis on individuals' responsibilities to their communities to counteract the supposed tendency of old welfare to pander to the inactive (Latham 1998, p. 387).

Latham lost the 2004 federal election, and subsequently the leadership of the ALP. Hence, he never had the opportunity to translate these ideas into practical reforms. However, the man that defeated him, Australia's second longest-serving Prime Minister (1996–2007), John Howard, was already advancing a view of Australian society that emphasised the value of spontaneous community, albeit in more colloquial and less overtly Third Way rhetoric. Howard did this by weaving neoliberal conceptions of individual self-reliance and spontaneous community with deep-seated myths about the unique virtues of the Australian national character, particularly the ideal of *mateship* (Dyrenfurth 2007; Johnson 2007).

The concept of mateship emerged in the late nineteenth century to refer to worker solidarity within the then-incipient labour movement. Howard followed a tradition of twentieth century conservatives in eschewing mateship's foundational link to class struggle, instead reinterpreting it a universal Australian capacity for spontaneous camaraderie and mutual aid in times of adversity. This mateship characteristic was purportedly born out of the harsh conditions experienced by settler farmers and pioneers during the initial years of colonisation (Australian Government 2020b), and cemented in mass military service that took place during the First World War. Mateship is thus now imagined as a quasi-natural safety net (Dyrenfurth 2007) that is situated within civil society rather than the State, and which could be relied upon by otherwise independent and enterprising individuals when unpredictable hardships befell them. In Howard's words:

> ...[mateship] talks of the spirit of helping people in adversity. We express mateship when we help people in floods. We express mateship when we help people in fires. We express mateship when we strive for days to rescue people who have been buried under the debris of ski lodges. We do it when we work hard to haul bodies out of train wrecks. It's an expression that refers to the willingness, the distinctive willingness of independently minded Australians to help their fellow countrymen and women in times of adversity.
>
> (Howard 1999 cited in Dyrenfurth 2007, p. 221)

As Jim Page (2002) highlights, mateship invokes a form of "affective solidarity:" an emotional bond and sense of obligation to others that is activated at times of adversity. There is thus a powerful resonance between the contemporary national mythology of mateship and the neoliberalised forms of solidarity discussed in Chapter 3 that are natural, spontaneous, and unmediated by the State (Muehlebach 2012). By exploiting these resonances, Howard helped naturalise neoliberal conceptions of the social in Australia, paving the way for the mobilisation of charity as a response to poverty that we discuss below.

Neoliberal ideas about spontaneous assistance and self-governing community continue to shape how society is conceptualised today by Australian political leaders. In classical liberal fashion, Australia's current Prime Minister and leader of the Liberal Party, Scott Morrison, firmly centres the individual when discussing Australian society. In a speech delivered in 2018 soon after he became Prime Minister, Morrison discussed the influence of Liberal Party founder and former Prime Minister, Sir Robert Menzies, on his own political views and values, stating that:

> Menzies' vision, and all of those who joined him, it all began and started with the individual. It's all about the individual, and the capacity and the value and sanctity, the inherent virtue of every single human being that has the privilege to call themselves an Australian whether by birth or by pledge.
>
> (Morrison 2018)

Importantly, however, whilst Morrison sees the individual as the moral and ontological basis of the social, the individual is not seen as an isolated atom engaged only in self-interested acts of market-based competition and exchange, as some accounts of neoliberal thinking would have it (Harvey 2007). Rather, the ideal society is one where individual freedom and self-fulfilment are made possible by the spontaneous bonds of self-governing community. Thus, Morrison's speech went on to state that:

> [Menzies] understood that for the individual to be successful in life, and to be able to realise what they wanted, to realise for themselves, they needed some very important things. If they were fortunate enough, they would have a family that loved them... Then there's the community... All walks of life. People from school, people volunteering for Emergency Services, people just getting together and crocheting. A community supporting itself. An individual can thrive in a community like that.
>
> (Morrison 2018)

In Morrison's ideal society, then, individuals are imbricated in webs of mutual obligation and solidarity that spring from their everyday interactions and relationships – "people from school, people volunteering for Emergency Services, people just getting together and crocheting." These relationships simultaneously bind individuals to others and make possible the pursuit of their personal projects.

This is precisely the understanding of community that Rose (1999, 2000) identifies as underpinning neoliberal (or advanced liberal in his parlance) modes of governing. As outlined in Chapter 3, neoliberalism entails a rescaling of conceptualisations of the social, driven by a move away from the State-mediated relations of the welfare era, and towards the supposedly pre-political bonds of community and the forms of ethical citizenship that pertain to it. The reader will recall that ethical citizenship emphasizes the ethical *duties* that flow from community membership, more so than the *rights* to social protection that correspond to the social citizenship of the welfare era. Morrison places these duties front and centre in his account of what makes an Australian citizen:

> As Australians, our goal is to make a contribution, not to seek one. It doesn't matter what walk of life you're in. We always want to look in our community... wanting to make a contribution rather than take one. See where they can contribute rather than whether they can take out. That is what creates a noble society. That's what creates a growing and benevolent society. A caring society. Always looking to see where you can make the difference.
>
> (Morrison 2018)

For Morrison, then, the ideal society is one comprised of ethical citizens whose *modus operandi* is to contribute to their community by taking responsibility for caring for those around them, and by eschewing the temptation to take out more than they put in.

Neoliberal understandings of the social thus permeate the worldview advanced by Australia's political leaders over the last few decades. This worldview places a premium on forms of sociality, solidarity, and citizenship that operate beyond the State in the quasi-natural domains of community and civil society. Alongside the withdrawal of the State discussed in the previous chapter, the cultivation of practices of charity is seen as key to the realisation of this worldview. As stated in Chapter 1, charity entails the voluntary gifting of one's time and resources to assist people outside of one's immediate family (Dean 2020; Dees 2012). It is thus taken as the paradigmatic embodiment of community supporting itself and of ethical citizens "wanting to make a contribution rather than take one," to use Prime Minister Morrison's (2018) words. We now turn to how the State and related political authorities seek to cultivate charity in order to make the neoliberal world view a reality.

Enrolling charity in poverty governance

In Australia, State and political actors go to great efforts to solicit, facilitate, and bolster the ostensibly independent and spontaneous acts of charity that they see as symbolic of the ideal society. As noted in Chapter 3, we conceptualise these efforts using Latour's concept of translation (Latour 1986, 1987, 2005). The reader will recall that translation refers to the strategies that actors employ to enrol others' support for their attempts to reassemble the social by aligning the interests of those others with the vision they are advancing. The remainder of this section will be used to document and analyse the translation strategies employed by Australian political authorities to enrol the charitable in poverty governance and thus cultivate the neoliberal social.

Funding to facilitate and supplement charitable giving

The withdrawal of the State from direct welfare provisioning, and the subsequent increase in the rates and depth of poverty, along with increasing rates of homelessness, are important conditions for the enactment of ethical citizenship and affective solidarity. These processes create the manifest social need that provides charitable responses to poverty with their *raison d'être* and their affective stimulus. They also get the State out of the way, creating a vacuum in welfare provisioning for community initiatives to fill (Lambie-Mumford 2019). This is not, however, a simple withdrawal or retrenchment of the welfare state. For while the State withdraws resources and support for social security and public services, it becomes increasingly active in providing material support for charitable initiatives.

Aggregate data on State funding to charity

In Australia, State funding to facilitate charitable responses to poverty and other welfare needs have increased drastically in recent years. To establish trends over time in government funding, we examined data from four instalments of the Australian Charities and Not-for-Profit Commission's (ACNC) 2019 Annual Information Statement Data, covering the 2014/2017 period. These administrative datasets contain annual information on charities' characteristics, size, finances, main activity, and beneficiaries. The ACNC data reveals that the Australian charity sector is expanding. Between 2014 and 2017, the number of charities grew by approximately 3.2 per cent, from 47,005 to 48,517. There were also substantial increases in government funding (expressed in $2017 AUD) to charities over this period, from ~$55.25 billion in 2014 to ~$60.52 billion in 2017, or a 9.5 per cent increase.

Critically, the data allows us to isolate charities that listed social services as their main activity. The number of such charities grew at a much faster rate than the sector: from 1,632 in 2014 to 3,508 in 2017, or a 115 per cent increase. Whilst social-service charities comprised 3.65 per cent of all charities in 2014, their share had increased to 7.43 per cent by 2017. At the same time, government funding to charities providing social services as their main activity over the 2014/2017 period increased more rapidly than the sector rate; from $4.49 billion in 2014 to $7.30 billion in 2017. A comparison of time trends in government funding to charities providing social services as their main activity and all other charities is displayed in Figure 5.2. The figure shows that revenue from government grants for social-service charities increased by 62.8 per cent between 2014 and 2017, while the analogous figure for other charities was a much smaller 5.5 per cent.

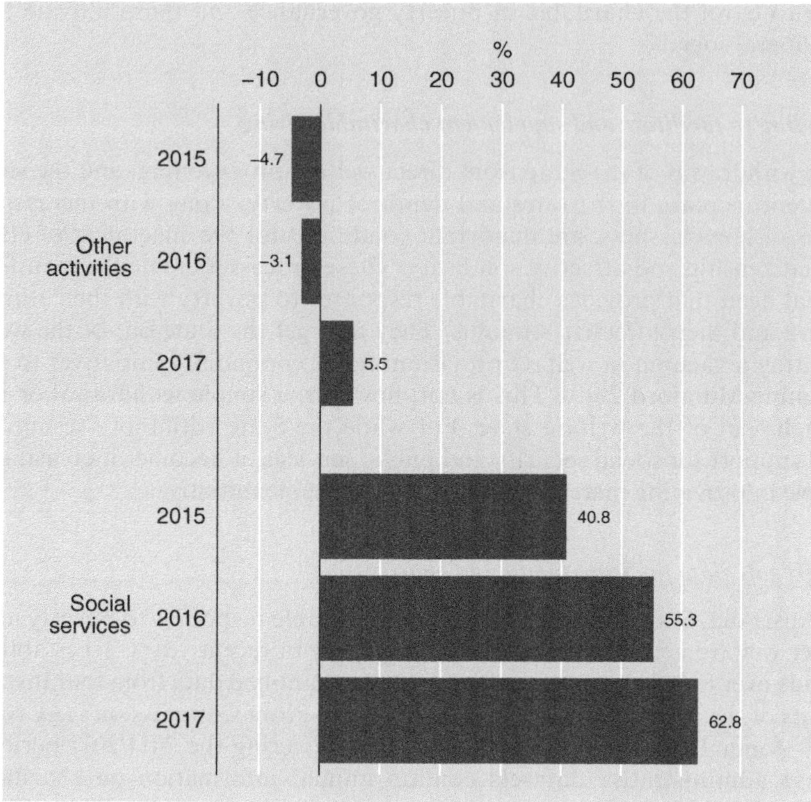

Figure 5.2 Trends in government revenue, by year and charity's main activity.

Notes: Data from the Australian Charities and Non-for-profits Commission (ACNC) Annual Information Statement Data, 2014/2017. All figures adjusted for inflation using the Consumer Price Index and expressed in $2017.

Rationale for funding charity: Federal examples

These data reveal the significant material investment that Australian governments make to enrol charity in their project of reassembling the social along neoliberal lines. Analysis of the rationale provided for specific examples of this funding shows that the government's aim in providing funding to charities is to instil communities with the capacity to manage poverty and disadvantage, and to move away from assumed dependency-producing forms of direct State welfare provision. At the Federal level, the Australian Government Department of Social Services (DSS) administers a range of initiatives that provide funding to facilitate community-based responses to poverty. One such initiative is the Strong and Resilient Communities Activity. The stated aim of this scheme is "to build strong and resilient communities by supporting local community organisations in their efforts to overcome disadvantage and solve complex social problems" (Australian Government 2018). The official statement goes on, noting that this funding:

> [H]elps to foster community cohesion by increasing people's sense of belonging and engagement. Grants help to strengthen the capacity of communities to become more self-reliant and empowered to address local issues.
> (Australian Government 2018)

Here, the funding of charity is rationalised as helping to cultivate the affective bonds that underpin community in the neoliberal imaginary ("people's sense of belonging and engagement"), and thus enhancing communities' self-governing capacities. Implicit in this aim of making communities more "self-reliant and empowered" is a desire to prevent their reliance on those more direct forms of State welfare support that are understood as creating passivity and dependence, and stifling communities' natural capacity for responsible self-governance (Rose 1999).

The aim of preventing welfare dependence is more explicit in the rationale provided by DSS for its national Emergency Relief program. As noted above, the State funds resources distributed to people in need via emergency relief, but it relies on the voluntary labour mobilised by charitable organisations to deliver these resources. The rationale provided by DSS for mobilising these charitable actors (the organisations and their volunteers) to deliver emergency relief is that these actors "build strong networks within their local communities to assist individuals to minimize potential dependence on assistance" (Australian Government 2020a). As with the example of the Strong and Resilient Communities Activity described above, the assumption here is that charitable initiatives have a unique ability to prevent dependence thanks to their embeddedness within self-governing communities, and that provision of relief directly by the State would squelch or undermine this ability by encouraging passivity.

Beyond building community capacity to manage poverty and prevent welfare dependence, State funding also aims to supplement and underwrite charitable responses to poverty, thus helping them to fulfil their role within the neoliberal social. This is evident in DSS's Food Relief program, where State funding is not only used to build the capacity of charities in terms of the distribution of food relief, but also to ensure that they can continue to provide food relief when donations fall short.

Food Relief, as formally set out by the Australian Government (2020c), aims to increase emergency relief organisations' access to a cost-effective supply of food items. Organisations are funded to ensure food items are available for service providers to deliver to individuals and families in need across Australia by:

- Receiving donated foods from farmers/manufacturers/retailers/other food redistribution services, and redistributing these foods to community organisations or other distribution centres where the food is needed

- Sourcing and transporting essential foods on a basis where food donations are insufficient
- Leading the development of local partnerships amongst food redistribution suppliers to improve access and distribution, especially in rural and remote communities.

Similarly, during the early stages of the COVID-19 pandemic in 2020, the Australian Government deployed public funds to address a shortfall in the supply of volunteers for the delivery of emergency relief, and to meet the rising demand for relief brought on by the pandemic. Funding of over $37 million was made available from April 2020 to Commonwealth-funded Emergency Relief providers to:

- Source, retain and increase workforce capacity, including volunteers – noting that coronavirus could impact workforce capacity, including volunteer support, for Emergency Relief providers
- Implement and extend home delivery services
- Provide financial and material assistance to those who are at imminent risk of not being able to pay a bill.

As these examples show, the State not only goes to great lengths to enrol charity in poverty alleviation, it also strives to guarantee and maintain its activities. This approach of using public resources to generate capacity within communities to address issues such as poverty is consistent with neoliberal understandings of the State's role as being one of creating the conditions for communities, and other self-regulating domains of society, to govern themselves (Foucault 2008; Rose 1999). The State's role is thus helping to build and maintain the neoliberal social, rather than mediating social relations and addressing social problems as it did in the welfare state era (Miller & Rose 2008).

Rationale for funding charity: homelessness charities

Another striking example of how State funding to charity is rationalised *vis-à-vis* the aim of bolstering community capacity for poverty relief is in the responses to homelessness of State and Territory Governments. At the same time, as government investment in social housing has been declining and private rental accommodation is becoming increasingly unaffordable (Pawson et al. 2020), there has been a proliferation of new charitable initiatives targeting the homeless in Australia (Parsell & Watts 2017). The most high-profile example of these initiatives is Orange Sky Laundry, a charity started by two young men from Brisbane in 2014 that aims to provide mobile hygiene amenities to people without homes. As noted in Chapter 2, Orange Sky began with the two people fitting washing machines and cloth dryers to vehicles and driving them into public spaces to wash homeless people's clothes. It later expanded to include vehicles with mobile shower facilities.

Orange Sky has rapidly expanded the size, capacity, and the geographical coverage of its operations. After commencing with one vehicle in one city, Orange Sky now operates 27 vehicles in 23 cities across all Australian states/territories, with 1,795 registered volunteers (Orange Sky n.d.). In 2018 Orange Sky expanded to New Zealand, and is currently pursuing expansion opportunities in the United States (Orange Sky n.d.). Along with private philanthropy, this growth has been facilitated by public funding from several Australian State and Territory Governments. In the financial year ending 30 June 2019, Orange Sky had a revenue of $6,077,462, of which $3,697,689 came from donations and $1,291,350 from government grants (Orange Sky 2020). In the State of Queensland, the emergence of Orange Sky appears to have inspired the State Government to create a new funding scheme titled Dignity First to support charities that "promote the immediate dignity of people doing it rough on our streets" (de Brenni 2016, p. 4828). Whilst Orange Sky was not explicitly cited as the impetus for the fund, it emerged immediately after Orange Sky rose to national prominence and was awarded the inaugural allocation of funding from the scheme with significant fanfare.

The Queensland Government's establishment of a permanent fund for charitable responses to homelessness illustrates a broader desire amongst political authorities to normalise and expand such responses. The New South Wales Government (2015), for instance, stated that their funding "provides significant support to Orange Sky Laundry co-founders... helping to deliver their vision of expanding nationally as quickly as possible." This desire is also evident in the rationale behind the Australian Government funding to charitable responses to poverty that we discussed above. By directing public money to supplementing charitable initiatives when they fall short, the Australian Government positions charity as the default mechanism through which Australian society will respond to growing poverty. This is done with no recognition of the State's role as a guarantor of people's basic needs, nor of the role that the withdrawal of the State from direct welfare provisioning has in creating the need for charity.

Symbolic recognition: creating exemplars and conferring ethical capital

The effort to normalise charitable responses to poverty is at the heart of neoliberal efforts to reassemble the social, and to establish forms of citizenship and solidarity premised on the spontaneous, affective, and ethical energies and bonds between citizens. In addition to the provision of material support, the normalisation of charity is pursued by the State and other authorities through a range of symbolic and discursive strategies.

One such strategy is the identification and celebration of specific charitable actors or initiatives as exemplars of ethical citizenship. An illustrative example of this practice is a recent trend of the State bestowing of national honours on bottom-up responses to homelessness through the highly prestigious Australian of the Year Awards. Presented by the Prime Minister as part of official Australia Day celebrations each year, the Australian of the Year Awards aim to highlight "the achievements and contributions of eminent Australians." It does this by "profiling leading citizens who are role models for us all" and who "inspire us through their achievements and challenge us to make our own contribution to creating a better Australia" (Australian of the Year Awards n.d.). These awards are thus used to promote particular conceptions of the ideal citizen.

In 2010, a Queensland school teacher, Jean Madden, was named "Queensland Young Australian of the Year" for her work establishing Street Swags (now Backpack Beds), a charity which provides custom-made portable camping beds to people sleeping rough. In 2016, Orange Sky Laundry founders, Nicholas Marchesi and Lucas Patchett, became the first dual recipients of the Young Australian of the Year Award, accelerating the expansion of their mobile laundry and shower initiative. More recently, Donna Stolzenberg, founder and CEO of the National Homelessness Collective, was named the 2021 Victorian Australian of the Year for her work in setting up various charitable initiatives aimed at helping the homeless. Stolzenberg's most recent initiative is the Kala Space, a second-hand clothing shop that employs homeless women, and where there are no set start or finish times in recognition of the vagaries of life on the street. However, Stolzenberg is also well known for launching The Period Project, a charity which distributes sanitary products to homeless women.

In each of these cases, the charitable are celebrated for exemplifying the socially coveted virtues of ethical citizenship, such as the spontaneous generosity and practical initiative they demonstrate in the face of manifest poverty and need. Stolzenberg is praised on the Australian of the Year website for her "generosity and resourcefulness" which "have provided practical solutions in Australia's most recent crises," such as the COVID-19 lockdowns (Australian of the Year Awards 2021). Madden was also celebrated for her generosity and innovation for establishing Street Swags (Dynamic Business 2012), as were Marchesi and Patchett, who then-Prime Minister Malcom Turnbull praised for their "very simple gesture, this simple idea, practical, innovative idea," which he believed "would go such a long way to raising health standards and restoring dignity to homeless people" (Turnbull 2016).

Beyond generosity and practical initiative, the charitable are held up as exemplars of how citizens can foster the affective bonds that are at the heart of (neo)liberal conceptions of social solidarity and the good society (Muehlebach 2012). Orange Sky's founders are at pains to highlight that the charity does more than meet a basic need: it creates human connection and companionship. As one of the charity's founders explained,

> The most important things that our vans carry around are not the washing machines or the dryers, it's not the detergent, it's not the volunteers – it's the six orange chairs [that people sit on whilst they wait for their laundry] which foster really positive and genuine conversation… That's where our service makes the biggest impact.
>
> (Tatham 2016)

Politicians are frequently enamoured with this sentiment (as are the media, as we show in Chapter 6), often explicitly identifying Orange Sky's capacity to create affective connections as a virtue that they wish to promote and normalise throughout Australia. For instance, then-Federal Labor Senator Claire Moore responded to the naming of Marchesi and Patchett as Young Australians of the Year with a gushing speech to parliament. In the speech, she stated that the true value of Orange Sky is its ability to create human connection and community: "Again, this is the link of having not just the laundry service available but the important element of engagement and having a conversation. Indeed, it is building community, load by load of washing." The Senator finished her speech by entreating Australians to recognise:

> …that we can be a part of it. That is the opportunity we have, not just through young Australians of the year but through building Australian community on every corner of every street and by ensuring that we treat people with the respect they deserve, and maybe having a chat with them while their laundry is being done by Orange Sky.
>
> (Parliament of Australia 2016)

Similarly, when launching the Dignity First Fund, the Queensland Housing Minister stated that "Orange Sky has been an outstanding example of our dignity first principles," which centre on promoting "a human approach to homelessness supports" (de Brenni 2016, p. 4828). According to the minister, it was important to encourage these kinds of "fresh approaches to the challenges people face," implying that State-led initiatives based on social rights, such as supplying social housing to prevent homelessness, are passé. Charity is valorised here for its ability to create affective connections that ground social solidarity in the spontaneous and quasi-natural bonds of community, eschewing the impersonal and pacifying mediation of the State.

As the embodiment of these values, recipients of accolades like the Australian of the Year Awards are positioned as paradigmatic examples of a way of being that all citizens should strive for. This was particularly true of Orange Sky's Marchesi and Patchett, who had won the highest honours of any of the exemplars discussed above. The Chief Minister of the Australian Capital Territory, Andrew Barr, described the two men as "amazing role models for our young people" (Australian Capital Territory Government 2017). Similarly, the Premier of Queensland, the state where Orange Sky first began, stated that:

> Their accomplishments are truly inspiring. They demonstrate not only amazing initiative and integrity, but determination to go above and beyond to make a difference, reminding us all of what it truly means to be a Queenslander.
>
> (Palaszczuk 2016)

As this quote illustrates, the charitable are positioned as revealing certain truths about who we are, and who we should be, as a society. In that manner distinct to liberal governmentalities (Rose 1999), the ethical citizen is positioned paradoxically as both our natural way of being, and as a goal that we are morally obligated to strive for.

In addition to promoting exemplars of ethical citizenship, the celebration of the charitable through official accolades also points to another symbolic strategy for cultivating ethical citizenship: the conferral of *ethical capital* on the charitable. The reader will recall from Chapter 3 that we use ethical capital to refer to the symbolic recognition of those who fulfil their obligations as ethical citizens. This recognition brings with it a certain amount of social prestige and an elevated social status, thus creating an incentive for citizens to engage in charitable acts. Accolades like the Australian of the Year Awards are one of the most pronounced examples of how the State confers ethical capital on charitable citizens. Another example is the official recognition of volunteers by political authorities through the Australian Government Certificate of Appreciation for Volunteers. The website hosting the Certificate states that:

> To help recognise [the] very important contribution [of volunteers], the Australian Government Certificate of Appreciation for Volunteers has been developed for use by Members of Parliament (MPs) and Senators. The certificate provides an effective way to formally acknowledge the efforts of outstanding and well-deserving volunteers in their electorate or state/territory.
>
> (Australian Government 2021)

As with the conferral of awards, the certificate enables political actors to bestow symbolic recognition on specific individuals for their performance of the virtues of ethical citizenship. Although not every volunteer will receive a certificate or an official award, these practices create public precedent for valorising the charitable and affording them elevated social status, which, in turn, encourages others to step up and perform their duties as ethical citizens. Indeed, the Australian Government explicitly teaches migrants to Australia that "compassion for those in need," as manifest through mateship and volunteering, is a requirement of citizenship that they are tested on

(Australian Government 2020b). As we show in the next chapter, the media play an important role in this process, both in terms of amplifying State efforts to celebrate the charitable and through their own efforts to identify and celebrate charitable citizens.

Cultivating the charitable through coordination and regulation

The final translation strategy that we will highlight here is the State's role in providing governance infrastructures for charitable activities in Australia. These infrastructures are largely regulatory in nature; however, this does not mean that they are about State control of the largely independent sphere of civil society. Rather, these infrastructures work to (re)configure legal and regulatory environments in ways that incentivise charity, and which provide the organisational resources and support that charity requires to play the prominent role in poverty governance that neoliberal reasoning imagines for it. Regulation is here primarily about enabling the practice of charity and fostering the organisations that administer it.

One way in which these governance infrastructures operate is by coordinating charitable responses to poverty as a means to enhance their efficiency and efficacy. The Australian Government, for instance, chairs a National Coordination Group (NCG) for all charities involved in the provision of emergency and food relief across the country. The stated aim of this group is to "analyse the impact of services, identify gaps and ensure that support is provided where it is needed." The Australian Government describes the NCG as follows:

> To ensure there is a collaborative, timely and coordinated approach to emergency relief and food relief across Australia, a sector-led National Coordination Group has been established, with representatives from the Emergency Relief, Food Relief and Financial Counselling sectors and the Department of Social Services (DSS). The National Coordination Group has been tasked to provide advice to Government and oversee opportunities to ensure the sector moves to more efficient models of operation, to better support emergency responses in the future.
>
> (Australian Government 2020d)

With the NCG, we see the State acting as a mediator and facilitator of the supposedly spontaneous energies and self-governing capacities of civil society. The Australian Government not only creates a forum wherein charitable organisations can identify shared challenges and seek to better coordinate their poverty-relief efforts, but it also plays an active role in guiding these deliberations.

The Australian Government also facilitates and mediates the coordination of charitable activities through the grant-funding activities described in the section on material support above. It does this by including criteria that favour proposals that include collaborations between different charitable organisations and activities:

> The grants place an emphasis on collaboration amongst organisations to develop whole-of-community approaches to emerging community challenges. They enable community organisations to innovate service delivery and work together to better respond to changing community need.
>
> (Australian Government 2020d)

Here, the State creates an incentive for charities to coordinate their activities in ways that they would likely not do if left to their own devices.

Beyond its more direct role in coordinating charitable activities through institutional arrangements such as the NCG, the State also facilities charitable activities indirectly by creating a conducive legal and regulatory environment for charitable organisations. The best-known example of this is the legal status afforded to organisations that are officially registered as charities. Under Australian law, an organisation may be registered as a charity if it can demonstrate that it operates on a not-for-profit basis and has "charitable purposes… that are for the public benefit" (Australian Government 2013, p. 4). A range of specific categories of charitable purpose are laid out in the *Charities Act, 2013*, including "advancing social or public welfare" by "relieving the poverty, distress or disadvantage of individuals or families" (pp. 11–12). Registered charities enjoy significant tax concessions, and are in many cases exempt from paying tax on their incomes, consumption, or fringe benefits. Additionally, people or organisations who donate to charities are able to deduct these from their own tax liabilities. These concessions play an important role in enabling charitable responses to social issues like poverty, as they incentivise and help make viable the setting up of organisations (i.e. charities) to coordinate and facilitate these activities.

Charitable activity is also facilitated by the State through its regulatory infrastructures. Government bodies, such as the Australian Charities and Not-for-Profit Commission (ACNC), oversee State-sanctioned charitable activities. However, in keeping with broader shifts in the practice of regulatory bodies engendered by the rise of neoliberalism (Clarke 2019; Tombs & Whyte 2013), these organisations see their primary aim as enabling and enhancing charity, rather than detecting and punishing bad behaviour (McGregor-Lowndes 2016). The ACNC states that one of its key aims is to "support and sustain a robust, vibrant, independent and innovative not-for-profit sector" (Australian Charities and Not-for-Profit Commission n.d.a), and that it commits to "a renewed focus on championing charities, working with them to become more effective, and helping them improve their governance" (Australian Government 2016a). At the same time, the ACNC downplays its prescriptive and policing functions: in response to claims that Australia has "too many charities" and that the State should play a greater role in regulating their proliferation and activities, the ACNC states that:

> Citizens have a right to freedom of association and this is something that we value in our society. Charities and not-for-profits are often the vehicles that citizens use to form associations and undertake activities. They are rightly independent of the State and a cornerstone of civil society.
>
> (Australian Charities and Not-for-Profit Commission n.d.b)

We see another example here of the indirect and facilitative role imaged for the State in the neoliberal social (Rose 1999). Rather than directly controlling the number and activities of charitable organisations, the State should create the conditions for their flourishing.

In performing this enabling role, regulatory bodies provide charities with a range of practical resources to meet their legal and regulatory requirements, including the establishment of a dedicated call centre and administrative guidance documents by the ACNC (McGregor-Lowndes 2016). This is coupled with a concerted effort by regulators to minimise red tape by removing unnecessary regulatory obligations imposed on charities, which are perceived as diverting them from their core work. So central is this crusade against red tape that the ACNC lists it as one of its core aims. It aims to, "promote the reduction of unnecessary regulatory obligations on the sector" (Australian Charities and Not-for-Profit Commission n.d.a). Similarly, the Australian Government (2016b) states that:

> The Department is delivering on the Government's commitment by streamlining processes for civil society organisations and removing red tape. This will enable the sector to self-manage and focus more on its work in the community.

Minimising the State's regulatory burden on private actors was an early preoccupation of neoliberal reform (Ayres & Braithwaite 1992), and one that persists today. Regulation is seen as one of the principal ways in which the State hampers the dynamic, self-governing potential of the market and civil society (Pusey 1991). Minimising regulatory activity to only that which is absolutely necessary, coupled with the aforementioned efforts to enable non-State actors to self-regulate (through advice, support, resources, etc.), is thus a key strategy through which the State seeks to enhance charitable activity.

Mediation and counter-translation

As we have shown, the State's efforts to translate the interests of (potentially) charitable citizens and align them with the project of neoliberalising the social are manifold and sophisticated. However, we cannot assume that these strategies necessarily succeed in their goal. As we argued in Chapter 3, translation is (at least partially) an open-ended process where enrolled actors act as mediators of the broader project (Latour 2005). This means that they have the capacity to both advance the project through the contribution of their unique capacities, and to resist or redirect it through practices of counter-translation, wherein they harness resources or infrastructures used to enrol them to advance their own projects or purposes.

When we look at how prominent Australian charities discursively position themselves in relation to poverty governance, we see that their relationship to the neoliberalising projects of government is complex. On the one hand, these organisations tend to reinforce the message that the value of charity lies in its capacity to advance community and ethical citizenship. This can be seen in how large national charities describe the act of volunteering to support their efforts to alleviate poverty. The St Vincent de Paul Society (2021a) describes volunteering as "a chance to give something back to the community" and "to make a difference in the lives of people who need assistance the most." Similarly, for The Salvation Army (2021a),

> Volunteering is an invitation to demonstrate our care for others in our local communities; it is the everyday embodiment of love in action. Those who give up their time so freely are some of the greatest contributors and advocates of Salvation Army mission and vision.

Participation in charitable activities is here represented as an *opportunity* to perform the virtues and duties of ethical citizenship, specifically the exercise of spontaneous compassion and care to people in need – "giv[ing] up their time so freely" to "care for others in our local communities." The act of volunteering is linked fundamentally to the spontaneous sociality of community, with the idea of State-mediated social rights being conspicuously absent.

These organisations also advance and reinforce the idea that the charitable acts they facilitate are about mitigating (welfare) dependence, as illustrated by their common refrain that they provide a hand up, not merely a handout.

> We help people in crisis meet their immediate needs, because we believe no one should have to go without the essentials. *But we want to offer more than just a hand out.* We believe that people possess a range of strengths and skills to overcome life's challenges. Our aim is to journey with individuals to find long-term solutions to their struggles.
>
> (The Salvation Army 2021b, emphasis added)

> The Society aspires to be recognised as a caring Catholic charity *offering 'a hand up' to people in need.* We do this by respecting their dignity,

> sharing our hope, and encouraging them to take control of their own destiny.
>
> (St Vincent de Paul Society 2021b, emphasis added)

Consistent with the political and policy discourses discussed above, charity is here positioned as antithetical to the kind of dependency that is associated with State welfare provision in neoliberal social imaginaries (Miller & Rose 2008). By providing people in need with a hand up, charity helps imbue communities with the capacity for self-reliance.

Yet, alongside these images of ethical citizens building self-reliant communities, charitable organisations also articulate a strong commitment to the principles of social justice, which are largely absent from government rhetoric, and indeed from the neoliberal conception of the social it advances. Anglicare Australia cites "equity and justice" amongst its core goals, and claim that their national network "strives for social justice, respecting the inherent worth of every human being with special concern for the vulnerable and disadvantaged." Similarly, The Salvation Army state that they represent "a mobilised force fighting injustice and inequality around the world without discrimination."

In some cases, this commitment to justice appears to mean little more than mobilising volunteers to address basic needs. Anglicare for instance states that:

> This year, once again, our Anglicare Australia Network members have gone above and beyond the call of duty in providing services that each, in their own way, contribute to creating a more just society. We thank them for all the hard work 'at the coal face' that makes it a task of joy and pride to represent.
>
> (Anglicare n.d., p. 7)

Importantly, however, the commitment to justice can also mean that charitable organisations take on a responsibility to go beyond manifest need to question the causes of poverty. For instance, the St Vincent de Paul Society states that:

> When we speak about social justice we go to the heart of what the St Vincent de Paul Society stands for. We are called, as Vincentians, to feed, clothe, house and assist our brothers and sisters who are forced onto the margins of society. We are also called to ask why they are left out and pushed out?
>
> (St Vincent de Paul Society 2021c)

Here, the engagement with the basic needs of the poor is linked to an overtly political practice of highlighting the social processes in which poverty is embedded. Alongside values like compassion and empathy, the St Vincent de Paul Society (2021b) lists advocacy as one of its key values, defining it as "working to transform the causes of poverty and challenging the causes of human injustice." Indeed, in the previous chapter we cited the St Vincent de Paul Society (2020) describing the below poverty line unemployment benefit as brutal for forcing people to struggle to survive. Further, in early 2021 when the Australian Government increased the unemployment benefit by less than AUD$4.00 per day, The Salvation Army publically criticised the government for failing to provide people with the necessities public resources to address disadvantage (The Salvation Army 2021c). These examples inspire our ideas for activism in our reimagination of what it means to be charitable (Chapter 9).

Consistent with previous studies (Cloke et al. 2017; Muehlebach 2012), this observation suggests that charitable actors can leverage their valorised position in neoliberal models of poverty governance to advance critiques of the poverty-generating tendencies of neoliberalism itself. Indeed, Australian charities play a key role in publicly highlighting the impact of the poverty-generating policies that we described in Chapter 4. For instance, in addition to enabling volunteers to provide frontline support to people in need, Anglicare Australia carries out a series of high-profile national surveys into the causes and experiences of poverty in Australia. The reports highlight the connection between the low rate of unemployment benefits, material poverty, and people's reliance on charitable support, including emergency relief (Anglicare 2020). Similarly, Anglicare's annual *Rental Affordability Snapshot* draws attention to the failure of Australia's housing system to provide housing that is affordable to people on low incomes, generating significant media attention and debate. The 2019 report placed government under-investment in social housing squarely at the heart of the issue, with the opening statement from the Executive Director proclaiming that:

> Australia is looking to the private rental market to provide housing for more and more people. As our governments walk away from social housing, more people must fend for themselves in a market that is out of control. With over 115,000 people homeless, we desperately need to increase the amount of social housing and put a roof over the head of every Australian.
>
> (Anglicare 2019)

The call for greater investment in social housing was reiterated in the 2020 report, which stated that "ending our social housing shortfall would be the most powerful way to tackle the rental crisis and boost regional economies." The Salvation Army (2021c) was unambiguous in asserting that the Australian Government's slight increase to the unemployment benefit "does not solve the problem."

The critiques of welfare state withdrawal offered by charities like The Salvation Army, St Vincent de Paul Society, and Anglicare cast their endorsement of ethical citizenship and bottom-up community in somewhat different light. Namely, these critiques and the dissatisfaction with dominant State policy that they represent suggest that they are advancing an alternative conception of the social to the neoliberal vision advanced by the State. Instead, it is a vision in which the ethical commitments and practical ingenuity of citizens and communities are paired with a welfare state that takes seriously its role in securing social rights by making sure the basic needs of all citizens are satisfied. Most large charities, similarly, are signed and publically visible participants to the Raise the Rate and Everybody's Home campaigns. We return to this alternative vision in Chapter 9, where we explore in greater depth the practices of counter-translation that are required to make it possible.

Conclusion

Charity's role in poverty alleviation is no accident. However, neither is it an automatic response to the withdrawal of the State from direct welfare provisioning and the subsequent rise in visible poverty (Lambie-Mumford 2019; Levitas 2012). Rather, the growth of charity is something that is actively cultivated by political and governmental actors as part of a broader project of reassembling the social in accordance with neoliberal ideals. As we have demonstrated in this chapter, neoliberal conceptions of the social emanate from the highest levels of Australian social and political life. They are put forward as both a reflection of the true Australian character, and as an aspiration that all citizens should strive towards. To make these ideals a reality, the State employs a series of translation strategies that provide material, symbolic, and legal/regulatory support to charitable responses to poverty, at the same time as direct welfare support is withdrawn in the ways described in Chapter 4. Through this process, charity is mobilised to cultivate the forms of self-governing community, ethical citizenship, and affective solidarity that comprise the neoliberal social imaginary.

Yet, we have also begun to demonstrate that the neoliberalisation of the social is not a *fait accompli*. Whilst prominent charitable organisations in Australia embrace charitable work as an opportunity to practice ethical citizenship and affective solidarity, they also demonstrate a commitment to questioning the social and political causes of poverty, and sometimes advance advocacy campaigns that critique and challenge welfare state withdrawal. This is a reminder that there is nothing essentially neoliberal about the practice of charity, and that efforts to reassemble the social are ongoing and open-ended, and thus open to redirection and harnessing alternative projects and ideals. In the next chapter, we turn to the question of public representations of charity, and the role of the media in cultivating and challenging images of the charitable as ethical citizens.

References

Anglicare n.d., *Stronger Together: Anglicare Australia*, viewed 13 March 2021, https://www.anglicare.asn.au/docs/default-source/default-document-library/annual-report-2017-18.pdf?sfvrsn=2

Anglicare 2019, *Anglicare Rental Affordability Snapshot: National Report, 2019*, Anglicare Australia, Canberra.

Anglicare 2020, *Ask Someone Who Knows: A Survey of Australians on Centrelink Payments*, viewed 13 March 2021, https://www.anglicare.asn.au/docs/default-source/default-document-library/asking-those-who-know—web-version.pdf?sfvrsn=0

Australian Capital Territory Government 2017, *Orange Sky Laundry to Serve Canberra's Homeless*, viewed 23 February 2021, https://www.cmtedd.act.gov.au/open_government/inform/act_government_media_releases/barr/2016/orange-sky-laundry-to-serve-canberras-homeless

Australian Charities and Not-for-profits Commission n.d.a, *About Us*, viewed 23 February 2021, https://www.acnc.gov.au/about

Australian Charities and Not-for-profits Commission n.d.b, *Are There Too Many Charities in Australia?*, viewed 23 February 2021, https://www.acnc.gov.au/for-public/understanding-charities/are-there-too-many-charities-australia

Australian Government 2013, *Charities Act 2013*, viewed 13 March 2021, https://www.legislation.gov.au/Details/C2013A00100

Australian Government 2016a, *Australian Charities and Not-for-Profits Commission (ACNC)*, viewed 23 February 2021, https://www.dss.gov.au/communities-and-vulnerable-people/programmes-services/australian-charities-and-not-for-profits-commission-acnc

Australian Government 2016b, *Civil Society*, viewed 23 February 2021, https://www.dss.gov.au/our-responsibilities/communities-and-vulnerable-people/programs-services/civil-society

Australian Government 2018, *Strong and Resilient Communities*, viewed 23 February 2021, https://www.dss.gov.au/our-responsibilities-communities-and-vulnerable-people/strong-and-resilient-communities

Australian Government 2020a, *Emergency Relief*, viewed 23 February 2021, https://www.dss.gov.au/our-responsibilities/communities-and-vulnerable-people/programs-services/emergency-relief

Australian Government 2020b, *Australian Citizenship: Our Common Bonds*, viewed 05 March 2021, https://immi.homeaffairs.gov.au/citizenship-subsite/files/our-common-bond-15112020.pdf

Australian Government 2020c, *Food Relief*, viewed 23 February 2021, https://www.dss.gov.au/communities-and-vulnerable-people/programmes-services/financial-wellbeing-and-capability-overview-of-changes/food-relief

Australian Government 2020d, *Emergency Relief National Coordination Plan*, viewed 23 February 2021, https://www.dss.gov.au/communities-and-vulnerable-people-programs-services-emergency-relief/emergency-relief-national-coordination-plan

Australian Government 2021, *Australian Government Certificate of Appreciation for Volunteers*, viewed 23 February 2021, https://www.dss.gov.au/communities-and-vulnerable-people-programs-services/australian-government-certificate-of-appreciation-for-volunteers

Australian of the Year Awards n.d., *Recipients*, viewed 23 February 2021, https://www.australianoftheyear.org.au/recipients/

Australian of the Year Awards 2021, *Recipient 2021 Donna Stolzenberg*, viewed 23 February 2021, https://www.australianoftheyear.org.au/recipients/donna-stolzenberg/2281/

Ayres, I & Braithwaite, J 1992, *Responsive Regulation: Transcending the Deregulation Debate*, Oxford University Press, New York.

Clarke, A 2019, 'The governance of mundane urban nuisances: Examining the influence of neoliberal reason on regulatory practices in Brisbane, Australia', *City*, vol. 23, no. 4–5, pp. 524–539.

Cloke, P, May, J & Williams, A 2017, 'The geographies of food banks in the meantime', *Progress in Human Geography*, vol. 41, no. 6, pp. 703–726.

Dean, J 2020, *The Good Glow: Charity and the Symbolic Power of Doing Good*, Policy Press, Bristol.

de Brenni, M 2016, *Record of Proceedings, Parliament of Queensland*, viewed 23 February 2021, https://www.parliament.qld.gov.au/documents/hansard/2016/2016_12_01_WEEKLY.pdf

Dees, G 2012, 'A tale of two cultures: Charity, problem solving, and the future of social entrepreneurship', *Journal of Business Ethics*, vol. 111, no. 3, pp. 321–334.

Department of Social Services 2017, *Discussion Paper: Financial Wellbeing and Capability Activity*, Australian Government, Canberra.

Dynamic Business 2012, *Social Entrepreneur Jean Madden on Charitable Business*, viewed 23 February 2021, https://dynamicbusiness.com.au/leadership-2/entrepreneur-profile/social-entrepreneur-jean-madden-on-charitable-business-06062012.html

Dyrenfurth, N 2007, 'John Howard's hegemony of values: The politics of 'mateship' in the Howard decade', *Australian Journal of Political Science*, vol. 42, no. 2, pp. 211–230.

Foodbank Australia n.d., *Foodbank Hunger Report 2019*, viewed 13 March 2021, https://www.foodbank.org.au/wp-content/uploads/2019/10/Foodbank-Hunger-Report-2019.pdf

Foucault, M 2008, *The Birth of Biopolitics: Lectures at the Collège de France, 1978–79*, Palgrave Macmillan, London.

Harvey, D 2007, *A Brief History of Neoliberalism*, Oxford University Press, Oxford.

Johnson, C 2007, 'John Howard's 'values' and Australian identity', *Australian Journal of Political Science*, vol. 42, no. 2, pp. 195–209.

Lambie-Mumford, H 2019, 'The growth of food banks in Britain and what they mean for social policy', *Critical Social Policy*, vol. 39, no. 1, pp. 3–22.

Latham, M 1998, 'Economic policy and the Third Way', *Australian Economic Review*, vol. 31, no. 4, pp. 384–398.

Latour, B 1986, 'The powers of association', in J Law (ed.), *Power, Action and Belief*, Routledge & Kegan Paul, London, pp. 264–280.

Latour, B 1987, *Science in Action: How to Follow Scientists and Engineers Through Society*, Harvard University Press, Cambridge.

Latour, B 2005, *Reassembling the Social: An Introduction to Actor-Network-Theory*, Oxford University Press, Oxford.

Levitas, R 2012, 'The just's umbrella: Austerity and the Big Society in Coalition policy and beyond', *Critical Social Policy*, vol. 32, no. 3, pp. 320–342.

McGregor-Lowndes, M 2016, 'Lawyers, reform and regulation in the Australian third sector', *Third Sector Review*, vol. 22, no. 2, p. 33.

Miller, P & Rose, N 2008, *Governing the Present: Administering Economic, Social and Personal Life*, Polity, Cambridge.

Mohan, J & Breeze, B 2016, *The Logic of Charity: Great Expectations in Hard Times*, Palgrave Macmillan, Basingstoke.

Morrison, S 2018, "Until the bell rings" – Address to Menzies Research Centre, viewed 12 March 2021, https://www.pm.gov.au/media/until-bell-rings-address-menzies-research-centre

Muehlebach, A 2012, *The Moral Neoliberal: Welfare and Citizenship in Italy*, University of Chicago Press, Chicago.

New South Wales Government 2015, *Orange Sky Laundry Services – Now Operating in Sydney*, viewed 23 February 2021, https://www.facs.nsw.gov.au/about/media/news/archive/orange-sky-laundry-services-now-operating-in-sydney

Orange Sky n.d., viewed 23 February 2021, https://orangesky.org.au/

Orange Sky 2020, *Orange Sky Australia: Annual Report 2019/20*, viewed 23 February 2021, https://orangesky.org.au/wp-content/uploads/2020/12/201202_Annual_Report_FINAL_with_Financial_Report.pdf

Page, J 2002, 'Is mateship a virtue?', *Australian Journal of Social Issues*, vol. 37, no. 2, pp. 193–200.

Palaszczuk, A 2016, *Media Statement. Queensland Government*, viewed 23 February 2021, http://statements.qld.gov.au/Statement/2016/1/25/outstanding-young-queenslanders-named-young-australians-of-the-year

Parliament of Australia 2016, *Adjournment: Orange Sky*, viewed 23 February 2021, https://parlinfo.aph.gov.au/parlInfo/search/display/display.w3p;db=CHAMBER;id=chamber/hansards/6b734b2a-e113-486c-bacc-822e11cbf7e6/0248;query=Id:%22chamber/hansards/6b734b2a-e113-486c-bacc-822e11cbf7e6/0000%22

Pawson, H, Parsell, C, Lui, E, Hartley, C & Thompson, S 2020, *The Australian Homelessness Monitor, 2020*, Launch Housing, Melbourne.

Pusey, M 1991, *Economic Rationalism in Canberra: A Nation-Building State Changes Its Mind*, Cambridge University Press, Cambridge.

Reddel, T 2004, 'Third way social governance: Where is the state?', *Australian Journal of Social Issues*, vol. 39, no. 2, pp. 129–142.

Rose, N 1999, *Powers of Freedom: Reframing Political Thought*, Cambridge University Press, Cambridge.

Rose, N 2000, 'Community, citizenship, and the third way', *American Behavioral Scientist*, vol. 43, no. 9, pp. 1395–1411.

Scanlon, C 2001, 'A step to the left? Or just a jump to the right? Making sense of the third way on government and governance', *Australian Journal of Political Science*, vol. 36, no. 3, pp. 481–498.

St Vincent de Paul Society 2020, *Briefing: Raising the Rate of Newstart*, viewed 22 February 2021, https://www.vinnies.org.au/page/Publications/National/Factsheets_and_policy_briefings/Briefing_Raising_the_Rate_of_Newstart/

St Vincent de Paul Society 2021a, *Making a Difference in Someone's Life*, viewed 23 February 2021, https://www.vinnies.org.au/page/Get_Involved/Become_a_volunteer/

St Vincent de Paul Society 2021b, *Our Mission*, viewed 23 February 2021, https://www.vinnies.org.au/page/About/Mission__Vision/

St Vincent de Paul Society 2021c, *Our Story*, viewed 13 March 2021, https://www.vinnies.org.au/page/About/St_Vincent_de_Paul_Society/#:~:text=When%20we%20speak%20about%20social,onto%20the%20margins%20of%20society

Tatham, H 2016, 'Orange Sky laundry launches on Sunshine Coast, tackling housing, employment with clean clothes', *ABC News*, https://www.abc.net.au/news/2016-04-13/orange-sky-laundry-launches-on-sunshine-coast/7323292

The Salvation Army 2021a, *Volunteering with the Salvos*, viewed 23 February 2021, https://www.salvationarmy.org.au/get-involved/volunteer-with-us/

The Salvation Army 2021b, *Doorways and Emergency Relief*, viewed 23 February 2021, https://www.salvationarmy.org.au/about-us/our-services/doorways-and-emergency-relief/

The Salvation Army 2021c, *A $24 Increase to JobSeeker Does Not Solve the Problem*, viewed 01 March 2021, https://www.salvationarmy.org.au/about-us/news-and-stories/media-newsroom/a-25-increase-to-jobseeker-does-not-solve-the-problem/

Tombs, S & Whyte, D 2013, 'Transcending the deregulation debate? Regulation, risk, and the enforcement of health and safety law in the UK', *Regulation & Governance*, vol. 7, no. 1, pp. 61–79.

Turnbull, M 2016, *Remarks at AskIzzy Launch, Melbourne*, viewed 23 February 2021, https://www.malcolmturnbull.com.au/media/remarks-at-askizzy-launch-melbourne

6 Representing charity

Introduction

This chapter presents the results of analyses of how the media represents charitable responses to poverty. In earlier chapters, we demonstrated how the State instigates policies that create poverty and the need for charity, and then employs a range of techniques to encourage and facilitate charitable responses to that poverty. We argued that these processes are part of a broader project aimed at reassembling the social along neoliberal lines. We showed how the State presents charity as an exemplar of the ethical citizenship and spontaneous community that are at the heart of neoliberal ideals and conceptions of the social. It does this by celebrating, not to mention funding, the charitable as ethical citizens for exercising spontaneous and ground up compassion. The ethical citizen is presented as not motivated by self-interest. The ethical citizen instead, does what the State does not do; what the State cannot do; and what the State ought not do.

The State, however, is not the only institution that shapes social citizens and guides their responses to poverty. Scholars have long recognised that the media is a highly influential institution with the power to regulate and shape society (Entman 1993). This insight has only increased in relevance with the rise of social media and the use of algorithmic targeting to influence people's attitudes and perceptions (Rebello et al. 2020). With its ability to disseminate large volumes of information rapidly and widely, the media has considerable power to shape how we think about and respond to social issues such as poverty (Bullock et al. 2001).

We know that editorial decisions, such as what issues are covered and how they are framed, have significant implications for how society understands poverty (Bullock et al. 2001; Chauhan & Foster 2014; Hodgetts et al. 2005). This, in turn, has the power to influence not only individual responses to the issue, but also overarching policy. As Darrin Hodgetts and colleagues argue, "policies are likely to be developed and implemented if policy makers consider there to be sufficient public support expressed through media coverage" (Hodgetts et al. 2005, p. 31). Indeed, existing scholarship draws links between media representations of poverty and the perceived responsibility of the State, suggesting that the absence of the State from media discussions of poverty leads to a lack of public expectation for the State to act on the issue (Hrast 2008).

This prompts us to ask how the media's treatment of charity contributes to the production of the neoliberal social and the forms of citizenship and solidarity that underpin it. Although there is a sizeable body of literature that examines media representations of poverty and the people who experience it, there is a comparative lack of literature examining media representations of charitable responses to poverty. The literature that does exist demonstrates that media representations of people who act charitably are highly positive, and foreground their morality and generosity (Hodgetts et al. 2005; Smith-Carrier 2020a). We extend this literature by demonstrating the role of media representations of charity in the broader project of reassembling the social along neoliberal lines.

To do this, we analysed news reports published online or in print in Australia's four national mainstream news media outlets – *The Australian*, *The Australian Financial Review* (AFR), *Australian Broadcasting Corporation News* (ABC), and *Special Broadcasting Service News* (SBS) – between 2014 and 2020. News reports were sourced from the Factivia media database, and were deemed eligible for inclusion if they focused on charitable acts towards the poor within an Australian context. We analysed a total of 111 news reports' representations of poverty, charity, and the people involved in the practice of charity. Findings from our analysis suggest that the media helps communicate to the public – and, indeed, to the State – collective social investment in the values and duties of ethical citizenship. It also helps perpetuate an image of society as retaining (or perhaps regaining) the affective and moral bonds of the lost *gemeinschaft* that haunts the modern cultural imaginary and which is targeted for resurrection by the neoliberal cultivation of community.

The characterisation of good

As we have demonstrated at length in earlier chapters, charity is valorised in public discourse as a positive and desirable means of contributing to society. In this section, building on existing work (Hodgetts et al. 2005; Smith-Carrier 2020a), we examine why charity is valorised in media discourse, despite its inability to address the underlying causes of poverty. We argue that the media constructs poverty primarily as a problem of inequalities in social status and esteem, with little attention paid to the role of material inequalities in creating a need for charity in the first place. The solution to inequalities in status – and, in turn, to poverty – is presented by the media as lying in the restoration of the dignity of the poor. Media reports celebrate charity's capacity to restore dignity to the poor by enabling their (usually temporary) symbolic reintegration into the normative order of society. The restoration of dignity is seen to be achieved through charities' provision of basic resources to address the manifestations of poverty and allow receivers of charity to feel and pass as normal. Dignity is also seen to be achieved through the human connections that charity engenders between the poor and volunteers, which provide the former with opportunities to feel included by a society that otherwise positions them as outcasts. Through the provision of dignity and opportunities for social reintegration, charity is positioned as a means through which the poor may be supported by their community to help themselves out of poverty and become contributing members of the community.

Charity as recognition

The idea that charity is a positive feature of society because it attends to the poor's immediate material needs and alleviates their suffering is widespread, and helps to contribute to society's valorisation of charitable responses (Smith-Carrier 2020b). Our analysis shows that the vast majority of charitable acts discussed in the media involve the provision of basic support to address the immediate needs of the poor, including food, clothing, and emergency shelter. The following excerpts illustrate media sentiment well:

> The service is a mobile drop-in centre, offering material aid such as food, clothes, internet access, or just a hot drink.
>
> (ABC 2015, Chatterbox Bus providing support for homeless, at-risk youth in Melbourne)

> Studio Thrifty 4 opened its doors in June in Albion and has since helped hundreds of Brisbane's homeless by providing them with items to make life on the street a little easier.
>
> (ABC 2017, Op shop Studio Thrifty 4 provides survival sacks for the homeless)

> Loaded with toiletry packs, food hampers and first-aid kits, they help those in need.
>
> (ABC 2018, 11yo Ashton Brown's dream of helping the homeless from a caravan comes true)

Some might argue that such initiatives are indicative of a society that values the redistribution of resources to help address material inequalities. However, as Katrien Boone and colleagues argue, trying to correct poverty by redistributing basic material resources to the people experiencing poverty (e.g. through food vans, clothing donations, and crisis accommodation) is insufficient for addressing the underlying conditions that drive poverty (Boone et al. 2018). So, while such initiatives may seek to redistribute material resources in ways that mitigate the symptoms of poverty, they overlook the necessity of redistributing resources in ways that prevent poverty from occurring in the first place (see Chapter 2).

Indeed, rather than positioning poverty as the inequitable distribution of resources, the media emphasises the centrality of status inequalities that are experienced as a significant burden by people living in poverty. Lamenting the status and power imbalances that exist between the haves and have nots, the media encourages the more fortunate of us to be mindful of these imbalances in our interactions with those we may wish to help. In a series of articles entitled *How to talk to a homeless person?* and *What's the best way to help a homeless person?* (SBS 2018), we are reminded of the metaphorical power imbalances that help to reinforce the marginalisation of people sleeping rough.

> There's no greater metaphorical power imbalance than looking down on somebody you are talking to. "If I feel comfortable, I will sit down next to someone or drop on my haunches."
>
> (SBS 2018, How to talk to a homeless person)

We are similarly reminded of the importance of viewing and treating those experiencing hardship as people – just like us – who may be different but are nonetheless deserving of respect and inclusion.

> See the person, not the stereotype... "Anything you can do to make them feel like a part of the community, and not isolated, and on the outer."
>
> (SBS 2018, What's the best way to help a homeless person?)

> They are human like the rest of us and they deserve that human respect no matter what their circumstances are... There's nothing that can reinforce you feeling marginalised like people just ignoring you.
>
> (SBS 2018, What's the best way to help a homeless person?)

The media's focus on addressing issues of status and social stigmatisation over those concerned with creating the social conditions for everyone to participate equally in society reflects a broader privileging of struggles for recognition in societal responses to inequalities. For Fraser (2000), the rise of identity politics has resulted in the recasting of social inequality as being fundamentally a matter of the misrecognition and devaluation of certain social identities. This leads to a reductive view of material/distributive inequalities where identity is all that matters, rather than as a relatively autonomous process that intersects with issues of status in complex ways. In this context, the media reduces poverty to a devalued identity, the remedy for which is presented as the restoration of dignity through charity.

A sense of dignity

The restoration of dignity emerged as a core theme in the media reports we analysed. Many of the charitable initiatives presented in the media were framed in terms of their ability to restore dignity by responding to the immediate needs of the poor and providing a sense of normalcy, as the following examples illustrate.

> It's enabling people to have choice as well. It's bringing a bit of dignity back into that space.
>
> (ABC 2015, Melbourne's Period Project for homeless reaches regional Victoria)

> "Choice is dignity," says Halas. "The fact that the clothes are new and the fact that they have choice provides a sense of dignity."
>
> (AFR 2020, How a not-for-profit is helping retailers deal with excess stock)

> Mr Bottrell said the caravans would serve as a vital foundation for homeless veterans to start getting their lives back on track. "It will give them a sense of more dignity," he said.
>
> (ABC 2018, Lismore Men's Shed volunteers tackle veteran homelessness by building caravans)

As the first two excerpts demonstrate, the idea of choice is commonly linked to the restoration of dignity. In these instances, the ability of charity receivers to choose the resources that they are given is positioned as a key factor enabling their agency and, in turn, providing them with a sense of dignity. Allowing charity receivers to choose their preferred articles of donated clothing, their preferred sanitary products, and their preferred meals, is positioned as an important means through which they may both exercise their agency and have their immediate needs met. Dignity is assumed to be achieved when immediate needs are addressed through charity in ways that are preferable to the receiver; the threat to dignity that charity itself represents is largely overlooked.

As we demonstrate in Chapter 8 with the experiences of people relying on charity, the sentiment that charity provides dignity for the poor contrasts with literature demonstrating the strong feelings of shame that people feel when they are forced to rely on strangers' kindness to survive (Parsell & Clarke 2020; Purdam et al. 2016; Smith-Carrier 2020a). Purdam and colleagues, for example, show how accessing free foodbanks can actually come at a very real cost for people experiencing poverty, despite most foodbanks offering a range of product choices (Purdam et al. 2016). As well as experiencing shame and stigma due to being dependent on others to fulfil a basic need, individuals who access foodbanks often experience negative impacts on their self-perception and sense of self-efficacy (Purdam et al. 2016; Smith-Carrier 2020a). Far from providing dignity, this can compound the shame of accessing charity and act as a barrier preventing people from accessing the support they require to subsist. This is particularly true for parents, who often fear that accessing foodbanks may cause others to doubt their ability to care for their children and result in the children being removed by child welfare services (Purdam et al. 2016).

The disconnect between the purported importance of charity for restoring the dignity of the poor and the evidence surrounding the links between charity and indignity suggest that there are other factors underpinning public perceptions of charity as an effective response to poverty. One such factor is the desire for people experiencing poverty to become more like – and, in turn, more acceptable to – the rest of society. This is evidenced, in part, through the news reports' focus on providing dignity by improving the physical appearance of people experiencing poverty (e.g. through the provision of showers, clean clothes, haircuts):

> He said the service provided around 200 free showers a month and brought immeasurable benefits to the people who used it. "It was just the dignity that they would get back and the feeling of community and not being judged."
>
> (ABC 2018, Homeless mobile shower bus appeals for funds to get back on the road)

> "We always give them a shower and clean them up and we give them clean clothes," she says, "just to give them some dignity."
>
> (ABC 2019, This 83-year-old nun calms down ice users in the emergency department at St Vincent's Hospital)

Dignity here is linked to social perceptions and acceptance. The media draws on the assumption that in order to have dignity, individuals must maintain an acceptable level of cleanliness and presentation. While a person experiencing poverty may indeed feel more comfortable being clean and clothed, the comfort of broader society seems to be an equally important factor. It is much easier for society to accept those who appear to be like us; making the poor acceptable to us is therefore an important first step in fostering human connections.

The human connections that charity engenders between the poor and volunteers are celebrated in the media for their ability to make people experiencing poverty feel more integrated into society. Earlier in this section, we demonstrated that the media highlights the importance of viewing and including those experiencing hardship as members of the community. This is arguably much easier to do once we have removed the physical manifestations of poverty, which often provoke feelings of discomfort and disdain. In encouraging us to "see the person, not the stereotype," the media also valorises charity for its efforts to change people perceived as fitting a stereotype into people who can be perceived as belonging to society. Restoring dignity is thus a means of re-establishing the affective bonds and identifications of spontaneous community (Rose 1999), which are perceived as disrupted by the status inequalities produced by poverty.

With dignity comes opportunity

Another important function of dignity, as it is constructed by the media, is its perceived ability to act as a catalyst for a person's journey out of poverty. When a person's dignity is restored, it is believed that barriers to employment and other opportunities are removed. With the removal of these barriers, there is little preventing individuals from helping themselves out of poverty.

> Her service is driven by the belief that "with hygiene comes dignity, and that with dignity comes opportunity"... something as simple as a shower has the ability to remove barriers relating to employment, access to housing and other pathways to advancement.
>
> (SBS 2016, What Australia can learn from this San Fran bus helping eradicate poverty)

> Just making tea and coffee and toast for someone can set them on a path where they feel better about themselves, and maybe able to engage in services – education and to find housing – and just be better equipped to be able to deal with what would be a hard day in front of them.
>
> (ABC 2016, Homelessness in Newcastle through the eyes of a volunteer helping those in need)

This reflects and reinforces the common idea that charitable acts should provide a hand up, not a hand out (see Chapter 5). Crucial to this idea is the importance of not only helping the poor to develop independence, but also helping them to actively change their own circumstances.

> "The best option is to give people who are struggling a chance to improve their own circumstances. This makes them feel better about achieving something.
>
> (SBS 2018, Unconditional charity: Why it's okay to give money to homeless people)

> ... giving people a gift of encouragement and lifting them up and helping them find a better way.
>
> (ABC 2016, Homelessness in Newcastle through the eyes of a volunteer helping those in need)

> ... most importantly, they get results. Why? Because they empower and equip the homeless with the skills and the ability to make real changes in their lives.
>
> (SBS 2020, How appearing on Filthy Rich & Homeless changed me forever)

The idea of charity as important for helping people in poverty improve their own circumstances reinforces an individualised view of poverty. It promotes the idea that poverty is something that people can overcome with a bit of dedication and support, and overlooks the important structural barriers that remain in place regardless of the amount of encouragement and motivation charity provides. Consistent with the political and policy discourses discussed in Chapter 5, charity is positioned as a means through which to promote and mobilise responsible self-governance on the part of the poor by re-connecting them to the supportive networks of community.

Charity and the State

In previous chapters, we discussed how conceptualisations of the social have shifted in response to increasingly neoliberal forms of government. Indeed, the move away from the State-mediated relations of the welfare era has been accompanied by an increasing focus on the supposedly pre-political bonds of community and the forms of ethical citizenship that pertain to it (Muehlebach 2012; Rose 1999). In this section, we ask how the media constructs the relationship between charity and the State, and whether it reflects or challenges dominant political discourses. We demonstrate that, although at times the media notes the limitations of current State responses to poverty, this is often positioned as an inevitable limitation of the State's ability to provide for its citizens. Charity – and, importantly, the people who act charitably – are thus positioned as crucial for filling the gap left by the State. In doing so, the responsibilities of the community are foregrounded, and the virtues of those who uphold these responsibilities are celebrated. This serves to reinforce the valorisation of the ethical citizen that we see in political discourse, and legitimises the State's withdrawal from direct provision of support.

The best thing in life is to help somebody else

As we showed in the previous chapter, neoliberal understandings of the social permeate current policy and political discourses in Australia. These discourses place a premium on forms of sociality, solidarity, and ethical citizenship that operate beyond the State in the quasi-natural domains of community and civil society. Thus, the State is increasingly reassembling the social by withdrawing from direct welfare provision and facilitating community solidarity and assistance to take its place. As we elaborated in Chapter 3, translation – the process through which the reassembling of the social is achieved – is key here (Latour 1986, 2005). Translation involves enrolling the support of people into, and through, the enactment of a particular definition of the social. Australian political authorities therefore seek to mobilise charitable responses to poverty by aligning the interests of community members to their neoliberal goals and worldviews.

As we have demonstrated in previous chapters, the government employs a variety of translation strategies to achieve this alignment, including perpetuating discourses that foreground citizens' ethical obligations to their communities.

Our analysis of Australian news reports suggests that the media reflects and perpetuates discourses surrounding citizens' ethical obligations to help support people in their communities who are experiencing poverty. One subtle but pervasive strategy for emphasising community ties and responsibilities is the use of possessive language to refer to people experiencing poverty.

> ... some of the city's most disadvantaged.
>
> (ABC 2015, Launceston soup van on a mission to make a difference for the disadvantaged)

> ... Sydney's needy and lonely...
>
> (ABC 2017, Malcolm Turnbull dances in the streets of Kings Cross while volunteering at Wayside Chapel)

> ... for our most vulnerable.
>
> (ABC 2017, Volunteers pitch in to stop Indigenous families being evicted from public housing)

By referring to people experiencing poverty as *our* poor or *the city's* poor, the reports imply that we are responsible for people experiencing poverty and are obligated to respond. Framing the poor in such a way may seek to mobilise communities to take responsibility for ameliorating the suffering of the needy, lonely, and vulnerable. Yet it also helps to construct the poor as passive recipients of charity who are dependent on others' support. Moreover, failing to refer to people experiencing poverty as people, identifying them instead purely by undesirable traits, renders them nothing more than objects on which we may bestow our magnanimity. We return to the significance of this point later in the chapter.

The community's moral obligation to support those experiencing poverty is further exemplified in the media reports' portrayal of volunteers. The reports frequently quoted and told the stories of the volunteers who act charitably towards the poor, most of whom spoke to the strong sense of moral obligation they felt to help those in need. Tropes like "giving back" and "making a difference" were commonly utilised both within volunteers' quotes and throughout the reports' commentary.

> "I believe that all of us have some degree of obligation to assist those in the community that aren't as well off as what we are," he said.
>
> (ABC 2015, Launceston soup van on a mission to make a difference for the disadvantaged)

> Asked why they all volunteer their time, she said that "with so many people struggling, it is the least they can do."
>
> (ABC 2015, Volunteers organise Christmas feast for those doing it tough in Parramatta)

> The best thing in life is to help somebody else; it's the best thing that I could do… is to help somebody else, and just knowing that you are contributing.
>
> (ABC 2016, Homelessness in Newcastle through the eyes of a volunteer helping those in need)

Giving back to the community is core to values of ethical citizenship and the foregrounding of the ethical obligations that community members have to each other over their rights to social protection (Rose 2000). Affective motivations like empathy and compassion are common and important to definitions of charity and ethical citizenship, and are promoted through the media. The media thus perpetuates the idea of the ethical citizen, who is intrinsically motivated to address an injustice or to help people in need by engaging in charitable acts.

To the ethical citizen, then, living up to their community responsibilities is not a chore, but is rather seen as an opportunity to give back and, moreover, an opportunity for which they are grateful. Participation in charitable activities is represented by the media as an opportunity to perform the virtues and duties of ethical citizenship, specifically the exercise of providing spontaneous compassion and care to people in need.

> It's a great opportunity to help people who really need it.
>
> (ABC 2015, Sydney's Homeless Connect offers helping hand to those in need)

> I hope into the future that this expands each year and we can look at what else we can do to assist the vulnerable people in our community.
>
> (ABC 2015, Free flu vaccinations to be offered to Canberra's most vulnerable)

> "I love the people. I love talking to them. I love asking them where they're from, asking them what they were doing before they were drinking," Ms Tapim said.
>
> (ABC 2020, Pilbara soup kitchen delivers nearly 10k meals a year and creates safe place to sober up)

As well as constructing charity as an opportunity for individuals to perform the virtues of ethical citizenship, the media also foregrounds the benefits gained by those who act charitably.

> Tutors learn from teaching too... Ms Simons said she was now weighing up teaching as a future career.
>
> (ABC 2019, Learning club making a difference for children and tutors)

> Speaking with people from all walks of life is not just about benefiting them ... we all have much to gain from interacting with our fellow community members.
>
> (SBS 2018, How to talk to a homeless person)

> In rescuing others, we rescue ourselves.
>
> (ABC 2017, Fatma Elzein: How this mother built a network of mums paying it forward)

Importantly, these benefits are not positioned as the motivation for acting charitably. As demonstrated previously, the ethical citizen is constructed as motivated to action by their morality and intrinsic values. The benefits of acting charitably, then, are positioned as desirable by-products, or rewards for the ethical citizens' moral behaviour. In this way, community members are encouraged to fulfil the role of the ethical citizen for moral and selfless reasons, but safe in the knowledge that they too will have something to gain. This helps to legitimise the State's withdrawal from welfare provision, and when considered in conjunction with the findings presented earlier into the chapter, suggests that the media positions community responses to poverty both as an effective way to fill the gap left by the State's withdrawal, and as beneficial enterprise for all involved.

When they won't... people like us will

Importantly, Latour (1987) reminds us that social actors are not mere dupes who will automatically respond to efforts to enrol their support for some project in the desired ways. Rather, social actors are active mediators who may eschew the roles imagined for them, and redirect the relationships, policies, and/or resources towards alternative ends. As we showed in Chapter 5, charity organisations may use the public prominence and proximity to poverty granted to them by neoliberal reforms as a platform from which to critique the consequences of those reforms, and/or campaign for direct State involvement in addressing poverty. This is reflected in the Australian media, which infrequently draws our attention to the limitations of current State responses to poverty, linking the problem to the State's inaction.

> The tragedy of homelessness that we see on the streets is a result of poor leadership and will continue unless governments make a stand and change polices, adds Smith of Homelessness Australia.
>
> (SBS 2017, Pop-ups don't work: Why homeless people deserve more than converted shipping containers)

> "This is just getting bigger and bigger, and there is no housing," the charity's John Lee said. Community activist Carmen Stewart agreed the region suffered from a lack of social housing.
>
> (ABC 2017, Good Samaritan offers to pay rent for homeless Murwillumbah flood victims)

Importantly, while the problem of ongoing poverty is at times linked to the failure of the State, the solution to the problem is rarely positioned as different or more effective forms of governance. On the contrary, the remedy to State failure is positioned as lying in community sociality, solidarity, and ethical citizenship.

> "We know we're not going to suddenly, magically have government be able to produce the hundreds of thousands of new homes that are needed," she said. "So, we need organisations like Uniting and other housing providers to take these exciting initiatives and provide appropriate housing for people."
>
> (ABC 2018, Pop-up shelter for homeless women makes use of Sydney building awaiting demolition)

> She said studies have shown volunteers are worth about $5 billion to the State's economy each year. "It's an incredible financial contribution and imagine if we didn't have that, what our taxes would be if we expected the same level of service," Ms O'Loughlin said.
>
> (ABC 2017, Census data reveals South Australia leads the States on volunteer percentage)

> This is a basic human right we are talking about. It is the responsibility of our governments to provide this basic necessity to its people… And when they won't, people like us will.
>
> (SBS 2016, What Australia can learn from this San Fran bus helping eradicate poverty)

In the above examples, the media simultaneously positions the limitations of the State as undesirable, yet largely inevitable. The State is seen as having the responsibility to provide for its citizens. However, this responsibility is accepted as a largely unfeasible expectation. As a result – and at the expense of pushing the government to do more to uphold its responsibilities – the media foregrounds community responses as the most viable solution for filling the gaps left by the State. Indeed, even when the media points out that the solution is affordable housing, it reports charitable acts such as sleep buses and pop-up shelters as endeavours that adequate replacements. There is little engagement in the media with the limitations of charitable acts to address structural resource limitations driven by State withdrawal.

Media representation implications

So far in this chapter, we have shown that the media portrays charitable acts towards the poor as an effective means through which to restore dignity and enable social reintegration, and as essential for *filling* the gap inevitably left by the State. In this section, we consider how these representations impact the lives and identities of those involved in charitable processes. We argue that the representations of charitable acts that dominate the media reify problematic identities of charity givers and receivers, which, in turn, exacerbates both status and material inequalities.

We show that charitable givers are upheld for their morals and virtues, and, in turn, accumulate ethical capital. For those who are forced to rely on charity for subsistence, the accumulation of such capital is often out of reach on account of their lack of material and social resources. The accumulation of ethical capital through engaging in charitable acts, then, represents a means through which the haves may further improve their social standing, while the have nots are unable to do the same. Further, in addition to their lack of access to ethical capital, receivers of charity are positioned by the media as pitiful and passive objects, thus reinforcing their marginalised social status.

The construction of charity receivers as passive objects through which ethical citizenship may be enacted means they are rarely engaged in conversations about their own needs, or in conversations about charity's ability to address those needs. Dominant views of charity as able to restore dignity and assist people to move out of poverty are therefore foregrounded, and the inability of charity to address the material inequalities that underpin poverty is minimised. This helps to depoliticise poverty and undermine the importance of changing the structural conditions that facilitate the material inequalities that pervade society.

Of talented, generous, and creative volunteers…

In the previous chapter, we showed how Australian Governments actively cultivate ethical citizenship, in part by valorising and creating exemplars of citizens who act charitably towards the poor. Through the conferral of honours and awards, governments uphold the charitable as ideal citizens and encourage others to emulate their values and contributions to the community. A similar trend can be seen across the Australian media, whereby the virtues of ethical citizens are foregrounded and lauded. Virtues such as generosity, community spirit, and dedication are made particularly prominent.

> "He does an amazing job and he is so generous for the timely support he renders," adds Kate.
>
> (SBS 2019, Transforming bottles into food: this family is recycling for charity)

> Henry hasn't only succeeded in feeding hundreds, if not thousands, of people; she's been a rock of support to a vulnerable and often marginalised community.
>
> (SBS 2020, The woman who travels around Melbourne to feed the homeless)

> Mr Gillies works 60 hours a week on six social initiatives he has founded...
>
> (ABC 2017, Mike Brady: Up There, Cazaly songwriter named Victorian of the Year)

By telling the stories of people who act charitably and highlighting their virtues, the media not only provides examples of ideal ethical citizens for the rest of society to emulate, but it also confers status to those who fulfil this ideal. According to Paul Lazarsfeld and Robert Merton (2004), the conferral of status is an important social function performed by the media. By presenting charitable acts and actors in a favourable light and giving them prominence of place, the media indicates their importance and the value society ascribes to them. Media attention also acts as a reward for those who embody the values of ethical citizenship, as it provides public acknowledgement of their good deeds. In doing so, the media helps to raise the social status of those who act charitably through its conferral of ethical capital.

In Chapter 3 we explained how we use the term ethical capital to refer to the symbolic recognition of those who fulfil their obligations as ethical citizens. This recognition brings with it a certain amount of social prestige and an elevated social status, thus creating an incentive for citizens to engage in charitable acts. As well as highlighting the virtues of those who engage in charitable acts, the media also confers ethical capital through its coverage of honours and award ceremonies. Indeed, there is much fanfare in the media surrounding the importance of recognising and celebrating those who act charitably towards the poor.

> The talented, generous, creative volunteers on the Gold Coast deserve to be acknowledged, recognised and praised, which is why we have this spectacular event.
>
> (ABC 2019, Is 8-year-old volunteer Taz Traill the Gold Coast's most generous kid?)

> Speaking at the awards ceremony in Melbourne, Brady said the honour came as a "complete surprise. [I'm] a bit stunned, really... but I'm also very proud," he said
>
> (ABC 2017, Mike Brady: Up There, Cazaly songwriter named Victorian of the Year)

> One Queenslander's passion and determination to ensure that every woman, no matter their circumstances, has access to sanitary items has been recognised nationally.
>
> (ABC 2017, How Share the Dignity makes sure every woman in Australia has pads and tampons)

Although not every volunteer receives media attention or recognition at an awards ceremony, these practices create public precedent for valorising charitable givers and elevating their social status, which, in turn, encourages others to step up and perform their duties as ethical citizens. Charity is thus not just portrayed by the media as important for restoring the dignity of the poor. It is also portrayed as important for facilitating the forms of social participation and ethical citizenship that sit at the heart of the neoliberal social.

This valorisation of charity and the ethical capital attached to it provides an additional avenue through which the non-poor may improve their social status. Importantly, people who rely on charity for subsistence generally do not possess the resources necessary to engage in charitable acts towards others or uphold the values of ethical citizenship. The accrual of ethical capital is therefore often out of reach for the poor – a group that already experiences significant marginalisation and low social status. When considered in conjunction with the shame and stigma that often accompanies the receipt of charity (illustrated in Chapter 8), we can see that far from addressing inequalities in social status, charitable acts have the potential to reify and further entrench the devalued identities of the poor and the lauded identities of those who act charitably towards them.

It means a great deal to them

Where the charitable giver is valorised in the media and constructed as an active and moral citizen, the charitable receiver is constructed as a pitiful and passive object through which ethical citizenship may be enacted. Representations of the poor as pitiful come through particularly strongly.

> It is about extending the hand of friendship to people who most have turned their backs on.
>
> (ABC 2015, Sydney advertising executive Stacey Bachelor makes a change as barber to the homeless)

> These kids barely get to smile because of the problems of poverty…
>
> (ABC 2016, Firefighters who battled Footscray's Little Saigon blaze raise funds to replace charity's lost presents)

> I can't even imagine how I'd feel about myself; how embarrassed, how ashamed.
>
> (ABC 2018, Share the Dignity ACT calls for more tampon and pad donations to help disadvantaged women)

As well as pitiful, charity receivers are also presented as passive. In contrast to the frequent quoting and foregrounding of the experiences of givers of charity, receivers of charity are rarely given a voice through the media (MacKinnon 2015), particularly when it comes to communicating the effectiveness of charitable responses. Indeed, when the media tells us about the benefits of charity, it is most often told through the perspectives of those providing the charity, rather than the perspectives of those receiving it.

> Co-founder Nicholas Marchesi said "Orange Sky Laundry's biggest feat was in enabling human connections… Without a regular dinner table, homelessness can be very isolating – a separation Mr Marchesi said the service was changing."
>
> (ABC 2016, Orange Sky Laundry launches on Sunshine Coast, tackling housing, employment with clean clothes)

> For us it's just a few hours of our time but for those families it's a lot more than that… I think for them it's going to mean a lot and just to have those presents under the tree on Christmas day, they will be happy.
>
> (ABC 2017, The Smith Family Christmas delivers thousands of gifts to disadvantaged children)

> For our young mums it adds a beautiful, personal touch and it's a one-stop shop for agencies like us.
>
> (ABC 2017, Charity helping new parents overwhelmed by pre-loved items, eager for warehouse space)

The foregrounding of the perspectives of charitable givers is problematic, not least because it is unlikely that a giver of charity will fully understand or discuss the potential negative implications of the charitable acts they are involved in. On the contrary, charitable actors spoke of the positive impacts of their work, even when they had not received explicit positive feedback. In instances where explicit positive feedback was not received, receivers' reactions to the charity were interpreted by givers as being positive and appreciative.

> It can be difficult for women to express appreciation for help with such a private issue, but Elaine Pollack from St. Benedict's Community Centre in Queanbeyan said their faces say it all.
>
> (ABC 2018, Share the Dignity ACT calls for more tampon and pad donations to help disadvantaged women)

> She was crying at how grateful she was – for something we take for granted.
>
> (SBS 2018, Giving homeless women sanitary products along with dignity)

As receivers of charity are positioned as passive and are rarely given the opportunity to speak about their experiences, dissenting views or critiques about negative experiences of charity are rarely made visible.

When the media does engage directly with people who receive charity, the quotes presented generally relate to how much they appreciate charity they receive. Again, critical voices are conspicuously absent from the media discourse.

> Steven Smith became the first Adelaide user of the free washing service and said it was welcome. "It means a great deal to the homeless, the needy."
>
> (ABC 2016, Orange Sky Laundry service for the homeless extended to Adelaide)

> … she is very grateful for the toy warehouse … "it's just such a big relief off our shoulders," she said.
>
> (ABC 2014, Christmas Toy Warehouse makes festive season brighter for Hunter families)

> "Thank God for Safe Night," Mr Kelly said. "They keep you through the cold winters."
>
> (ABC 2020, Homeless being turned away as cool weather pushes Safe Space shelter to capacity)

As we discuss more fully in Chapter 9, the construction of the passive yet appreciative recipient contributes to social expectations that the poor will humbly and gratefully accept any charity that the charitable decide to offer. The actual impact of charity from the perspective of the charitable receiver is not made visible; nor, indeed, is it positioned as an important factor to consider. Thus, rather than recognising the poor as full and complex subjects with the agency to define and articulate their own needs, they are constituted as objects of pity, and as passive and one-dimensional subjects who are a mere symbolic and material resource through which others can demonstrate their commitment to the values of ethical citizenship.

By focusing on all the ways in which acting charitably can help givers enact their ethical citizenship, attention is diverted away from the actual needs of people experiencing poverty, as well as from the structural processes that produce those needs. The additional silencing of the voices of those who receive charity as a means of survival acts as a barrier preventing society from understanding – much less improving – our responses to poverty.

Conclusion

The media is an important relay for dominant ideas about how society is, or should be, assembled (Entman 1993). It not only amplifies discourses promoted by politicians and other influential social actors, it also holds up to the public an idealised representation of how good citizens behave, and how social problems can and should be addressed. In this chapter we have demonstrated that, although representations are not uniform, the media is a powerful conduit for idealised images of the neoliberal social and the role of charity therein. On the basis of this, we conclude that the media plays a key role in the cultivation or translation (Latour 1986) of charity, and its enrolment in the project of reassembling the social along neoliberal lines.

This chapter has demonstrated how charity is valorised in the media for the restoration of dignity to the poor and thus addressing the inequalities of status between the poor and better-off members of society. Charity is represented as meeting basic needs and as creating opportunities for recipients to be recognised as "people," with minimal attention paid to the structural drivers of their poverty, including the role of the inadequate levels of social protection provided by the State. Indeed, the role of the State is largely eclipsed by celebratory accounts of the good works being done by self-governing communities, fuelled by the ethical commitments and affective motivations of charitable citizens. The State's absence is sometimes mentioned, but usually in ways that take its inaction as a regrettable but largely expected and accepted feature of the way contemporary (neoliberalising) societies operate.

We have also begun thinking through the implications of the model of charity that is represented and celebrated in political and media discourse – a task that we will continue and refine throughout the rest of this book. The media valorisation of charity provides an important opportunity for people practicing charity to accrue ethical capital for their good works; this opportunity is not extended to charity recipients. Instead, recipients are positioned as pitiful and passive subjects whose agency is restricted to the discrete choices and opportunities for self-improvement afforded to them by charitable citizens. As such, they are positioned as incapable of reciprocating with their own acts of care and thus attaining recognition as full citizens.

At the same time, however, the media representations discussed here lacked the usual demonising and blame attributing representations that permeate media representations of the poor (Bullock et al. 2001; Chauhan & Foster 2014; Esmark & Schoop 2017). Whilst charity recipients are certainly positioned as socially subordinate, they are constructed as objects of pity, rather than scorn; and as grateful, rather than selfish and lazy, subjects. Indeed, their treatment is significantly more generous than that of the dole bludger that we described in Chapter 4. One possible reason for this is that these kinds of demonising representations of the poor are inconsistent with their role as targets of the compassionate care of ethical citizens. It would be difficult for the media – or indeed an authoritative actor – to glorify the assistance the charitable provide if that assistance was going to people who do not deserve it.

In the chapters that follow, we explore these and other themes through the meanings, practices, and relationships of the people involved in day-to-day charitable encounters. We show how the model through which charity is enacted in practice is conditioned in important ways by the policies and discourses discussed in this and the previous chapters. However, we also show how the desire to help and the (sometimes) authentic encounters between providers and recipients of charity point towards the ways in which this model can be transformed to better meet the needs of the recipient.

References

Boone, K, Roets, G & Roose, R 2018, 'Social work, poverty and anti-poverty strategies: Creating cultural forums', *The British Journal of Social Work*, vol. 48, no. 8, pp. 2381–2399.

Bullock, H, Wyche, K & Williams, W 2001, 'Media images of the poor', *Journal of Social Issues*, vol. 57, no. 2, pp. 229–246.

Chauhan, A & Foster, J 2014, 'Representations of poverty in British newspapers: A case of 'othering' the threat?', *Journal of Community & Applied Social Psychology*, vol. 24, pp. 390–405.

Entman, R 1993, 'Framing: Toward clarification of a fractured paradigm', *Journal of Communication*, vol. 43, no. 4, pp. 51–58.

Esmark, A & Schoop, S 2017, 'Deserving social benefits? Political framing and media framing of 'deservingness' in two welfare reforms in Denmark', *Journal of European Social Policy*, vol. 27, no. 5, pp. 417–432.

Fraser, N 2000, 'Rethinking recognition', *Left Review*, vol. 3, pp. 107–120.

Hodgetts, D, Cullen, A & Radley, A 2005, 'Television characterizations of homeless people in the United Kingdom', *Analyses of Social Issues and Public Policy*, vol. 5, no. 1, pp. 29–48.

Hrast, M 2008, 'Media representations of homelessness and the link to (effective) policies: The case of Slovenia', *European Journal of Homelessness*, vol. 2, pp. 115–137.

Latour, B 1986, 'The powers of association', in J Law (ed.), *Power, Action and Belief*, Routledge & Kegan Paul, London, pp. 264–280.

Latour, B 2005, *Reassembling the Social: An Introduction to Actor-Network-Theory*, Oxford University Press, Oxford.

Lazarsfeld, P & Merton, R 2004, 'Mass communication, popular taste, and organized social action', in J Peters & P Simonson (eds.), *Mass Communication and American Social Thought: Key Texts 1919–1968*, Rowman & Littlefield Publishers Inc., Lanham, pp. 230–241.

MacKinnon, M 2015, 'Representations of homelessness in 'The Australian' newspaper, 2008–2012', *Australian Journalism Review*, vol. 37, no. 1, pp. 165–176.

Parsell, C & Clarke, A 2020, 'Charity and shame: Towards reciprocity', *Social Problems*, https://doi.org/10.1093/socpro/spaa057

Parsell, C & Watts, B 2017, 'Charity and justice: A reflection on new forms of homelessness provision in Australia', *European Journal of Homelessness*, vol. 11, no. 2, pp. 65–76.

Purdam, K, Garratt, E & Esmail, A 2016, 'Hungry? Food insecurity, social stigma and embarrassment in the UK', *Sociology*, vol. 50, no. 6, pp. 1072–1088.

Rebello, K, Schwieter, C, Schliebs, M, Joynes-Burgess, K, Elswah, M, Bright, J & Howard, P 2020, *Covid-19 News and Information from State-Backed Outlets Targeting French, German and Spanish-Speaking Social Media Users*, viewed 24 February 2021, https://comprop.oii.ox.ac.uk/wp-content/uploads/sites/93/2020/06/Covid-19-Misinfo-Targeting-French-German-and-Spanish-Social-Media-Users.pdf

Smith-Carrier, T 2020a, 'The (charitable) pantry is bare': A critical discourse analysis of Christmas food hamper programs in Canada', *Critical Policy Studies*, https://doi.org/10.1080/19460171.2020.1722190

Smith-Carrier, T 2020b, 'Charity isn't just, or always charitable: Exploring charitable and justice models of social support', *Journal of Human Rights and Social Work*, vol. 5, pp. 157–163.

7 The meaning of helping

Introduction

So far in this book, we have shown how the meaning and function of charity in contemporary Australian society is shaped by processes that are largely external to the day-to-day practices of care and support that charity comprises. In doing this, we have challenged the idea that charity is a *sui generis* phenomenon that is driven purely by the ethical commitments of volunteers and the needs of the poor. We have argued instead that both charitable giving and the poverty that it responds to are cultivated as part of a broader project to reassemble the social in accordance with a neoliberal worldview. We have demonstrated this by analysing how the need for charity is created through welfare reforms that restrict people's ability to meet their basic needs through direct State support. We also show how the State cultivates charity through a range of material, symbolic, and governmental strategies, and how it is supported in these activities by media representations of charitable giving. Yet, in doing this, we have said little about what all this means for how charity is practised in day-to-day encounters between charitable volunteers and people experiencing poverty.

Previous research shows that these day-to-day encounters have meaning and dynamics that cannot be simply read off, or deduced from, the political, discursive, and institutional contexts in which charity is enacted. For instance, Cloke et al. (2010, 2017) demonstrate how the practice of charity involves a degree of performative improvisation, wherein people delivering and receiving charity respond in strategic and creative ways to the spaces and encounters in which charitable care takes place. In this process, people make meaning of their actions and experiences by drawing on the quotidian discourses and ethical codes of everyday life, often eschewing political or organisational narratives about giving being a civic obligation (Cloke et al. 2017). Others highlight how volunteers' understandings and practice of charity are shaped by their projects of self-formation (Allahyari 2000) – which are in turn shaped by their own biographies and social positioning (e.g. their class locations) – and how they understand their role in responding to those in need (Parsell & Clarke 2020).

Given this, it is imperative that we ground our understanding of charity, and our prescriptions for its transformation, in how it is enacted, experienced, and understood by the volunteers and recipients whose day-to-day encounters bring it into being. In this and the following chapter, we thus turn our attention to answering the following questions: how is the practice of charity, and its role in societal responses to poverty, understood by the people who actually provide and receive it? How do their experiences relate to the positioning of charity in the broader field of poverty governance and the normative understandings of the social that it is connected to? What do they tell us about the opportunities to transform charity so that it is better able to meet the actual needs of charity recipients?

We argue that the experiences of providers and recipients reveal a tension at the heart of contemporary practices of charity, a tension which points to both the fundamental limitations of the contemporary approach and the opportunity to cultivate an alternative approach that is organised around the needs of recipients. In what follows, we show how this tension arises from the enrolment of charity in the production of the neoliberal social, and the structural position in which this process places providers and recipients. On the one hand, volunteers desire to make a difference in the lives of the poor but find their efforts frustrated by their limited capacity to address the underlying structural drivers of material poverty; drivers which, as we showed in Chapter 4, are linked to social policy decisions to limit State welfare provisioning. On the other hand, recipients of charity experience significant shame due to their passive and dependent position in the charity encounter, a position which excludes them from the norms of ethical citizenship by preventing them from engaging in reciprocal acts of care. Volunteers can exacerbate or mitigate this shame, depending on how they see their own role in the charity encounter. In the final chapter, we show how volunteers have the capacity to minimise the shame that people experience, and how this, coupled with their desire to truly help people who are poor, provides an opportunity to transform the practice of charity and decouple it from the neoliberal project.

This chapter focuses on the perspective of the provider of charity. We present findings from ethnographic research we conducted with volunteers engaging in the practice of charity in Queensland, Australia. The ethnographic data include in-depth interviews with 26 volunteers who provide charity and approximately 200 hours of observations of the provision (and receipt) of charity. We sat in when people requested and volunteers provided charity. The research was conducted at three support centres in Southeast Queensland, where people experiencing poverty present and ask volunteers for charitable assistance. Assistance available at the support centres includes food, clothing, furniture, and supermarket vouchers. There is also the potential to receive more significant support, such as financial assistance for short-term accommodation, electricity, and other utility bills (Parsell & Clarke 2020).

In what follows, we describe how volunteers are motivated primarily to make a difference in the lives of people experiencing poverty, as well as their recognition that they have limited capacity to achieve this in many cases. We also describe the different ways in which volunteers make sense of, and respond to, their limited capacity to make a difference. Some volunteers recognise the structural drivers of people's poverty – drivers that are largely beyond the control of charitable citizens – and respond by focusing on making whatever small difference that they can. Others, however, project their failures onto people who experience poverty, and respond to this by focusing on assessing the validity or the true nature of their needs. We then show, in Chapter 8, how these different approaches can either mitigate or exacerbate the shame experienced by charity recipients.

Making a difference

Our interviews with volunteers who engage in the practice of charity demonstrate that they are animated, beyond anything else, to make a difference in the lives of people who are poor. As such, their capacity to make a difference was central to whether or not they found the act of giving personally satisfying. Responding to a question about the best part of providing charity, a volunteer named Amir remarked:

> Every now and again, and I won't say it happens a lot, but every now and again you go home thinking I've made a difference to somebody's life.

At the same time, Amir explained how making a difference is so important by recognising that:

> Sometimes you go home thinking, I couldn't help that person and that really sucks.

Others saw making a difference as the moral duty of the charitable. For instance, when asked about the motivations behind charitable giving, Betty explained:

> Well, that's probably a personal thing, I think. Everyone's reason would be different. If you asked why should I be here, because I think every now and again I make a difference to somebody's life and that's the best you can hope for. It doesn't happen often. You maybe ease their pain for a bit and sometimes you just fluke it and you do make a difference to someone's life.

As these remarks show, volunteers are personally invested in the project of helping people in need and their inability to meet that need meant that they were personally affected by the suboptimal outcomes that they achieved.

Thus, our participants were emphatic that the satisfaction of their own desires and projects is bound up with their ability to achieve outcomes for charity recipients. This contrasts with to the argument that charity is fundamentally driven by the desire for salvation or self-realisation on the part of the giver and eschews the needs of charity recipients (see Chapter 2). When asked why they engaged in charitable giving, volunteers consistently invoked what Elizabeth described as the "simple" goal of helping people in need:

> To help people, really. That's all it comes down to. I mean, there's no big grand plan or anything… I suppose I just want to give a bit of ease in the suffering a little bit, I suppose, and give some people a glimmer of hope, a bit of light.

Yet volunteers' motivation to benefit others did not mean that they receive nothing themselves. We consistently heard volunteers describing the benefits that they gain from feeling as though they are helpful. A volunteer named Karl spoke for many when he said that the best part of providing charity was "the satisfaction of most people when they leave. I suppose being able to help people who are hungry." Thus, volunteers derive benefits from providing charity, but their personal benefits are intrinsically related to their capacity to be helpful to others. No one in our research gave any sense that they are satisfied with providing charity simply on the basis of their righteous motivations. No one, similarly, articulated a "robotic duty" to help (Brooks 2004, p. 6). They are all driven by – and the basis of their satisfaction drawn from – the first order commitment to make a difference in people's lives, albeit not the consequentialist calculations promoted by Singer (2015) to achieve the "biggest positive impact."

Volunteers often spoke about the joy and pleasure that they attain from feeling as though their charity helped recipients. People thus thought about what need and charity meant, and they framed their charity in terms of the outcomes they can achieve by themselves. They felt good when they achieved a positive outcome, and bitterly disappointed when they were unable to help people who they saw as in true need. Dianna described the unpleasant part of volunteering as:

> Feeling that you're helpless. Basically, we are helpless. In the long term, we don't really help them, I don't think.

These feelings of disappointment bring us to another crucial aspect of volunteers' meanings and experiences regarding the provision of charity. Many volunteers spoke about how their desire to help and make a difference is often frustrated by their limited capacity of charitable giving – e.g. the provision of basic resources to meet people's immediate needs – to address the deep structural poverty faced by charity recipients. Elaborating upon her remarks noted above, Dianna explained how she felt that her capacity to help people is ultimately limited and partial.

> I mean, it's not like obviously counselling one-on-one because you can't follow-up. You don't know what happens to the people once they leave here... So you hope that something like that helps that person take another step forward.

This volunteer recognises that the capacity of the charity per se to make an enduring/long-term difference is limited and, moreover, difficult to assess. Nevertheless, she hoped that helping people meet their basic needs can ideally contribute to an individual's broader life progress, helping them, as she commented, to "take another step forward." This belief that charity was still worthwhile despite its recognised limitations was a consistent theme amongst the volunteers in our research. However, the way in which volunteers made sense of this experience and belief differed in important ways.

The importance of doing what we can

Some volunteers respond to the limitations of charity by focusing on making whatever positive difference they can for charity recipients, no matter how small or seemingly insignificant. Aileen was the supervisor for her local charity area; she expressed this sentiment particularly clearly.

> AILEEN: But the thing that I always say is that if someone comes here, you never let them go away without some sort of a card or food, even if it's only a $10 card. So they can go down to [the supermarket], buy a chicken and a loaf of bread if they want.
>
> RESEARCHER: Yep. And why is that? Why do you always want to see them receive something if they come?
>
> AILEEN: Well, just they come and I just feel – oh, I say to all the people here, "Don't let them leave with nothing." They've made their way here and the money that we give them is really, it's minuscule.

The volunteer highlights the importance of trying to provide some assistance to all people, even if what is provided is limited or "miniscule," so that some level of practical benefit is realised for the recipient. She went on to explain that her commitment to make whatever small difference she can is driven by a sense of duty to help her follow human beings – a sentiment that reflects the discourse of ethical citizenship, with its focus on ethical bonds and duties, discussed in the previous chapters of this book. However, contrary to that discourse, the volunteer also linked her commitment to helping despite its limits to the fact that the people that she helps have few other options for assistance or relief within contemporary society. Noting that many of the people she helps are homeless, Aileen explained how people sleeping on the streets are reliant on unemployment benefits that are too low to meet their basic need, and that they often present to charity asking for help after the council has "disposed their belongings left in public spaces." Aileen's co-volunteer interjected and remarked, if we don't help, "where are they going to go?"

In constructing what helping through charity meant, many volunteers like Aileen and her co-volunteer just quoted are aware that people present to charity in need after they have been excluded from government support. Helping through charity was understood as being minimal. However, it was also necessary because it constituted a last resort for people with nowhere else to go. Thus, same as the perspective of the large charitable organisations discussed in Chapter 5, some individual volunteers also premised their charitable giving on an awareness of the structural drivers of poverty and the failures of neoliberal welfare policy to ensure that all people can meet their basic needs.

This understanding of what charity is – making a small difference to an individual in lieu of adequate public support – was a common theme identified in our research. The below passage comes from Vicki, who explained to us what she understood as the meaning of her efforts to help people in need, and what motivated her to help. Similar to the previous example, Vicki highlights the importance of trying to do something for everyone who presents in need, despite her recognition that her charity will likely only address the symptoms of a much larger problem:

> Just sending people out knowing at least we did something for them today. It's a bit like that starfish. Just walking along the beach and picking up a starfish and throwing it back in. There's millions of them and someone says, "Why would you bother? There's millions of them. What does it matter?" and you say, "It made a difference to that one." So they threw it back. So, as I said, making a difference for people, even if it's alleviating the burden for a day. But the downside, if the question is coming, is just simply you walk out and say, "I've only just taken a little bandaid on a very big cut."

Our research with people providing charity revealed that they are not simply animated by helping people in need, they are also deeply engaged in thinking about what helping people in need means, including – as we show below – the nature of people's needs. They grapple with the individual and societal issues that drive people to seek charity, on the one hand, and they think about the best way that they, as individual volunteers providing minimal resources, can help meet that need, on the other hand. As Vicki recognised, her desire to make a difference by "alleviating the burden for a day" took into account that the assistance she provided did not address the person's underlying need; as she put it, her intervention constitutes "a little bandaid on a very big cut."

Although volunteers are conscious that their attempts to help people who are poor are significantly constrained, this does not mean that they accept these constraints as simply "the ways things are." Rather, they routinely express frustration about these constraints and a desire to do more. Elizabeth, introduced above, described the charity she contributed to as "keeping a family from being worse off," but ultimately Elizabeth believed the assistance she provided people living in poverty was "the very bottom rung of the ladder." In the below interview excerpts, Pavel and Wayne articulate their desire for themselves and the charity they volunteer with to do more to help those in need:

PAVEL: We're not really helping them beyond showing them the door, and they do need a lot more help than that. Getting additional housing would be great. That's been an ongoing issue for some time. Even in my short years, short time here, there's been a few failed attempts at getting additional housing. I just hope that that will actually come off so that we can actually say that we've actually acquired accommodation.

WAYNE: I think sometimes we have so many restrictions. We can't pay rent, we can't do this. Certain people, we know they're homeless but we can't just put them in a motel because you're bandaiding the problem. The other 364 days are going to be on the street.

Here again we see volunteers seeking to reconcile their desire to make a difference with their limited capacity to address the structural drivers of poverty – in this case, the limited supply of affordable housing. Thus far, we have shown how some volunteers manage this tension by focusing on making whatever small difference in people's lives that they can, which often amounts to consciously alleviating the immediate burden of poverty. Yet, not all volunteers responded to the frustrations of their efforts to make a difference in this way.

A desire to assess for true need

In contrast to those volunteers who expressed an awareness of the structural nature of the poverty experienced by charity recipients, there are others who believe that the problems that people presented with are driven by their poor choices. These volunteers, too, are frustrated when they cannot do more to address what they saw as the underlying problems that drive people to seek charity. However, they tend to attribute that problem to the poor themselves, for instance by ascribing it to bad behaviours or greed, rather than to the lack of public support for people experiencing material hardship. For these volunteers, the precondition for truly helping therefore becomes engaging in a thorough assessment of a person's situation in order to determine what their true needs are. That is, the provision of charity – i.e. what is provided and to what value – is subsequently determined by volunteers' assessments of whether a person's needs really are what they claim them to be, and whether a charitable response is indeed appropriate.

Given this, the desire to help and make a difference is in some cases understood by volunteers as requiring a degree of paternalism and conditionality in the delivery of charity. For example, a volunteer named Phillip expressed concern that other volunteers continued to provide a specific individual with charity, when this did not correspond to the individual's true needs. Phillip said the individual is:

> On [Disability Support Pension] and lives in public housing. He should have plenty of money. Why can't he afford food? We should decline to see him until he has received budget training.

Phillip went on to assert that his co-volunteers should refer the recipient to financial counselling. If the recipient does not attend, when he comes in, say "no budget training [signals with his hands waving goodbye]." The implication here is that the individual's true need is not material charity, but rather training on how to better manage their finances. The volunteer's role – as understood and articulated by Phillip – thus becomes one of discerning true need through an exhaustive assessment of the recipient.

Other volunteers similarly grappled with dilemmas about how to help people when they determine that their needs are generated by poor choices. Le explained:

> Yes, it does become judgemental. You have people that smoke and you say, "Well, if you did not smoke you would have $30 extra which you could use." You look and say, "Also, in the past you've spent money that could have been put aside. You've spent money on tattoos, piercings." They have had their priorities wrong. They've had needs and wants mixed up.

Another volunteer, Andrea, likewise linked people's need for charity to their poor choices. Andrea saw his role as helping people in need to include supporting them understand and change their choices:

> Anybody who smokes, I just tell them, "Nobody can afford to smoke. There's two reasons. Financial and health. You're in a situation where you can't afford to smoke."

As these examples show, many volunteers see the assessment of true needs as integral to helping people and making a difference. They held this belief despite the fact that assessing people's needs can lead to paternalistic and sometimes cruel behaviours on the part of volunteers that are not in themselves helpful. For instance, Dennis recalled how when he started volunteering he was encouraged to attend the charity support centre to work with different volunteers to get a feel for the process. Dennis described the, "misfortune of working with a few vile people. They wanted to make the client cry; if you didn't cry, you wouldn't even get a teabag, but if you did cry, you could have anything."

Volunteers who are concerned with assessing people's true needs often expressed a belief that people seeking charity are, as Phillip said, "just trying to take what they can." For instance, Jude is a volunteer we shadowed at a support centre; she described one family as too choosy for exercising discrete choices – for example, refusing food and accepting only supermarket vouchers. Jude stated that:

> I haven't recorded it yet, but I will in a minute that we won't be providing services for these people for the next three months, and I won't even feel bad.

In response, a co-volunteer added, "no, you shouldn't feel bad." Another volunteer, Sebastian, believed that assessing need was important in order to detect "charity hoppers." When asked to explain what a charity hopper is, Sebastian asserted:

> They fudge the truth, which is in itself a problem. I think people who use charities, it's probably a generalisation, but they tend to fudge things in their life or exaggerate them because they think, and again, it's human nature, it doesn't just happen in charities, but they're looking to give you the maximum. "Oh, I feel really bad for you. Let's do everything we can for you." So, that's going to happen.

Others still believe assessing need is necessary to prevent charity being used to support people's addictions. As Phillip stated:

> [Some recipients are] just going to go and sell those vouchers on the street for cash or drugs or whatever. That they're not going to be using them at the shop, what they're intended for. That's the downside, when you see people who do use and abuse the system. That's the worst of it.

These volunteers believe that many charity recipients are trying to exploit the system and their goodwill. Reflecting this sentiment, a volunteer named Ian said that, "the biggest problem is we don't have a lie detector, and that's a problem."

On the basis of these concerns, volunteers developed various strategies for assessing need. Some simply relied on instinct: as Graham put it, "you can tell in five minutes who's taking you for a ride." Others developed more elaborate assessment strategies. Le described his method as follows:

> I'll always ask if they want bread, because my first impression is, if they won't take bread, well, they're not hungry. Some of them, "No, I don't want bread." You think, "Wait a minute, if you're really hungry you'd take bread." Because I don't think they're desperate enough. The ones that are genuinely desperate they'll say, "Okay, I'll eat pantry food."

As with the observation about provoking crying to elicit a positive charity response, we can see the meaning that volunteers ascribe to recipients' circumstances – whether they are truly hungry or lying to exploit their positive intentions – drives their approach to helping. The belief among volunteers that some recipients are trying to exploit their goodwill reduces their motivation to help. Sebastian explained that:

> Well if I think someone's really pulling the wool over my eyes, I probably wouldn't be as generous to them. Well, I know I'm not as generous to them.

Thus, the positioning of the self in the process of providing charity has important flow on consequences. When someone seeks to access a resource that they are voluntarily given and do not have an entitlement to, it confers the giver with a prerogative to decide whether they are truly deserving of it. Much has been written about how charity has distinguished the deserving from the underserving poor (Katz 1986; O'Brien 2015). This work articulates deservingness with reference to the moral and religious behaviours of recipients: whether they misuse alcohol, are single parents, or attend religious ceremonies, for instance. These distinctions between deserving and undeserving are thus drawn to monitor and control normative behaviours; that is, charity is seen as a means for the well off to ensure that the poor are behaving as they should. Our research, by contrast, has identified the meaning of separating the deserving from the undeserving, not for the sake of the recipient – how they should or should not behave, but for validation of the charitable's mission of making a difference. It is their desire to truly help a person, to meet their true need – and feeling frustrated when they cannot – that drives volunteers motivation to assess for deservingness: the emotional passion to meet a person's need through helping relies upon the charitable's belief that the recipient has a legitimate need that they can meet.

We have shown how deservingness assumes significance because it is central to the meaning that some volunteers attribute to their efforts to help. They want to identify the deserving, and distinguish them from the underserving, not primarily out of a desire to enforce certain behaviours among the poor, but because they see the classification as significant to whether they, as volunteers, can realise their desire to be truly helpful. Assessing true need is a consequence of motivation to truly help the needy.

However, it is also important to recognise that the desire to assess people's true need is also the product of a failure on the part of this group of volunteers to recognise the policy and other structural processes that produce and maintain poverty. Whilst the volunteers cited in the previous section recognised that people access charity because of the inadequacy of State welfare provision to meet basic needs, those concerned with assessing true need tend to individualise the problem and associate it with the behaviours of charity recipients. This is not to say that charity recipients do not ever make choices that appear contrary to their own interests or try to extract what they can from charitable providers. As Matthew Desmond (2016) argues, some people experiencing poverty are willing to spend money on what many would consider to be excessive luxuries because they feel that frugality and budgeting make little difference to their situation. Reflecting on the choice of one of his research participants to use her monthly food stamp allowance to purchase lobster on her wedding anniversary – a choice which left her reliant on a local food charity for the rest of the month – Desmond explained that:

> People like Larraine lived with so many compounded limitations that it was difficult to imagine the amount of good behavior or self-control that would allow them to lift themselves out of poverty. The distance between grinding poverty and even stable poverty could be so vast that those at the bottom had little hope of climbing out even if they pinched every penny. So they chose not to. Instead, they tried to survive in color, to season the suffering with pleasure.
>
> (Desmond 2016, p. 219)

Thus, whilst the desire to assess people's true needs is understandable given volunteers' motivation to genuinely help people, it is based on a fundamental misrecognition (Fraser 2000) of charitable recipients and their circumstances. We take up this point in Chapter 9, where we argue that charity can only become an effective aspect of societal responses to poverty if it recognises and addresses the structural basis of poverty and eschews the idea that people experiencing poverty are passive and incompetent subjects.

Listening, not judging

The drive of some volunteers to assess people's true needs raises an important set of questions: how is need determined, by whom, and to what end? In the above examples, volunteers positioned themselves as arbiters of the truth about people's needs. Moreover, they did so out of a concern that *their* project of making a difference was being hijacked by charity recipients who were not interested in improving their lives, and instead used charity to support irresponsible or deviant behaviours. This understanding of charity, and the relationship between giver and recipient therein, is consistent with the neoliberal worldview discussed in earlier chapters, wherein the poor are positioned as fodder for the charitable's performance of ethical citizenship (see Chapter 4). Despite the concern with determining people's true needs, it is the charitable's needs that are elevated in this mode of practising charity; and the poor must play by their rules if they want to receive any support at all.

Yet, not everyone embraces the role of assessor of true needs. As we noted above, many volunteers recognise the links between people's need for charity and the limited support provided by the welfare state, and other structural processes that contribute to poverty. This group tends to be much more open to people experiencing poverty's own determinations about what their needs are – or at least open to letting those people determine how they navigate their poverty and the support available to them. They thus renounce what they describe as the "judgemental" practice of assessing who was worthy of their support. As Aileen put it, "we don't judge people. We see them as individuals, as equal."

Interestingly, the avoiding of judgement did not necessarily mean that volunteers took recipients' accounts of their needs and circumstances at face value. Many still suspect that recipients want vouchers, often to sell for cash, and they embellish or fabricate their stories to achieve this. As Stephen put it:

> No, you can't afford to be too mean. I interviewed one this morning. You could write a book on her case history. [Wallet] stolen, we gave her [vouchers to travel] to pick the car up. But when you look back on her story [wallet] was stolen in May. But, as [our president] said, a lot of the stories are made up stories. But we're not to judge.

For this group, the crucial variable is not whether they assess the recipient's account of their needs as true or not, but rather how they (the volunteer) understand their own role in the charity process. As we saw above, this group often see their role as making whatever small difference that they can for recipients, despite recognition that their capacity to help is structurally limited. There is also a recognition that volunteers do not necessarily have the capacity to understand the full complexity people's circumstances, making judging people a fraught exercise. For instance, reflecting on the possibility that people fabricate stories to access resources from charities, Elizabeth stated, "if they're not desperate in that way, then they're desperate in other ways. So, it's not for me to judge anyway."

There is a sense here, then, that people experiencing poverty should be afforded a degree of agency in the charity encounter, and in terms with what they do with the resources on offer. Rather than the volunteers determining what people should get and what they should do with it, they take a non-judgemental stance and help people in whatever small way they can. In some cases, this amounts to trying to make people feel welcome and accepted in the support centre. For instance, Amir described his approach to people who present at his centre as follows:

> Look, "come in." "Hi, how are you? A bit colder outside than here," or, "A bit warmer outside." If there's a little kid with them, "How are you buddy?" Really make it warm. Instead of people come cap-in-hand, "What do you want?" Make it welcoming where people say, "I'm welcome here. I'm valued. I feel good about being here."

Others eschew the scepticism that they have regarding recipients' accounts and make an effort to actually listen to their stories. For instance, Pavel described how he shifted over time from the judgemental approach to listening to people as he came to recognise the structure circumstances surrounding people's poverty.

> When I first came, I was hard on people. Probably because I've worked all my life to get what I want, I thought, "Well, these people out here, they should be doing the same as me." Then you're here for a period of time [and you realise] there's no jobs, [benefits] not paying much… So, over the last couple of years, you listen to people. I never used to listen to them basically. "What do you want? What are you here for?" But now I listen to their story.

Another volunteer, Chen, expressed the view that listening "and encouraging people to tell their story" is the most significant thing volunteers can do, because people seeking help really want "someone to listen to them." Similarly, Dianna said the best interviewing technique as being "to listen."

With the focus on listening to people, making them feel welcome, and being non-judgemental, we see a way of practising charity emerge that places recipients and their needs at the centre of the charitable encounter. This approach contrasts with the discourse of ethical citizenship, with its positioning of people who are poor as passive objects upon which the charitable exercise their civic obligations. Instead, the volunteers discussed in this section afford people who are poor a degree of agency in the definition and pursuit of their own needs through the charitable encounter. It thus provides another example of what we are calling counter-translation (see Chapter 3): the process wherein the charitable harness to their positioning on the frontlines of poverty governance for the pursuit of projects that are at odds with those advanced by the political elites seeking to enrol the charitable in reassembling the social. In Chapter 9, we reflect on how counter-translation can form the basis for a transformed model of charity that places the needs of the poor at its centre.

Conclusion

We conclude by reflecting on how this chapter helps advance thinking about what it means to help people who are poor through charity. The ethnographic data shows that people are motivated to give their time, energy, and intellect to benefit others. We found great diversity in how volunteers providing charity thought about helping people; different understandings of people's needs; and contrasting approaches to enacting the helping process.

Their individual motivations to help, when thought about collectively, represent an encouraging indication that society cares for people living in poverty. Care is both an essential part of the functioning of society and an element of a good life. Providing and receiving care are part of the dynamics that constitute society. For Marian Barnes (2012, p. 3), "care is so fundamental to our capacity to live together that we simply cannot see its significance." The type of care that is evidenced through the charitable efforts to help people in poverty represent, as Tronto (1993, p. 9) observes, "both a moral value and a basis for the political achievement of a good society."

We have to infuse our understanding of what it means to help someone who is poor through charity with some optimism. Our optimism for what the practice of charity represents for society, however, is limited. Engster (2007) acknowledges, similar to what we presented in this chapter, that some level of care can be provided by individual charity, but ultimately "the State remains important in care ethics for overcoming the well-known shortcomings of private organizations" (Engster 2015, p. 25). Our research with volunteers providing charity clearly demonstrated their structurally constrained position to achieve justice, given that the resources required to meet the needs of people seeking help were well beyond their grasps. Indeed, many volunteers understood that the poverty that they were addressing was tied to trends in welfare provisioning, such as below-the-poverty-line unemployment payments and limited availability of social housing.

Volunteers providing charity were deeply attuned to the profound limitations of what their charitable care could achieve. They understood that people's need for care was of a greater magnitude than what they could fulfil. It was the societal injustices that drove the needs of people seeking charity, including what society does not provide as a matter of social rights, that animated some volunteers to give up their time to try, as best as they could, to help those in need. Volunteers voiced these challenges well, with their analogies of throwing one starfish back in the water to make a small difference to one person, and reflections on the rhetorical question of "where are they going to go?" if the volunteers didn't provide some help. They recognised how their practice of charity was limited, but they understood their charity to be a means to provide some practical assistance and show people that they mattered, particularly because society had failed to do so.

It was the desire to *truly* help people in need through providing charitable care that created the conditions for some volunteers to be actively involved in assessing for *true* need. The desire to help through charity meant that volunteers wanted to be sure that the people they were helping actually needed the help. If volunteers providing charity believed that people's needs were driven by their bad choices, many of them still espoused a commitment to meet a need. However, they assumed that people needed advice about behavioural change: to stop smoking or undertaking financial counselling, for example. Assessing for true need was not principally about policing transgressive behaviours, but rather about how the charitable understood the meaning of helping people in need.

This chapter has helped us think about how the practice of charity to people who are poor sits within a broader system of poverty governance, shaped by the neoliberal translation strategies discussed in Chapters 3, 4, and 5. The system withholds societal resources and generates the need for charity. It then cultivates a model of charity where those excluded from resources are prevented from participating in a process where they can exercise their agency and contribute in ways that challenge their passive position. Receiving charity through a model of care that positions recipients as passive creates the conditions for them to be distinguished as *other* than the giver. Their status as other is reinforced through a process of articulating – or exaggerating – their needs for care, with an inability to provide care themselves.

Our analysis in this chapter, of course, only provides a partial and on its own unsatisfactory answer to the question, "what does it mean to help someone who is poor through charity?" We have provided an indication of what volunteers providing charity want to achieve, how they go about trying to help, and the importance of listening to and creating the conditions for people who are poor to be listened to and articulate what is meaningful for them. Without engaging deeply with the first-hand experiences of those people receiving charity themselves, we know little about whether they are helped and what being helped through charity means. As Tronto (1993) observes when articulating the principle of responsiveness in the provision of care, we cannot simply ask the caregiver how they would like to be cared for to identify whether the care they provide satisfactorily responded to the recipient's need. On recognition of the power differences that exist between the provider and recipient of charity, together with the likelihood that the two parties share different ideas on what charity, care, and help mean, we need to understand how receiving charity is experienced, and what recipients understand as the meaning of being helped. A lack of responsiveness to the recipients of care means a lack of care (Tronto 1993).

By taking seriously the experiences and perspectives of people on the receiving end of charitable care, we can develop a more sophisticated understanding of what helping (them) means. The reimagination of charity that we outline in Chapter 9 relies upon a deep understanding of what it means to be poor and the subject of one's charity. By engaging with people who are poor in receipt of charity, we can reimagine charity along the lines that St Francis' Peace Prayer emphasises, "for it is in giving that we receive." Helping people who are poor through charity requires starting from the position and experience of people in poverty. It is this experience that we now engage.

References

Allahyari, R 2000, *Visions of Charity: Volunteer Workers and Moral Community*, University of California Press, Berkeley.

Barnes, M 2012, *Care in Everyday Life: An Ethic of Care in Practice*, The Policy Press, Bristol.

Brooks, A 2004, 'Faith, secularism, and charity', *Faith & Economics*, vol. 43, pp. 1–8.

Cloke, P, May, J & Johnsen, S 2010, *Swept Up Lives? Re-envisioning the Homeless City*, Wiley-Blackwell, Chichester.

Cloke, P, May, J & Williams, A 2017, 'The geographies of food banks in the meantime', *Progress in Human Geography*, vol. 41, no. 6, pp. 703–726.
Desmond, M 2016, *Evicted: Poverty and Profit in The American City*, Crown Publishers, New York.
Engster, D 2007, *The Heart of Justice: Care Ethics and Political Theory*, Oxford University Press, Oxford.
Engster, D 2015, *Justice, Care, and the Welfare State*, Oxford University Press, New York.
Fraser, N 2000, 'Rethinking recognition', *New Left Review*, vol. 3, pp. 107–120.
Katz, M 1986, *In the Shadow of the Poorhouse: A Social History of Welfare in America*, Basic Books, New York.
O'Brien, A 2015, *Philanthropy and Settler Colonialism*, Palgrave Macmillan, Basingstoke.
Parsell, C & Clarke, A 2020, 'Charity and shame: Towards reciprocity', *Social Problems*, pp. 1–17, https://doi.org/10.1093/socpro/spaa057
Singer, P 2015, *The Most Good You Can Do: How Effective Altruism is Changing Ideas about Living Ethically*, Yale University Press, New Haven.
Tronto, J 1993, *Moral Boundaries: A Political Argument for an Ethics of Care*, Routledge, New York.

8 The meaning of being helped

Introduction

In the shadow of the giver of charity – that glorified cultural hero whose spontaneous and compassionate acts are celebrated as the paradigmatic example of ethical citizenship and the lost *gemeinschaft* – stands the charity recipient. The presence of the charity recipient – a person whose poverty and suffering places them at the mercy of the generosity of others – is largely taken for granted in the representations and practices surrounding charity that we have discussed in the pages of this book. Their presence has been one of a silhouette, an empty signifier upon which various needs and characteristics have been projected, usually as a side effect of the practical and discursive construction of self-governing communities comprised of ethical citizens. Their existence is, of course, integral to both the charitable enterprise and to the project of reassembling the social along neoliberal lines that we have outlined in this book. As we argued in Chapter 5, people experiencing poverty are positioned as a resource for the production of neoliberal solidarity and ethical citizenship, in that their existence is necessary to provide spontaneous giving and thus a *raison d'etre*. Yet, recipients' experiences of receiving charity, and the social processes that shape these experiences, are either assumed or shrouded over in our rush to apprehend the magical process of charitable giving. This chapter aims to bring these forgotten experiences to the fore.

In the previous chapter, we argued that analysis of the interaction between providers and recipients of charity reveals a tension at the heart of the prevailing model of charitable giving, and also an opportunity for charity to be transformed. In that chapter, it was the perspectives of the charitable that were scrutinised. In this chapter, however, we explore this tension and opportunity from the charity recipients' perspective. Drawing on the experiences of recipients, we show how they are driven into reliance on charity by grinding poverty, which is in turn driven (at least in part) by the inadequate welfare support they receive from the State. They experience this position of dependence as deeply shameful, as they are aware that relying on others places them outside of the norms of responsible self-governance that are promoted by the discourses of ethical citizenship. We argue that the shamed status of the recipient is a by-product of efforts to enact the neoliberal social, for the realisation of ethical citizenship through charity is sustained by the creation of a population who are compelled to act in ways that contradict prevailing ethical norms. As such, they are also excluded from participation in ethical citizenship by their inability to reciprocate the generosity shown to them. To use the words of Australian Prime Minister Scott Morrison (2018), they are taking from their community, rather than making a contribution to it.

We also highlight how the charitable can exacerbate or mitigate people's experiences of shame, depending on which of the approaches to practising charity outlined in Chapter 7 they adopt. We show how recipients experience attempts by the charitable to assess their true needs as shame inducing. This is because these actions of volunteers problematise – implicitly or explicitly – their capacity to look after themselves responsibly, thus bringing their perceived failure to live up to prevailing norms to the fore. However, recipients also highlighted ways through which volunteers can create a sanctuary from shame, by avoiding judgements associated with ethical citizenship and instead allowing people to articulate their needs and circumstances in their own words. Although this practice does not address the structural positioning of recipients that causes shame, we argue that it points to the potential of an alternative model of charity that is built around the agency and experiences of the charity recipient.

Grinding poverty and surviving on charity

One of the most striking aspects of the experience of our research participants is how central a role charity plays in their day-to-day lives. Across three support centres where people come to access charity (inner urban of a large capital city, a coastal small city, and an inland regional city), we found that accessing charity was a routine survival strategy for people experiencing poverty. Amongst the 59 people accessing charity with whom we conducted in-depth interviews, and the many others with whom we engaged in fleeting conversations at the charity support centres, it was rare to meet anyone who told us that it was their first time seeking charity. This reality stands in stark contrast to political discourses on charity, which construe poverty as a temporary personal crisis and charity as a pathway to self-sufficiency (see Chapter 5). Instead, our participants described accessing charity as a routine practice, and a central feature of their strategies to survive deep and enduring poverty with limited State support.

Gough's experience provides a powerful example of how and why people incorporate charity into their survival strategies. Gough described how he accesses charity on a routine basis and has done so for several years. He cites his inability to cover the cost of his basic needs with his unemployment benefit payments as the key reason for this, noting how accessing charity helps him ensure that he does not go hungry.

GOUGH: Yeah. I usually come once a month, depending on how much money I've got left after Newstart. You're allowed here once a month. Maybe maximum I've been here is probably about six or seven times a year.
RESEARCHER: And how long have you been doing that?
GOUGH: When did I get released from prison? 2016. So, on and off for three years.
RESEARCHER: What drives your need to come here?
GOUGH: Yeah. Well, to put it bluntly, "fuck all" money. Rent is $500 a fortnight and I get paid $680 with rent assistance. So after that, because I don't have a license, top up my [public transport card], and once food's gone I've pretty much got "fuck all."
RESEARCHER: So each fortnight you have $180.
GOUGH: $180. You've got $30, oh no, $40 a fortnight for transport, so that's $140, and then I'm spending probably about $100 a fortnight on food and there's $40 for entertainment costs. So, I might buy a six-pack of beer, I might buy a bottle of wine maybe, I don't smoke, or I might go to the movies or something like that.
RESEARCHER: And how can you survive on $100 in food?
GOUGH: You know what to buy at [supermarket]. Sometimes it doesn't last and you have to come here. And sometimes, yeah, you can make it. You'll make $50 a week last eating noodles, and tuna, eggs... As long as I pay rent and I've got a roof over my head, I'm happy. I don't mind going hungry for a few days.
RESEARCHER: And do you do that? Are you going hungry for a few days?
GOUGH: I haven't for a long time, but yeah, I have done before. That was probably before I sought help from different [charities]. Because before then I was too embarrassed or too proud, or something. Once you get over that fact, it's a lot easier. Because yeah, prior to going to prison I was working full-time and all that. And you hit rock bottom.

As we showed in Chapter 4, unemployment benefits in Australia are paid well below the poverty line, and few people can access social housing – and thus avoid unaffordable private rents – due to limited government investment in housing stock. The experience of people like Gough suggests that, somewhat ironically, the limiting of State welfare provision to avoid welfare dependency pushes people into dependency on charity.

Other participants similarly described relying on charity for extended periods as a result of deep and persistent poverty and its attendant struggles. Pauline, a woman in her mid-30s, told us about her reliance on charity for the past 13 years since the birth of her first child. During this period, Pauline described her life as characterised by intersecting problems and associated stress. Pauline was a "stay-at-home single-parent" with three children aged three, five, and 13. She lived in a private rental property on the outskirts of a regional city, where rents are more affordable than Australia's large cities and coastal areas. In responding to a question about her experience accessing charity, Pauline explained:

> When my eldest was younger I couldn't work because of mental health. I had post-natal depression and everything and then it ended up in a domestic violence situation with my littlie's father and then it became acute post-traumatic stress. I want to work, I want to do these things, but now my children have high needs as well. So, I have to work with them daily and myself. I don't have the time or the energy to even go and work. I can't even keep up with my day. Everything is overwhelming… Four years ago I was pregnant and homeless with two little kids that were missing their stepfather and upset.

In the context of these life stressors, Pauline described charity as one of the few supports she has available to her:

> The only help I had was community services, different community services like Vinnies. When you've got post-traumatic stress and you're a single parent and then you've got school ringing you saying, "Why are your kids not at school? You're late every day." You being hounded by this or you've got that stress happening, you've got minimal groceries or energy to cook dinner. Some days you just sit there like a zombie and you can't do anything. Then you've got legals coming at you because your kid is not going to school and someone is reporting you to Child Services because you're a recluse.

It is difficult to overstate the magnitude, complexity, and intersectionality of the life problems that Pauline confronts. Her experience appears extreme: single parenthood, domestic violence, homelessness, children with disabilities, post-traumatic stress, inability to get children to school, and concerns about child protection authorities. Yet, many of the charity recipients who participated in our research reported frequently experiencing similar life stressors to Pauline. It is these stressors, and indeed enduring material poverty, that are significant in trying to grasp how people experience and make sense of charity. Pauline for example, sought charity because, "I need food vouchers and things weekly"… "I've got holes in my pants"… "I've got no proper shoes;" even:

> I don't have nappies for my son. So, like last night, I'm putting towels under him. I can't afford nappies.

It is this profound need for basic necessities and extreme life problems that make Pauline's experience of charity meaningful. She explained that the charity she received from various organisations was "the only help I had." Pauline's life experience also helps us understand her short but telling response to our follow-up question, "what aspects do you find helpful?"

> That they're willing to help. I'm at my lowest.

As Fiona McKay and colleagues have shown, whilst charity is a "normal and necessary part of the lives of many" (McKay et al. 2020, p. 2405), it is often falls short of meeting their needs. Charity does not meet the multiple needs Pauline has; it does not even meet her basic needs. Pauline still does not have nappies for her youngest son; she continually struggles to feed and clothe herself and her three children. Yet, it does provide her with some basic relief, and this is what keeps her, like many others, coming back.

Other participants are more successful in meeting at least their basic needs through charity, although they often go to great lengths to do so. A particularly striking example of this was provided by Malcolm, a man aged in his early 50s that we met when he was using an inner-city charity. Malcolm had moved around Australia throughout his life, but had been living in boarding houses and a social housing property in a large capital city for about five years. Malcolm spoke extensively about how his life was on hold, as he was going through legal proceedings. Although Malcolm described periods of earning "good money" in construction in remote Australia earlier in his life, he had not worked for several years and relied on unemployment benefits. From Malcolm's approximate $600 unemployment benefit each fortnight, he said he spent about $300 on rent, $145 on medication for chronic health problems including hepatitis, and $70 on child support. We asked Malcolm, "So how do you get by for a fortnight? … How do you survive?"

MALCOLM: I eat at [x charity]. So every day I get two meals from [x charity].
RESEARCHER: Just down the road here?
MALCOLM: Yeah.
RESEARCHER: Can you front up there and they'll feed you there?
MALCOLM: They give you just a sandwich and a piece of fruit and maybe a packet of chips and that sort of thing and that's enough for me for the morning. And then after lunch it's a different crew. You're only supposed to get one meal a day. But because it's a different crew, I'm onto that one, so I can go and get one for the afternoon. And then Sunday there's a lunch, Monday, there's a dinner, and Wednesday there's a dinner.
RESEARCHER: So it's three sit down meals there a week?
MALCOLM: Well, one of them is a sit down, which is Wednesday, and it takes two hours. It's really stretched out because they feed you. Whereas the other ones, you line up, you grab your food, go out and sit down, line up to get dessert.
RESEARCHER: So it's more of a grab-and-go kind of thing?

MALCOLM: Yes. It's really much quicker and I don't know why they don't just do the same thing. But it's an outing for a lot of people. It's a get together. The other one is [y charity]. On Monday morning, Tuesday morning I go there for breakfast, and I can go for lunch if I want. But I usually just get a lunch from [x charity].

RESEARCHER: So you've got [x charity], two, three, four times a week, depending on whether you get a meal or sandwiches?

MALCOLM: Five days a week, two meals a day.

RESEARCHER: So you go there five days religiously?

MALCOLM: I live right just next door to it. I live next door to it, so it's no problem just to walk past there. So, basically five days a week. One of them is a hamburger day. I don't like waiting for that so I go down to [charity y], and get something to eat there. And then after lunch I'll get a meal from [x charity]... So basically, I'm surviving on that. The cards [supermarket vouchers] that I get from these guys [Vinnies] could be for razor blades, toothbrush, soap, toilet paper, all the main things. And then, if I can afford to, I'll buy a little bit of fruit or vegetables or something and that's the end of $30. It's not much.

Like Gough above, Malcolm's experience shows how people experiencing poverty incorporate charity into their strategies for surviving on inadequate welfare payments. His experience also shows how surviving on charity is a complex and time-consuming practice, one that requires the navigation and sometimes subversion of the rules surrounding charity access. Indeed, everyone we spoke with – volunteers and recipients alike – recognised that although there are resource and time limits placed on charity use, people usually work around these. Malcolm explained how he waits for a different crew of volunteers to access a second meal for the day. Another person, Jacqui, described how she works around policy through a personal connection with a generous volunteer. Referring to the volunteer, Jacqui said:

> She gets me an appointment anytime, even though I've been here tonnes of times. They say, "This is your last time for so-and-so." But if I ring up a month down the track and I'm struggling, they will serve me. They won't turn me away.

People routinely – and for some like Malcom, systematically – accessed charity, including pushing the boundaries of the charity policy, because of extreme need and lives characterised by deprivation, and inadequate public support.

People access charity to survive but, like many volunteers (see Chapter 7), they understand that what they obtained is minimal, and sometimes not enough to even meet their basic needs. There is very little sense amongst participants that charity helps build a capacity for self-reliance or offers any kind of pathway out of poverty. This is contrary to the neoliberal discourses around self-governing communities that accompany government endorsements of charitable responses to poverty that we discussed in Chapter 5. A person who frequently uses charity and appreciates the resources provided captures this well. Echoing the sentiment of some volunteers mentioned in the previous chapter, he said, "it's a bandaid approach, without it being disrespectful. That's how it feels."

The experience of charity as a "bandaid" – i.e. as addressing the symptoms rather than causes of a problem – reinforces our argument that charity is currently geared more towards the production of ethical citizenship and affective solidarity than to meeting the needs of people experiencing poverty. People's reliance on charity is generated by social policy that limits State welfare support to people in need, rendering them structurally dependent on the spontaneous compassion of ethical citizens. In the next section, we show how people experience this structural position within the neoliberal social as a deeply shameful one.

Charity as a source of visceral shame

People feel a visceral shame asking for and receiving charity. This shame is manifest in people's descriptions of their experiences accessing charity as "horrible" and "anxiety provoking." These feelings mean that many people do what they can to put off accessing charity, despite feeling compelled to access it by their material circumstances. Julia accessed charity on the day we met her, but only out of desperation. Julia is a married woman in her 60s. The day before we met Julia, a friend drove her to the charity support centre carpark, but Julia was too ashamed to walk inside and ask for help. The next day Julia did go to the charity and ask for help:

JULIA: So this time I've just got no food. I've just ran out of everything. It's the most degrading thing to have to do. Honestly, you feel like a real bum. It's horrible.

RESEARCHER: So how did you deal with that feeling of still coming in today?

JULIA: Well, my friend brought me in yesterday and I said, "No, don't worry about it. I won't do it." Then when I got home I thought, "Oh god, we've run out of sugar, run out of this, run out of that," I thought, "I've got to. I've got no food until Wednesday." So, I had to bite the bullet and phone her up and said, "Will you take me?"

Julia's experience resonates with that of many others we encountered in our research: asking for charity is a shameful experience, but one that people will endure when they are desperate. Another participant, Christian a male in his 30s, illustrates similarly both the shame and the challenge of asking for charity:

> When people come here, I can't speak for everyone, but they don't really want to be here. They have to be. And sometimes we put it off thinking,

> "No, I won't go to Vinnies. I went there three months ago"... But now you've got to eat your own pride. That's easy to say, "Just go and see Vinnies." It's not always easy.

We found that people will endure the shame of charity when the alternatives are worse. Although we do not suggest that this is a simple rational calculus, there is a conscious decision-making process at play. People put themselves through shame when confronting more distressing realities, such as not being able to feed their children. Using charity is a last resort, and a step taken based on people's assessment of their situation and the consequences of not asking for charity. The experience of Tanya, a young woman with dependent children, illustrates this:

> It's always going to be humiliating and daunting. I don't think that that's going to change. I guess it's only out of absolute necessity that people like me go, "Well, you either suck it up and go get humiliated for a few hours and get food on the table for your children, or you don't get food on the table for your children. What's it to be?"

Another participant, Penny, who also has dependent children, spoke about balancing shame and family responsibility. Penny explained how she prioritises looking after her children over avoiding the shame she invariably experiences when accessing charity:

RESEARCHER: Do you think that coming in today is something that you feel quite happy to share with [extended family] or is it something that you might keep to yourself more?

PENNY: It's probably something I'd keep to myself, because my family are judgemental. Even though they're not willing to help, they wouldn't like me reaching out to get help somewhere else.

RESEARCHER: So what is that sense of judgement? What is that like for you?

PENNY: It's not very nice. But I've got to look after my kids before I worry about what people think.

Penny and Tanya explicitly frame tolerating the shame of asking for and receiving charity with reference to fulfilling a responsibility to feed their children. We can see an obvious gender dimension here, with Penny and Tanya underscoring the consequences to their children and their responsibility to provide for them as mothers. However, at a more fundamental level, their experiences resonate with those of other people in our research. People feel shame asking for charity, but they ask for it anyway because they feel compelled by their material circumstances.

Thus, even though charity is an enduring feature in many people's lives, we found that people do not present to volunteers and ask for help easily or automatically without first trying to identify alternatives. As Julia remarked, "sometimes we put it off thinking, no, I won't go to Vinnies. I went there three months ago." People need to be experiencing significant suffering, or the imminent threat of it, before they will ask for charity. Thus, consistent with the scholarly understandings of charity outlined in Chapter 2, charity is indeed experienced by people as a practical resource to meet an immediate need and relieve suffering. The reluctance that people reported about accessing charity and the desperate situations that drove them to ask for help contrast with some of the experiences from volunteers presented in Chapter 7 where they believed recipients were trying to carelessly take what they did not need.

It is because people's needs are so fundamental to day-to-day life – food for their children, or even petrol in the car to drive them to school – that they are willing to ask for help. Insofar as these needs are created by the limiting of welfare support available to people, we can see how the poor, too, are enrolled in the project of reassembling the social along neoliberal lines. Policy settings that deny people the means to meet their necessities for survival through universal social protections compel them to access charity despite their aversion to the shame associated with it. Their interests – meeting their own and their families' basic needs – are thus brought into alignment with the project of cultivating a society where poverty is address by self-governing communities comprised of ethical citizenship, with minimal direct welfare provision by the State.

Perversely, the same neoliberal worldview that requires people to access charity to meet their needs also creates the conditions for them to be shamed by it. Thomas Scheff's (2003) work shows how the experience of shame integrates the self and society. People feel shame when they fail to live up to their own values, which are conditioned by, and attuned to, the values that circulate in their social milieu. As we have shown, political and public discourses surrounding charity are infused with the values of ethical citizenship, which foreground people's responsibility to look after themselves and others, and to avoid becoming a burden on their community (Muehlebach 2012; Rose 2000). These values permeate the social milieu of people who rely on charity to meet their basic needs, meaning that they are well aware that their reliance on the generosity of others is in breach of prevailing social standards. Yet, the limited support available through public welfare means that people feel that they have few alternatives to charity, meaning that they must live with an enduring sense of shame.

The sense that shame is a product of failing to meet prevailing social standards came through strongly in people's accounts. Michaelia is a woman in her 40s with dependent children. Like many others, Michaelia described the shame of asking for charity, which she referred to as "humiliating." She described the source of this shame with reference to her belief that others will attribute her need for charity to a failure to manage her personal affairs responsibly:

> You're sort of going, "Well, I don't have any money for food because I have bills." It just sounds like you're not managing your money. You're wasting it on something, because where else is it going, and you get paid every fortnight and where has it gone, and all that sort of stuff.

For Michaelia, accessing charity is interpreted as a signal of personal failure, "seeing self negatively" (Scheff 2003, p. 254), which is grounded in the fear that others will perceive her this way. A male interviewee in his early 20s, Bob, expressed a similar sentiment: "it's a pride thing, I suppose. If you're self-sufficient it gives you a bit of self-esteem and so it's a blow to your self-esteem having to ask for help."

The shame of charity that we have presented to this point has little, if anything, to do with the actions of volunteers and the way in which they deliver charity. Indeed, some people were adamant that their experience of shame is not due to the actions of others. As Larissa, a female participant aged in her 20s, put it:

> You never feel good. No one is making you feel that way, it's just yourself, I think. You just don't want to be here. You don't want to be in this situation.

Larissa's experience resonates with findings from Kayleigh Garthwaite's ethnographic research in the United Kingdom. Garthwaite (2016, p. 280) found that "stigma was produced not from how people were treated at the foodbank, but instead through what other people would think, or through how people using the foodbank perceived themselves." For many people, then, shame arises from their structural position vis-à-vis others and prevailing social norms, more so than from overt stigmatisation by others. Yet, this does not mean that the practices of volunteers, and the dynamics of the charitable encounter, had no influence on recipients' experience of shame. Indeed, we found that the approach of volunteers did indeed contribute to shame in many cases – either exacerbating it or alleviating it. It is to this dimension of the experience of receiving charity that we now turn.

The charitable exacerbating shame

Charity can be provided in ways that exacerbate the underlying shame that people already experience due to their structural position as dependent upon the generosity of others. Charity is enacted through a dynamic interaction between the volunteer and the recipient, and the norms of ethical citizenship feature as an unspoken subtext in these interactions. As we show in this and the following section, the degree of shame experienced by charity recipients is shaped by whether and how volunteers invoke this subtext, and the assumptions they make about recipients concerning these norms. We found that the shame recipients feel is exacerbated when volunteers focus on assessing their true needs. As we showed in Chapter 7, many volunteers understand their project of making a difference in people's lives as requiring them to rigorously assess people's situations and discern what their true needs are. This often involves a questioning of people choices and motives, and we show here how this questioning problematises (implicitly or explicitly) people's capacity for responsible self-governance.

Bronwyn, a pregnant woman with two children in her late 20s, including a nine-year-old son who she said "probably eats twice as much as what I eat," described the food she received from charity as helpful, but the process of obtaining help shameful. Bronwyn experienced volunteers assessing her need and passing judgement on her capacities as intrusive and incongruent with her sense of self. In Bronwyn's words:

> I found it a little, tiny bit interrogating because they were looking at the rent that I'm just about to move into and they said, "How are you going to afford that?" and I said, "Well, I'm still working and I'm very good at budgeting. I can afford it." But I just felt like it was a little bit. They sort of doubted that I could afford it.

Bronwyn was at pains to explain that her need for help was a product of searching for a new house to accommodate her growing family in a location where access to affordable housing is limited: "on the coast, there's nowhere you can get that's under $350 for three bedrooms." She likened the process of volunteers going through her income and expenditure as "interrogating," and she felt that their approach ignored her capacities:

> I don't go wasting my money. I know how to prioritise my money and I'm still here, like in a pickle. That just goes to show even people who don't waste their money… can still get into trouble.

Bronwyn's experience shows how the assessment process undertaken by some volunteers exacerbates shame by invoking questions about people's capacity to look after themselves and their families responsibly. Assessing for true need involves the questioning of people's choices, which implicitly problematises their capacity to make responsible choices. There is an assumption of deficiency in regard to the charity recipient, and this assumption foregrounds the fact that, by requesting charity, the recipient stands in breach of the norms of ethical citizenship.

As we showed above, people seeking charity are already highly sensitive to being perceived as deficient by others, and are reluctant to access charity unless absolutely necessary out of fear of such judgements. When volunteers question their choices or offered unsolicited advice, people's insecurities about being judged are triggered, leading to intensified feelings of shame.

Kevin was a 35-year-old male with a son he did not see. He said he had a diagnosis of "agoraphobia and depression and anxiety and God knows what else." Referring to the charity where we met Kevin, he reflected, "as much as I don't like to admit it, I've been seeing these guys regularly for probably three years now." Kevin juxtaposed his experiences at the charity, where he said he never walks away empty handed or feeling judged, with another charity organisation that he feels the process of asking for help is shameful. Kevin recounted an experience at another charity that he recently contacted to seek help:

> They basically make you feel like an idiot for not realising how long you had to wait before you'd get more help. At this point in time, with everything else that's going on, I don't really need any more stress, and that's what I like about Vinnies. I can come here, it's easy to deal with people, they're always friendly, and I leave here with something that helps me and *no lecture*. That's the biggest argument with the [x charity]. You go in there and they try and lecture you about how you could do better, how you should be doing better. One of the [volunteers at x charity] said to me, "You're 35. You should have your shit together and not be relying on other people to help you."

As Kevin explained, being lectured by volunteers positions him as an inadequate and inferior subject who is failing to live up to society's standards of responsible self-governance. This exchange leads to feelings of shame that compound the hardships that he is experiencing. This in turn makes it even more difficult to ask for help, despite high levels of material need, and leads to the avoidance of certain charities that come to be seen as judgemental. For Gough, who we introduced at the beginning of this chapter, being asked why he needed charity stopped him from asking for help. He said that the questioning at some places that provide charity make it an intolerable experience. Gough explained:

GOUGH: [S]ome [charities], you call and they make you feel like you're a, well, a dipshit or a loser. They don't make you feel comfortable, so you don't go back.

RESEARCHER: I know it must be hard to talk about that, because it sounds pretty awful, what do they do to make you feel like that?

GOUGH: They just ask you, "Man, why do you need this? Why? Why?" And it's like, well.

RESEARCHER: Oh, is that right?

GOUGH: So they've got no real empathy and they go, "Well, why do you need this? Why do you need that? Why don't you do this? Why don't you do that?" I snapped one day and I said, "Look, it's fucking hard enough for me to ask for assistance without you fucking making me feel like a piece of shit."

In this exchange, Gough recognises that asking for charity is already a shameful act – "hard enough for me to ask for assistance" – and he makes it clear that volunteers delving into his personal problems only work to make this difficult task more challenging. As Gough recalled it, volunteers further reinforced the shame he felt by suggesting that he behaved differently: "why don't you do this." The shame was compounded, as the questioning of volunteers delved into Gough's problems, on the one hand, and assumed, on the other hand, that the cause of Gough's problems were his own making and the solution was for him to change his behaviour. As we noted in a previous chapter, such an approach entails a fundamental misrecognition of the circumstances that drive people to access charity, and we contend that shame is fundamentally bound up with this process of misrecognition.

One woman, Terri, powerfully illustrated this experience of misrecognition. Terri left an abusive relationship and required material support. She spoke about some volunteers at charities that are rude and judgemental. On one occasion, when a volunteer was rude to Terri when she asked for help, she said "I just walked out." Terri's principal concern is that the volunteers judged her situation on the basis of limited knowledge. In doing so, they overlooked the circumstances that produced her need for charity in the first place, and her agency in navigating those circumstances.

> They shouldn't assume why you're here because you just can't get your shit together. I don't think they should make that assumption. I'm here because I made a choice that I'm not going to put up with bad behaviour anymore, someone drinking and yelling at me.

It is well accepted by scholars that domestic violence is a structural problem: both the experience of violence, and the deprivation and hardship experienced by women when they leave a violent relationship, are grounded in ongoing structural inequalities between men and women (Kuskoff & Parsell 2020). Women who leave a violent partner often struggle to find affordable housing for themselves and their families, and many find themselves reliant on inadequate welfare payments following the loss of a partner's income (Frost & Meyer 2019). By questioning Terri's choices, volunteers elide these structural factors, as well as the agency and strength she (and many others) show by choosing to leave despite the lack of support. Shame is thus not only generated by people's structural position but also by whether or not that position is recognised by volunteers and society more broadly.

The charitable mitigating shame

Just as the actions of volunteers can exacerbate the shame recipients feel when accessing charity, they can also help to mitigate it. In the previous chapter we described how some volunteers eschew the judgemental approach of assessing true needs in favour of an alternative approach that involves listening to people's stories and helping relieve their suffering in whatever small ways possible. Charity recipients described how this approach helps them overcome the shame associated with asking for help, as it involves recognition of their circumstances and the hardships they face.

In some cases, the mitigation of shame is achieved simply by the absence of judgemental questioning and unsolicited advice. A woman accessing charity described her experience as positive simply because, "I think that's the biggest part of it all, someone not making you feel guilty [for] what you're doing." Participants associate the avoidance of judgement with being treated in a person-centred way, wherein volunteers engage them in their full human complexity rather than focusing solely on their (perceived) problems and deficiencies. Marise, a woman in her 40s who disclosed having a borderline personality disorder, contrasted her experiences accessing charity with her interactions with the Australian Government social security office (Centrelink). For Marise, volunteers at the charity support centre where we met her convey "genuine empathy." When asked to elaborate on this, Marise said the volunteers:

> Don't treat you like a dead shit, basically. When you walk into Centrelink, "What's your [welfare number]?" [The volunteers at the charity] treat you like a person.

Similarly, another participant who regularly accesses charity stated, "you can just come in and vent to them and have a cry. As I said, there's no judgement passed." As with volunteer practices that exacerbate shame, the non-judgmental and person-centred approach is meaningful to charity recipients by virtue of its relationship to pervasive social norms that position receipt of charity as a shameful act. As noted above, people present to charity in the knowledge that asking for help is in breach of the social expectation that ethical citizens will "make a contribution, not take one" (Morrison 2018). They are thus haunted by the possibility that they will be judged negatively by others for their reliance on charity. When volunteers eschew this opportunity to judge, and instead treat charity recipients in person-centred ways, they create a temporary sanctuary from the shame that comes from relying on the generosity of others (Bowpitt et al. 2014).

Along with the suspension of judgement, people receiving charity also valued being listened to by volunteers. Paul, a man aged in his early 50s, explained how he feels significant shame when seeking charity due to his struggles with a gambling addiction. He said:

> I just feel a bit of shame because I had money and I blew it in the pokies [poker/slot machines] and I just feel bad coming in and asking for a food voucher. I knew if I didn't go to the pokies I wouldn't have had to do it. I just feel a bit ashamed at the moment.

Notwithstanding his sense of shame, Paul praised the volunteers he encountered, stating that they "really do give a fuck; they do care." When asked what makes him feel this way, Paul explained that it is the fact that volunteers take the time to converse with him and listen to him explain his circumstances on his own terms. "They actually sit down and have a yarn [chat] to you. When you sit down and get the food voucher they'll just sit and have a yarn and see how you're going." Paul contrasted this experience of being listened to with his experience at another charity provider that he now refuses to visit because he feels that the volunteers "judge you... They look at you and think, Why are you here?"

For Paul, then there is an important difference between being assessed and being listened to, in terms of both the shame each elicits and his willingness to present for help. Being assessed entails having one's problems brought into focus, obscuring other aspects of people's understandings of their self and their circumstances that they feel help explain their situations. Thus, people appreciated volunteers who, as one participant put it, "don't... pry into too much of your life." Similarly, Pauline, whose situation we discussed above, explained how she experiences charity as positive when it provides relief for her problems without focusing on her problems. She said the volunteers she engages with are people who:

PAULINE: Give up their free time to help other people and they do not judge you. It is the difference between life and death, truly... I know when I've been that low and I thought nobody cared, just to have someone say, "Yes, we will help you," and say nothing else. Not, "How did you get yourself into this situation? What's wrong with you?"

RESEARCHER: So, that sense of not being asked questions and not being judged is very important?

PAULINE: Yeah. There's enough holes in us. That stuff gets in. People say, "Don't let it affect you." Clearly things have affected us. There's holes everywhere... So, to have people like this when you think you've got nothing and nothing is going your way, one good thing, one yes when you've had 100 no's is enough to keep you above the line. It matters. These people matter.

In this exchange, Pauline does not discount her problems; she is open and reflective about them: "there's holes everywhere." What she rejects is, rather, being assessed: the requirement that she lay out her problems for inspection by a stranger.

In contrast to this experience of assessment, being listened to is experienced by charity recipients as being given the space to represent themselves and their circumstances on their own terms and without fear of judgement. This experience is described well by Anne, who explained the positive attributes of the charity we met her at as follows:

> [It's] just the way that they are. They can sit down, and they try to give you advice without a lecture, they don't tell you that you're doing the wrong thing or anything. They just understand. *I can speak freely to them*. Whereas at other places you get that little bit anxious.

In Anne's reflection, we can see a subtle distinction between being listened to, wherein she can disclose aspects of her circumstances to volunteers without judgement ("I can speak freely with them") and assessment, wherein disclosure of circumstances leads to "a lecture" and being told "that you're doing the wrong thing." The former is experienced as a moment of recognition, with recipients perceiving that volunteers understand the complexity of their circumstances. The latter, on the other hand, is experienced as a moment of misrecognition, where people feel that their complex lives are reduced to set of discrete personal problems that form the basis of negative judgements and a sense of shame.

Positive experiences of accessing charity – when volunteers go out of their way to listen to recipients and provide refuge from shame – demonstrate that volunteers have the capacity to mitigate the structurally induced shame experienced by charity recipients. These experiences put empirical pressure on the claims of scholars like Sennett (2003), who describe charity as fundamentally condescending. Although Sennett's assertion is indeed consistent with some of our findings, it does not account for how people's experiences accessing charity can be fundamentally shaped by how volunteers engage with them and offer help. Thinking about charity as a dynamic interaction opens up the possibility for it to be experienced – and indeed practised – in multiple ways.

Responding to need or creating the needy

The foregoing discussion in this and the previous chapter outlines how charity recipients can be constructed as passive and deficient subjects by approaches to charitable giving that are harnessed to the production of the neoliberal social and its promotion of ethical citizenship. The duties of ethical citizenship presuppose the existence of people in need, in relation to whom communities of ethical citizens can enact compassionate care. This need is produced, in part, by social policy decisions that restrict direct welfare support to poverty inducing levels. However, we have shown here how the status of charity recipients as the needy can be (re)produced and reinforced in the charitable encounter through approaches to giving that require recipients to articulate their needs and the problems underpinning them. In many cases, people must present a compelling account of their needs before they can access charities' resources. Thus, charity is about more than meeting basic needs (see Chapter 2); it is also about the construction of the poor as needy subjects upon whom the charitable can perform their ethical duties.

Whilst the process of disclosing problems may confirm the recipient's position as needy, it is largely ineffective at convincing the charitable of anything meaningfully related to the provision of charity. As we demonstrated in Chapter 7, volunteers rarely believe the nature and detail of the information conveyed to them by recipients. The process of disclosing one's problems might serve to confirm the assumption that people are needy, but it is an inadequate and unreliable measure to provide the volunteer with information they can use to assist people. On the contrary, a charity assessment model that requires recipients to narrate their problems creates the conditions for volunteers to assume that the problems people present with are in fact the result of personal deficiencies. This process of articulating need necessarily distracts the conversation – the assessment – away from the policy decisions that in fact produced people's needs (and where its solutions lie).

As showed above, the positioning of charity recipients as deficient, needy subjects burdens them with a profound sense of shame. The experiences of people accessing charity make it clear that they neither enjoy disclosing personal information about their problems to a stranger nor volunteers asking about them, or prying. The shame that people feel about needing help means that they access charity reluctantly, and they only ask for help when they deem their situation to be dire. When volunteers probe into people's problems, it only serves to exacerbate the underlying shame. Even worse, recipients find unsolicited advice from volunteers about the behaviours they need to adapt or change to address their problems as tantamount to an unhelpful lecture. As we have suggested, this type of assessment is problematic in and of itself, as people routinely described not frequenting a charity, and therefore not accessing vital resources to survive, where they are assessed, lectured, and shamed. Further, and recognising that charity can be positive over and above any resources provided when recipients feel recognised and not judged by volunteers, the assessment process of volunteers, which can feel like an interrogation, subverts the realisation of a positive connection. In fact, the model of problem disclosure and assessment is counterproductive to the development of a connection between the needy and the charitable. Ironically, then, the model of charity where assessing true need assumes primacy can actually undermine the affective bonds that neoliberalism positions as core to social solidarity, despite the production of such bonds being integral to the realisation of neoliberal conceptions of the social (Muehlebach 2012).

In addition to foregrounding and reifying recipients' problems, the prevailing model of charity is similarly limited because it relies upon a passive recipient. Indeed, the model that requires one to only disclose problems, and nothing else, explains the approach that does not try to engage the recipient in a way in which they can contribute as capable people. That charity model therefore provides little explicit capacity for people to give back or otherwise practice the care that is central to the performance of ethical citizenship. It makes sense that a charity model that exclusively relies upon the recipient to be seen as a problem does not offer the opportunity for them to give and exercise agency beyond their problem status. As a needy group with problems, the charity model does not consider how they can make valuable contributions by providing help.

On this basis, we argue that the assessment process is unnecessary and counterproductive to the objective of helping people in need. As we showed in Chapter 4, the poverty experienced by many charity recipients is generated by welfare policies that ensure that people without income from employment live well below the poverty line. Given that the charitable are unable to address this structural underpinning of people's problems, the assessment process is largely a futile and degrading exercise. People accessing charity realise that volunteers cannot grasp the complexity and fullness of the problems they may experience, nor grasp the circumstances that drive people to charity. Moreover, questions about people's need for help ignore what is far more important to know about the recipient's situation to provide genuine help. This was powerfully exemplified by Terri's experience above about accessing charity because of the decision she made to leave an abusive relationship.

Notwithstanding these limitations, the fact that some volunteers practice charity in ways that recipients experience as mitigating their shame shows that an alternative model of charity is not only possible, but in fact exists. By abandoning judgement and truly listening to recipients, these volunteers both create a sanctuary from shame and open themselves up to the complex personal and structural realities that push people into poverty. Augmenting the empirical experiences from the previous chapter with the experiences presented here, we can see that when volunteers try to engage recipients as people in ways that transcend assessment of true need, the positive dimensions to charity shine. In doing so, these data from the perspectives of volunteers and recipients provide a rough sketch of what a model of charity that has the needs of the poor as its organising principle might look like. In the next and final chapter, we discuss the possibility of transforming charity based on this and other lessons established through the book.

References

Bowpitt, G, Dwyer, P, Sundin, E & Weinstein, M 2014, 'Places of sanctuary for 'the undeserving'? Homeless people's day centres and the problem of conditionality', *The British Journal of Social Work*, vol. 44, no. 5, pp. 1251–1267.

Frost, A & Meyer, S 2019, *Domestic and Family Violence: A Critical Introduction to Knowledge and Practice*, Routledge, Abingdon.

Garthwaite, K 2016, 'Stigma, shame and 'people like us': An ethnographic study of foodbank use in the UK', *Journal of Poverty and Social Justice*, vol. 24, no. 3, pp. 277–289.

Kuskoff, E & Parsell, C 2020, 'Preventing domestic violence by changing Australian gender relations: Issues and considerations', *Australian Social Work*, vol. 73, no. 2, pp. 227–235.

McKay, F, Haines, B, Beswick, H, McKenzie, H & Lindberg, R 2020, 'The prevalence, severity and experience of food insecurity in Australia: An investigation of food aid use', *Health and Social Care in the Community*, vol. 28, no. 6, pp. 2399–2407.

Morrison, S 2018, "Until the bell rings" – Address to Menzies Research Centre, viewed 12 March 2021, https://www.pm.gov.au/media/until-bell-rings-address-menzies-research-centre

Muehlebach, A 2012, *The Moral Neoliberal: Welfare and Citizenship in Italy*, University of Chicago Press, Chicago.

Rose, N 2000, 'Community, citizenship, and the third way', *American Behavioral Scientist*, vol. 43, no. 9, pp. 1395–1411.

Scheff, T 2003, 'Shame in self and society', *Symbolic Interactionism*, vol. 26, no. 2, pp. 239–262.

Sennett, R 2003, *Respect in a World of Inequality*, W. W. Norton & Company, New York.

9 Transforming charity

Charitable society

We live in an age in which charity is not only a core part of society's response to poverty, but also central to society's understanding of itself. Providing charity to the poor is a deeply evocative practice that operates as a signifier of a range of enduring social ideals: from selfless gifting, to compassion for others, to the power of community and human connection (Dean 2020; Dees 2012; Kymlika 2001). These properties render charity highly attractive to both a culture longing for connection and meaning in an otherwise fragmented and impersonal modern world, and to political projects seeking to reassemble the social in particular ways. Charity is therefore much more than the isolated act of giving; it is a deeply social and relational phenomenon from both the bottom-up and the top-down. In this book, we have endeavoured to analyse and evaluate charity in terms of its relationships, and to show how its public meanings and political uses impact the lives and practices of people experiencing poverty and of the people who seek to help them.

We have argued that the contemporary meaning and practice of charity is shaped in important ways by attempts to harness charity to the broader project of reassembling the social along neoliberal lines. We have shown how the State, with support from the media, seeks to enrol charity in the production of the forms of ethical citizenship and affective, community-based solidarity that comprise neoliberal conceptions of society. It does this, on the one hand, by creating a need for charity through social policies that limit and restrict access to State welfare supports, such that people experiencing poverty are forced to rely on charity to survive. On the other hand, the State cultivates charity by providing extensive material, symbolic, and regulatory support to the charitable. The media supports this process through the generation and amplification of representations of charity as paradigmatic of self-governing community and the charitable as exemplars of ethical citizenship.

These efforts to harness charity to the production of the neoliberal social have important implications for how charity is practised and experienced by charity providers and recipients. Recipients are driven into reliance on charity by grinding poverty and the inadequate welfare support that they receive from the State. Although charitable volunteers have a genuine desire to help people overcome poverty, their charity is limited to the provision of basic resources to meet immediate need, leaving the structural drivers of recipients' poverty unaddressed. This gives rise to a model of charitable practice in which recipients feel a deep sense of shame for their failure to live up to the norms of ethical citizenship. Within this model, frustrated volunteers exacerbate this shame by requiring charity recipients to account for their problems and demonstrate genuine and persistent need, leading to the misrecognition of recipients as the authors of their own suffering. The model is thus one where the actual needs and lived experiences of the poor are shrouded over, and they are positioned as mere fodder for the ongoing performance of ethical citizenship on the part of volunteers.

Yet, there are also instances where the charitable challenge this model of charity and the neoliberal worldview that underpins it. We have presented instances where either large charitable organisations or individual volunteers have leveraged their position on the frontlines of poverty relief to foreground the structural drivers of poverty and to question the social policy decisions that contribute to it. We have also shown how some volunteers seek to re-centre the needs and experiences of the poor through practices of recognition, such as listening to their stories without judgement or assessment and striving to lighten the burden of their poverty in whatever small ways possible. We have referred to these as moments of *counter-translation*, as they point to the ways in which efforts to enrol charity in the production of the neoliberal social can be reversed to prioritise the needs of the poor and advocate for structural change. For us, these instances of counter-translation point to the possibility of a transformed model of charity where the needs and desires of people in poverty are located front and centre in efforts to reassemble the social, rather than being incidental to it.

Where to from here?

While the neoliberalised model of charity discussed in this book is historically novel, charitable responses to poverty are far from new. Charity to the poor has endured for millennia, and for at least 300 years it has sat alongside State provision. Johnson (1996) was correct in remarking that the Whiggish view of history erroneously assumed that charity would fade as modernity took hold. Despite the advent of modern welfare states in the twentieth century, people who are poor continued to rely on charity to some extent, and people who are well-off continually showed that they want to help others by providing charity (Johnson 1996). In addition, charity remained a socially valorised and desirable practice (Dean 2020). Recent increases in reliance on charity are thus part of a much longer historical process where charity has ebbed and flowed – or, indeed, changed in terms of its function and meaning – while remaining a consistent feature of societal responses to poverty. If you are poor, charity is not going away anytime soon; if you are not poor and have a social conscience, engaging in charity will be presented to you as an attractive opportunity for you to practice your values and/or your duties as a citizen.

The stickiness and pervasiveness of charity mean that we cannot avoid it. It is a mistake to ignore charity on the belief that society ought to progress to an enlightened state, where science and evidence should inform what we do rather than the compassion and emotion that fuel charity (Dees 2012). Perhaps we should not be surprised about the stickiness and pervasiveness of charity. Writing more than 100 years ago, the Russian anarchist Peter Kropotkin argued that people have long exhibited the desire to connect with and help one another. In his words,

> The mutual aid tendency in man has so remote an origin, and is so deeply interwoven with all the past evolution of the human race, that it has been maintained by mankind up to the present time, notwithstanding all vicissitudes of history.
>
> (Kropotkin 2009, p. 223)

Although we are today (rightly) cautious of the kind of claims about "human nature" that Kropotkin makes, it is difficult to deny that acting charitably towards others and sharing resources, particularly in immensely inequitable and unjust societies, is a deep and enduring feature of social – and indeed human – life.

Yet, acting charitably, or helping someone who is poor, can mean many different things and assume many forms. Thus, the pertinent question is not whether or not charity is an appropriate response to poverty, but rather whether particular models of charity are better at helping meet the needs of people who are poor than others, and whether the prevailing model can be improved. Is it possible to transform charity such that the shame, misrecognition, and glossing over of structural processes that we have described in this book are mitigated? Is it possible to do so while retaining the popular will to help others and desire for social connectedness that charity represents? Even more optimistically, how can charity break free from its traditional function of ameliorating the symptoms of poverty and become a force to eliminate poverty?

In this chapter we outline a set of principles that we believe should underpin a transformed model of charity and its place in society. These principles respond to the failures of the contemporary (neoliberalised) model of charity that we have analysed in this book, while taking advantage of the opportunities for reworking charity around the needs of the poor that are manifest in the charitables' desire to help address social inequalities and in the instances of counter-translation identified above. We argue that the transformation of charity must involve (i) reframing what we praise as desirable care to, and concern for, people who live in poverty; and (ii) altering the model of charitable care provision to one based on recognition, solidarity, and reciprocity.

Reframing charity

The ultimate aim of charity must be to address the inhumane injustice of poverty. Here, we propose that the first step in transforming charity requires the recasting of ideal charitable action to be more than a response to the symptoms of injustice, and *also* a force to change the structural systems that generate it. Central to our argument is that we need to move from ameliorative charity to transformative charity. This shift is necessary for two reasons. The first reason is that poverty is a social injustice, and one that is widely recognised as inhumane. Indeed, the existence of poverty is at odds with both secular human rights and religious beliefs that all people are created in the image of God. Whether motivated by faith or something else, citizens working to change oppressive structures embody charitable care in its most fundamental form.

Regardless of how poverty is defined and measured, its existence harms human and social life. Saunders (2011) explains that the Australian and OECD poverty lines reflect what people require to experience an acceptable standard of living and to participate in the customs and activities of society. This is consistent with Marshall's (1950) theory of social rights, wherein the State has a responsibility to enable people to live according to prevailing social standards by providing an adequate level of welfare, administered through a respectful system. Marshall contended that income from the State not only reduces financial inequalities, but also promotes equality of status.

The experience of poverty thus entails the inability to participate fully in society. Living in poverty means not only feeling socially isolated and stigmatised, significant as these are (Walker 2014), but also living with the threat of violence and persecution (Lister 2004). The experiences of people using charity that we presented in the previous chapter resonate with these established insights. People resort to charity because they have no money for food, no money for housing, and no money for clothing or nappies for their children. Many access charity because they have no other supports, including after they have left abusive relationships. Their experiences powerfully convey how poverty subverts a person's capacity to feel part of society, let alone contribute to it, as a dignified citizen. This indignity and lack of control over one life's basic processes is exacerbated by the fact that, as the OECD (2010, p. 128) argues, Australia's below-poverty-line unemployment benefits prevent people from "look[ing] for a suitable job" and thus meeting their needs in socially acceptable ways.

The second reason for shifting from an ameliorative to a transformative model of charity – one that challenges the structural conditions that cause poverty – is that poverty is not inevitable. In wealthy countries, for example

Australia, we have both the knowledge and wealth to end poverty. In this book, we advocate for a charity model that pushes the charitable to do more than respond to the consequences of poverty because we know what causes poverty and we know how to end it (Brady 2019). The growth of homelessness and increasing depth of poverty in Australia are a direct consequence of policy decisions. We must confront these policy decisions when we think about charity and how it could be reimagined. The rate of the unemployment benefit means that recipients live below the poverty line. Similarly, defunding social housing creates a homeless population. Successive governments have administered policies that create the conditions for people to present to charity seeking food and shelter. Governments can act differently. In Chapter 4, we presented evidence of the buoyant and world-leading macro-economic conditions that Australia has enjoyed for a generation. We also demonstrated how Australia drew on some of this wealth in response to COVID-19, where cash transfers to unemployed people effectively doubled and immediately reduced poverty – for a short term – on an unprecedented scale in recent history (Phillips et al. 2020).

When assessing charity to people in poverty, we must appreciate that we are not confronted with two options: providing charity or accepting the *status quo*. Rather, we can both provide charity to help alleviate the burden of poverty while, at the same time, advocating for governments to end poverty by addressing its causes through improved policy. Moreover, as a society, we should only celebrate charitable action when it is coupled with efforts to end poverty, rather than celebrating it based on the motivations and ethical sentiments of the charitable. This is not to say that people's motivations do not matter. Chapter 7 illustrated how volunteers are motivated to make a difference in the lives of the poor through charitable giving. Such motivations are necessary and valuable. However, for the charitable to truly make a difference, they must engage in and be praised for actions that work to solve poverty.

Our position rejects cynical assertions from political leaders that poverty will always be a feature of modern social life (Perusco 2010). Our recasting of what constitutes ideal charitable action likewise rejects the claim of the co-founder of the Australian charity, Orange Sky Laundry, that solving homelessness is impossible (Edmistone 2020). As Poppendieck (1999) observed in the United States, progressing ameliorative charity can serve to subvert society's willingness to fund and progress policy that ends poverty by sending the message that we are already doing all we can. This is a concern that Australia has grappled with since at least the middle of the twentieth century (O'Brien 2015). To adapt an analogy from Karl Marx, we need to be careful that charity does not become the new "opium of the people."

There is a profound incongruence between what people living in poverty presenting to charity need and what current models of charity provide. Recipients and some volunteers, as we illustrated in Chapters 7 and 8, are well aware of these structural deficiencies. People need affordable housing, yet they are offered mattresses in carparks or mobile showers; they need a liveable income, and instead are provided with a food voucher and a lecture about how they ought to live differently. Even if people equally need companionship and social connections, their poverty and the demonstrable distinctions and power dynamics between the giver and the receiver render these relations difficult to achieve. Poverty is the absence of resources to live in accordance with prevailing societal standards. Although charity is an enduring feature in the lives of many citizens experiencing poverty, current charity models are unable to provide people what they require to live a dignified life as a citizen – let alone provide them with the resources and capabilities necessary for them to autonomously exit poverty.

How, then, can charity move beyond addressing the symptoms of poverty (ameliorative charity) to help address the structural causes of poverty (transformative charity)? In what follows, we outline three possible ways for transformative charity to operate.

Charity as innovating and pushing the State

Arguments for charity draw on ideas of subsidiarity, ground-up action, and the vibrancy and ethics of community and citizens that charitable action represents (Pope John Paul II 1991; Smith & Lipsky 1993). Some see charity as desirable because they believe the welfare state is an intrusive and ineffective imposition in people's lives (McKnight 1995; Shapiro 2007). Our argument for recasting appropriate charitable action as that which addresses the structural causes of poverty recognises that local action, instead of an exclusive and distant centralised State, does have a lot to offer society and indeed to people who experience societal injustices. However, it also recognises that the centralised State, the resources it holds, and its capacity to address structural inequalities is fundamental to achieving justice (Fitzpatrick et al. 2020).

We therefore see local charitable care as having a valuable role to play, not in the absence of the centralised State, but rather in agitating for changes to centralised systems. Local community and charitable action is vital, as many argue, but core to their charitable activities is work to challenge and push the centralised State to address the structural problems that local communities experience, but are ill-equipped to address by themselves. It is not a question of whether ground-up and local charity is desirable. As Kropotkin (2009) before us, we take it as self-evident that citizens showing concern for and acting to help their fellow citizens is both deeply ingrained in the structure of society and positive. Rather, it is what local volunteers do that matters. At the same time as his ideas were contributing to the design and establishment of the modern welfare state, Beveridge (1948) argued that charity should spearhead innovations that the State is reluctant to pursue. In this way, charity can take on some of the characteristics of the progressive settlement house movement, whereby charity is "an experimenting and reforming body," rather than a phenomenon that is concerned with "things as they are" (Briggs & Macartney 1984, p. 136).

Raising expectations of what constitutes commendable charitable care

Given that poverty is an affront to justice and dignity, and that current approaches to charity are inadequate to meet the needs of people living in poverty, we need to set the bar higher – much higher – for what constitutes *commendable* charitable care. Because many people living in poverty have so few resources, society celebrates any charitable act that is seen to give someone something – anything – that they do not have. As we showed in Chapter 6, the media lauds any charitable care that is seen as responding to the symptoms of poverty, even when it acknowledges State failure as the underlying cause of the problem.

The changes to charity that are envisioned here require, fundamentally, changes to societal expectations about what is desirable action towards people in poverty. The celebration of the acts of the charitable – such as designing and volunteering in charities to wash the clothes of the poor on the streets, or temporarily accommodate people in mattresses in inner-city carparks – serve to set dangerously low expectations about what is commendable behaviour. The media's uncritical celebration of the charitable for washing someone's clothes, along with the prestigious government awards, not to mention millions of dollars in direct State funding, sends a clear message to society that any charitable act towards the poor is good, regardless of the outcomes it produces. Moreover, the positioning of this type of charitable action sends a message to citizens of what the ideal citizen looks like. It is difficult to imagine the existence of the waitlist for people to volunteer in charities that wash and accommodate homeless people in public places if these charities and their volunteers were not positioned as ideal citizens.

To transform charity so that it can contribute to justice in an unjust world, we need to transform what we as society deem to be laudable charitable action. To transform charity so that it contributes to achieving justice, we must evaluate individual charitable acts and charity organisations in relation to the nature of the problem they address, its causes, and available options to solve it. To be truly charitable, one must work towards addressing the injustices that prevent people from living dignified lives as citizens. As a society, we need to celebrate (and fund) actions that contribute to justice, not actions that potentially soothe injustices and possibly even perpetuate them. This is a difficult task. As Bloom (2016) notes, empathy motivates charitable action to do good, but our empathic focus is structured by what we see in front of us. Preventing social problems from occurring in the first place by achieving structural change is less likely to be lauded than direct action to help a poor person in the here and now (Dees 2012). Society must celebrate the citizens who work towards ending or preventing the injustice of poverty, and not exclusively glorify the charitable for responding to the symptoms of systems failure (Schoenfeld & Mestrovic 1989).

Charitable care as a form of activism

A transformed charity model to end poverty by confronting the political institutions where poverty is embedded and where it may be addressed will inevitably require political activism. This locates charitable organisations in a vulnerable place, as it is unlikely that governments will bestow prestigious awards upon citizens whose (charitable) actions directly challenge them. Similarly, the political advocacy to challenge unjust systems runs the risk of threatening the continuation of government funding (Hasenfeld & Garrow 2012). However, if the charitable are motivated to help people in poverty, political activism is unavoidable.

Our argument here questions the supposedly neat distinction between charity as a direct act of compassion, on the one hand, and political activism to change institutions as something other than charity, on the other (Monforte 2020). The definition of charity as the voluntary act to help someone, including helping by giving one's time, leaves room for charity that includes volunteers freely giving their time to change institutions through which people's poverty is caused. If the distinction can be made between charity as an act of help by giving a hungry person food, or charitable actions to help someone who is hungry by changing social conditions so they can purchase their own food, surely the latter charitable act is a truer realisation of charity's meaning. Here, we extend the proverb that give a person a fish and you feed them for a day; teach a person to fish and you feed them for a lifetime. We argue that transforming charity is about the charitable challenging systemic inequities that prevent a person from accessing the river so they can fish.

This proposed transformation of charity, including what the charitable do and what society recognises as valued charitable behaviour, addresses Durkheim's concerns that person-to-person "charity has no moral value in itself and cannot by itself constitute the normal end of moral conduct" (1961). This is because this type of interaction "merely maintains the conditions which made charity necessary in the first place" (Durkheim 1958). We have to think about and recognise what constitutes charitable care in more ambitious and optimistic ways than what it currently involves. It is ambition for change and optimism for human life that drive a transformed model of charity that involves activism.

In Chapter 2 we drew on the multiple arguments that illustrate how faith can motivate charitable care, such as helping people who are poor as an example of living according to God's will. Our argument in this chapter, that helping people who are poor requires the charitable challenging the structures that produce poverty through activism, can likewise be supported by theology. In his book *A Theology of Liberation*, Gustavo Gutierrez (1988) compels Catholics to radically disrupt the political institutions that cause oppression. For Gutierrez, Catholics are required to fight these structural causes of poverty because it is impossible to live according to faith and at the same time be complicit in injustices that oppress people.

Gutierrez explains that it is "God who intervenes in history in order to break down the structures of injustice;" indeed, "was not Christ's first preaching to proclaim the liberation of the oppressed?" (Gutierrez 1988, p. 69). He goes on to argue that a failure to challenge structural oppression is equivalent to exercising direct action *against* the oppressed. In contrast, tackling structural inequalities is necessary for the realisation of God's Kingdom on earth:

> The struggle for a just world in which there is no oppression, servitude, or alienated work will signify the coming of the Kingdom. The Kingdom and social injustice are incompatible (cf. Isa. 29:18–19 and Matt. 11:5; Lev. 25:10ff. and Luke 4:16–21). "The struggle for justice," rightly asserts Dom Antonio Fragoso, "is also the struggle for the Kingdom of God."
>
> (Gutierrez 1988, p. 97)

For those whose charitable actions are motivated by Christianity, Gutierrez provides a radical and compelling argument to raise the bar for what constitutes helping people who are poor. He is adamant that "God wants justice, not sacrifice" (Gutierrez 1988, p. 111). Following this, it is the Christian duty to bring about justice, which, in turn, is to bring about the Kingdom of God. Gutierrez thus puts pressure on the assumption that helping people in poverty, if motivated by Christianity, means that a person is living according to God's will, regardless of the outcome. He asserts that this only occurs when the help provided also involves challenging the structural oppressions that are the source of people's poverty.

Although Gutierrez's presents a provocative theological position to push Christians, many people who provide charity, both within the literature and in our research, are not animated by Christianity or any faith. In our research, many people explained their desire to provide charity as the simple and secular commitment to help people in need because it is the right thing to do. They expressed their charity as part of their desire to live a meaningful life. For the many people motivated to act charitably for secular reasons there are of course a myriad of principles to draw on to substantiate the transformation of charity described above, including Marshall's (1950) social rights, and more broadly people's inalienable human rights. Here we present human rights as secular, but recognise that some scholars argue that the United Nations Declaration of Human Rights is actually embedded in, and exists because of, the Christian theological doctrine that all people are equal before God (Holland 2019).

The literature on the ethics of care is likewise important. Scholars recognise that care encompasses far more than interpersonal actions among family, between clients and professionals, or even between volunteers and recipients (Barnes 2012; Engster 2015; Tronto 2015). Contemporary scholars firmly place care as a public issue, where holistic expressions of care need to encompass the societal distribution of resources and public policy that ensures universal coverage of benefits. In short, we need to think about the provision of care at the societal level in ways that identify who needs care and who provides it, and how the roles and motivations of both parties are driven by social processes. Care is as much a social and political act as it is an interpersonal act. Caring for people through charitable actions has to be understood and indeed realised at the societal level through activism to change societal conditions.

As we showed in Chapter 5, the State's efforts to valorise the charitable as ideal/ethical citizens drew on secular ideas of community and affective social bonds. In the Australian context, desire for these kinds of bonds is often expressed in terms of the apparently uniquely Australian virtue of *mateship*. Implicit in the mateship narrative is the normative ideal that mates care for each other. Citizens are lauded for providing charitable care as the embodiment of Australia's commitment to and manifestation of mateship. In the same way that Gutierrez pushes Catholics to act charitably by challenging oppressive structures as living according to God's will, we argue that positioning the charitable as people who work to disrupt Australia's poverty causing institutions are demonstrating what Australians celebrate as true mateship. After all, as Prime Minister John Howard remarked, mateship has a "hallowed place in the Australian lexicon," defining it as "the spirit of helping people in adversity" (Dyrenfurth 2014). Indeed, Australians assumes a "quasi-religious admiration for mateship," which is premised on a nostalgia for collective egalitarianism (Dyrenfurth 2015).

If Australians cherish mateship as the expression of the ideal citizen, and mateship is about helping their fellow citizens achieve an egalitarian society, then true mateship requires citizens to challenge the systems that create adversity. To draw on a cognate ideal of the Australian character, charitable care must fight systems of oppression and structures that drive disadvantage because this is necessary to enable all Australians to experience the mythical "fair go," a land where gender, class, and family privilege are unimportant to success (Huang 2017).

Transforming the charity model

Above, we argued that the first step in transforming charity is predicated on the belief that the ultimate act of charity is to address the inhumane injustice of poverty. This position encourages the charitable to examine what constitutes care, and, in turn, to actively work towards changing the unjust systems that produce poverty through innovative practice and activism. Our advocacy to transform charity, however, similarly recognises the valuable role of citizens providing direct charitable care to their fellow citizens. We thus advocate for a continued role of direct charitable care, alongside charity expressed through political action to achieve structural change. Charitable care to people in poverty encompasses *both* addressing structures that cause poverty and meeting people's immediate needs, albeit through a transformed model of charity. Here, we introduce our ideas for transforming the day-to-day practice of delivering charitable care.

Recognition

A transformation of charity is required because, through the current model, the position, experience, and interests of its recipients – that is, people living in poverty – are insufficiently considered. As we showed in Chapters 7 and 8, the prevailing model of charity encourages the misrecognition of recipients. Through funding requirements and public sentiment, people using charity are positioned as vulnerable individuals experiencing a temporary personal crisis (Department of Social Services 2017; Parsell & Watts 2017). Their poverty is assumed to be driven by individual failure and this status represents a totalising identity of personal vulnerability (Fraser 2013). Through this construction, poverty and vulnerability are treated as intransigent social facts and their structural causes largely ignored.

This model of delivering charity relies upon, and practically facilitates, the misrecognition of the recipient. The charity recipient accesses charitable care through a process where they are not only required to account for their need for charity, they are also reduced to those needs. The model is exclusively directed towards the recipient articulating what is wrong with them, and the charitable expend considerable time and effort assessing the veracity or otherwise of the recipients' claims and providing them with basic resources to ameliorate their suffering. People are therefore often not given the time and space to articulate the structural circumstances behind their personal problems or their strength and ingenuity in navigating these circumstances. To be misrecognised in this way is to be institutionally positioned as inferior, not just to be looked down on, rather to be denied "the status of full partners in interaction, capable of participating on a par with the rest" (Fraser 2000, p. 114).

The harnessing of charity to the cultivation of ethical citizenship serves to reinforce the misrecognised state of charity recipients. The existence of a population of vulnerable individuals is required to provide ethical citizens with an object upon which to exercise their care and compassion towards. As we demonstrated in Chapters 5 and 6, volunteers are celebrated for their charitable care, while recipients are presented as the (sometimes grateful, but mostly silent) passive object of these caring acts. As such, recipients are not themselves provided with the opportunity to perform the duties of ethical citizenship, nor would they have the capacity to do so given that their material circumstances mean that they are required to dedicate their energies to meeting their basic needs. They therefore experience significant shame for failing to live up to societal norms, and this shame is exacerbated by volunteers questioning them about their reliance on charity.

The critique of the prevailing model of charity presented here is not a critique of the charitable. In our fieldwork we identified numerous examples where volunteers sought to listen to recipients' accounts of their circumstances on their own terms, and then tried to help them in whatever ways they could. Many volunteers were not driven to help people in poverty out of pity, but instead from a sense of empathy for their structurally conditioned situation and recognition of their shared humanity. However, despite the intentions and actions of the charitable, the current charity model is ill-suited to realise the interests of recipients.

Within the current model of charity, the charitable give, and the poor receives. The model dictates two distinct positions:

> Serving the dinner only signals your differences from them. You are serving; they are receiving. You are volunteering; they are there out of necessity.
>
> (Dees 2012, p. 329)

Through a model where they are only permitted to receive care, the recipients lose power at the same time as the charitable gain it. The transformation of the charity model, centred on the primacy of the recipient, requires recognition of people in poverty beyond their state of poverty and the needs that bring them to seek help. It also necessitates a disruption of the distinction between the helper and the helped. In Fraser's (2000) words, it requires bringing about recognition, through both changed cultural assumptions and access to resources, so that people can interact with others as peers. The fundamental change underpinning a transformed charity model involves, as one of our charitable volunteers noted, positioning recipients of charitable care as "as equals."

As equals, the transformed charity model will facilitate solidarity and reciprocity between the helper and the helped. It is not only symbolically seeing people as equal that can create the conditions for reciprocity and solidarity. A transformed charity model that includes activism to challenge oppressive systems, as outlined above, practically conveys to recipients that the charitable locate poverty as embedded within unjust social structures, not as a personal attribute of an othered recipient. It is towards the model's transformations to foster solidarity and reciprocity that we now turn.

Solidarity

Our reimagined model of charity relies upon solidarity between the helper and the helped. It is a form of solidarity, however, that differs from the affective solidarity of community promoted in neoliberal conceptions of the social. Notwithstanding our critiques of affective solidarity, the willingness and, in many cases, desire of the charitable to engage firsthand with people experiencing poverty does indeed provide the opportunity for connection and solidarity between the two parties. For, it brings together people who occupy often quite different positions in the social world, and who may not otherwise have the opportunity to grasp the perspectives and experiences of the other. These kinds of encounters open up the possibility of the formation of what Iris Marion Young (1986) calls "communities of difference," where the diversity of group members becomes a resource for mutual recognition, mutual growth, and the imagining of a shared future.

However, as we have shown, this outcome is not an automatic consequence of encounters between the charitable and the poor, even when these encounters are driven by compassion and a desire to help on the part of the former party. Indeed, the charitable often fail to grasp the structural and experiential basis for the differences they perceive between themselves and the people they are trying to help. This, in turn, leads to misrecognition, blaming and, from the recipients' standpoint, shame, which threaten rather than enhance the bonds of solidarity. For us, this points to the fundamental inadequacy the charitable's affective motivations or ethical commitments *alone* to produce solidarity.

What, then, will it take for the possibility of solidarity that arises from acts of charity to be realised? First, we contend that it requires openness, reflexivity, and a structural literacy on the part of the charitable. In Chapter 8 we showed the power of open and non-judgemental listening on the part of volunteers to mitigate the shame experienced by recipients and provide them with a sense that their circumstances, struggles, and strengths were truly recognised. These are moments where volunteers are reflexive about the differences between their own social position and experiences, and those of the people they are trying to help. In doing this, they suspend, and achieve a critical distance from, the norms of self-reliance, personal responsibility, and contribution to the community that circulate in their milieu and which they might otherwise apply as standards for themselves or those like them. Moreover, they deploy, or enable themselves to develop, a literacy of the structural circumstances that compel people to access charity, such as the low rate of unemployment benefits or the undersupply of affordable housing in Australia. Incipient forms of such a literacy were demonstrated by many of the participants in our research, as we outlined in Chapter 7, and were derived from their reflexive engagement with the stories told to them by charity recipients, pointing to the very real possibility to cultivating such practices in a transformed model of charity.

Second, we contend that charity can only contribute to solidarity when the affective and ethical motivations of the giver are translated into political consciousness and action of the sort that we described earlier in this chapter. On the one hand, this kind of politicised charity sees the charitable working *with* and *for* people experiencing poverty, rather than *on* them as passive objects. It involves listening to their stories, recognising their struggles, and using the socially valorised position of the charitable *qua* ethical citizens to speak out on their behalf. On the other hand, politicised charity advocates for the restoration and refinement of a political and intuitional basis of solidarity when it calls for adequate public welfare provision to guarantee the social rights of all people. It therefore transcends neoliberalism's reduction of solidarity to the ethical and affective bonds of community, and seeks to enact a definition of the social wherein solidarity is grounded in the institutionalisation of material and political equality through a democratically controlled State apparatus. As Arendt (2006) observed, this type of solidarity may be animated by the actual or perceived suffering of the oppressed. It is not, however, guided by it.

Third, for charity to contribute to solidarity, charity recipients must be provided with the opportunity to practice reciprocity. As we discussed in Chapter 2, scholars have long pointed to the unidirectional nature of charity as the basis of its shame inducing or "wounding" character (Douglas 1990; Mauss 2011; Molm 2010). Without the ability to practice reciprocity, people receiving charity find themselves in a passive and subordinate position, and this contributes to their being misrecognised as incapable or irresponsible subjects. We therefore advocate for the creation of opportunities for charity recipients to practice reciprocity within both the structure and representation of charity. This may involve opportunities for people experiencing poverty contribute as volunteers in the charitable care of others when – or, indeed, if – they have the capacity to do so. However, we think it should also involve a broadening of the understanding of what it means to practice reciprocity.

We showed in Chapter 8 that recipients of charity often experience grinding poverty, and many dedicate significant time and energy into finding ways to meet the basic needs of themselves and their families. For many, this involves enduring the shame of asking for help from charities so that they can provide for others, usually other members of their family. In these instances, receiving charity is in its own way an act of giving – and even sacrifice. It thus corresponds to what scholars refer to as "generalised exchange," wherein "each actor gives benefits to another and eventually receives benefits from another, but not from the same actor" (Molm et al. 2007, p. 206). It is not a simple model of A gives to B, and then B gives something of equal value to A. Rather, it is a complex model that recognises the interwoven yet open-ended nature of social relationships.

The argument for charity to foster reciprocity is premised on the desire and significance of people in poverty to maintain pride and self-worth. To be able to give, and not just receive, is critical for not only people's capacity to feel part of society, but also to be seen by others as full members of society. As the Peace Prayer of Saint Francis makes clear, "for it is in giving that we receive." Reciprocity is, as Sennett (2003, p. 219) observes, "the foundation of mutual respect." Although some people accessing charity appreciated the support of volunteers, none of them experienced their passive receipt of charity as a means to realise mutual respect. By being able to reciprocate – whether by directly participating in charity as volunteers or through recognition of their acts of generalised exchange – people in poverty can benefit practically from the resources they receive and benefit symbolically and socially by giving back.

While ambitious, we believe charity can be transformed to meet these three conditions for the production of solidarity. If achieved, *this* kind of solidarity is truly valuable and will provide us with a legitimate reason to celebrate charity. For this kind of solidarity works to undermine arbitrary distinctions between the ethical citizen and the vulnerable poor. It rests on the dignity of all people and principles of equal worth. Through solidarity, a diversity of perspectives and positions in society can operate together to challenge power structures where poverty is embedded. In these ways, charity driven by solidarity is consistent with the reimagination of charity as a project that also works to address the structural problems that led to people requiring charity in the first place. In turn, the reimagined charity model that requires expressing care through addressing the systems that cause people's poverty will facilitate solidarity. The model of solidary is based on collective efforts to fight societal injustices that oppress people in poverty, rather than the charitable model of care that relies upon the continuation of an impoverished population. This position is critical to promoting solidarity, or a democratic common purpose and responsibility to care (Tronto 2015).

Charity that promotes solidarity is thus based on recognition of people in terms of universal citizenship. Brunkhorst (2005) outlines a conceptualisation of solidarity that is central to the transformed model of charity envisioned here. It is a mode of solidarity that promotes individual freedom, while at the same time recognising that:

> Strangers are bound to one another by a universal bond of civility and can be brought into relations of reciprocity.
>
> (Brunkhorst 2005, p. 3)

It is the citizen coming together in a community of difference, but for the collective good, that represents charity's true value in society. As Brunkhorst recognises, the diverse citizens in our vision of solidarity come together to provide charitable care, not as the well-off giving to the poor, but rather as members of society interested in ending the structural conditions that create poverty. The reimagined vision for charity, especially through a transformed mode of charitable care, represents a fertile environment for volunteers and recipients to come together to progress societal transformations.

Conclusion

Offering advice about how to achieve realistic utopias, Bregman (2017, pp. 263–264) states, "if we want to change the world, we need to be unrealistic, unreasonable, and impossible." Bregman offers these thoughts on the basis that many of the institutions of a just and fair society that we take for granted today were once utopic, initially rejected ideas. Yet progress towards a utopic society requires people to change unjust institutions, no matter how unrealistic doing so may seem.

In this chapter, we have set out a vision for changing charity that many will see as unrealistic, unreasonable, and impossible. Indeed, the online comments rejecting critiques of charity's limitations presented in the epigraph of Chapter 1 demonstrate how many may interpret the transformation of charity outlined here. However, and reflecting on Wright's (2013) call for emancipatory social science to explain how solutions are viable and achievable, the ideas for transformation sketched in this chapter build on a strong evidence base about what society can achieve. These ideas are not only viable and achievable in terms of available resources and knowledge, but they are rather transformations to charity to change systems, instead of responding to symptoms, perfectly aligned with our research showing that volunteers are motivated to genuinely help people in need. Indeed, and more importantly, these transformations to charity – and the recasting of praiseworthy charitable action to be one that addresses poverty – is what people who live in poverty actually need.

Being fully conscious, however, that people in poverty are desperately in need of resources and social connections in the here and now, our ideas for transforming charity seek to make those resources available through a process that mitigates shame. The transformed charity model is not simply designed to mitigate shame, however. It can contribute to a community of difference progressed through principles of solidarity and reciprocity. Diverse social groups coming together for mutual support and connections and, in doing so, contributing to greater democratic engagement and participation, is core to what many see as the true worth of charity to society.

Although a lofty ideal, a transformed charity model can benefit society, the charitable, and people living in poverty. These benefits of charity rely upon recognition of people in poverty, solidarity among the helper and the helped, and indeed structures to break down distinctions between them through cooperation and reciprocity. Our vision for a transformed charity is to better enable citizens to come together to support each other and collectively work towards addressing social injustices.

References

Arendt, H 2006, *On Revolution*, Penguin, New York.

Barnes, M 2012, *Care in Everyday Life: An Ethic of Care in Practice*, The Policy Press, Bristol.

Beveridge, W 1948, *Voluntary Action: A Report on Methods of Social Advance*, George Allen & Unwin LTD, London.

Bloom, P 2016, *Against Empathy: The Case for Rational Compassion*, The Bodley Head, London.
Brady, D 2019, 'Theories of the causes of poverty', *Annual Review of Sociology*, vol. 45, pp. 155–175.
Bregman, R 2017, *Utopia for Realists: And How We Can Get There*, Bloomsbury, London.
Briggs, A & Macartney, A 2011, *Toynbee Hall: The First Hundred Years*, Routledge, Abingdon.
Brunkhorst, H 2005, *Solidarity: From Civic Friendship to a Global Legal Community*, Translated by J Flynn, The MIT Press, Cambridge.
Dean, J 2020, *The Good Glow: Charity and the Symbolic Power of Doing Good*, Policy Press, Bristol.
Dees, G 2012, 'A tale of two cultures: Charity, problem solving, and the future of social entrepreneurship', *Journal of Business Ethics*, vol. 111, no. 3, pp. 321–334.
Department of Social Services 2017, *Discussion Paper: Financial Wellbeing and Capability Activity*, Australian Government, Canberra.
Douglas, M 1990, 'Forward: No free gifts', in M Maus (ed.), *The Gift*, Routledge, London, pp. ix–xxiii.
Durkheim, E 1958, *Socialism and Saint-Simon*, Antioch Press, Yellow Springs.
Durkheim, E 1961, *Moral Education*, Free Press, Glencoe.
Dyrenfurth, N 2014, 'Mateship: Secular Australia's religion and how John Howard hijacked it', *The Sydney Morning Herald*, https://www.smh.com.au/national/mateship-secular-australias-religion-and-how-john-howard-hijacked-it-20141217-129c7t.html
Dyrenfurth, N 2015, *Mateship: A Very Australian History*, Scribe, Brunswick.
Edmistone, L 2020, 'The men behind Orange Sky charity empire', *Courier Mail*.
Engster, D 2015, *Justice, Care, and the Welfare State*, Oxford University Press, New York.
Fitzpatrick, S, Pawson, H & Watts, B 2020, 'The limits of localism: A decade of disaster on homelessness in England', *Policy & Politics*, vol. 48, no. 4, pp. 541–561.
Fraser, N 2000, 'Rethinking recognition', *New Left Review*, vol. 3, pp. 107–120.
Fraser, N 2013, *The Fortunes of Feminism: From State-Managed Capitalism to Neoliberal Crisis*, Verso, London.
Gutierrez, G 1988, *A Theology of Liberation*, Orbis Books, New York.
Hasenfeld, Y & Garrow, E 2012, 'Nonprofit human-service organisations, social rights, and advocacy in a neoliberal welfare state', *Social Service Review*, vol. 86, no. 2, pp. 295–322.
Holland, T 2019, *Dominion: The Making of the Western Mind*, Little Brown, London.
Huang, Y 2017, *Intergenerational economic mobility in contemporary Australia: Is Australia still the land of the "fair go"?*, PhD Thesis, The University of Queensland, St Lucia.
Johnson, P 1996, 'Risk, redistribution and social welfare in Britain from the poor law to Beveridge', in M Daunton (ed.), *Charity, Self-Interest and Welfare in the English Past*, Routledge, Abingdon, pp. 225–248.
Kropotkin, P 2009, *Mutual Aid*, Cosmo, New York.
Kymlicka, W 2001, 'Altruism in philosophical and ethical traditions: Two views', in J, Phillips, B Chapman & D Stevens (eds.), *Between State and Market: Essay on Charity Law and Policy in Canada*, McGill-Queen's University Press, Toronto, pp. 87–126.
Lister, R 2004, *Poverty*, Polity, Cambridge.

Marshall, T 1950, *Citizenship and Social Class*, Cambridge University Press, Cambridge.

Mauss, M 2011, *The Gift: Forms and Functions of Exchange in Archaic Societies*, Martino Publishing, Mansfield Centre.

McKnight, J 1995, *The Careless Society: Community and its Counterfeits*, Basic Books, New York.

Molm, L 2010, 'The structure of reciprocity', *Social Psychology Quarterly*, vol. 73, no. 2, pp. 119–131.

Molm, L, Collett, J & Schaefer, D 2007, 'Building solidarity through generalized exchange: A theory of reciprocity', *American Journal of Sociology*, vol. 113, no. 1, pp. 205–242.

Monforte, P 2020, 'From compassion to critical resilience: Volunteering in the context of austerity', *The Sociological Review*, vol. 68, no. 1, pp. 110–126.

OECD 2010, *OECD Economic Surveys: Australia*, viewed 22 February 2021, https://www.oecd-ilibrary.org/economics/oecd-economic-surveys-australia-2010_eco_surveys-aus-2010-en

Parsell, C & Watts, B 2017, 'Charity and justice: A reflection on new forms of homelessness provision in Australia', *European Journal of Homelessness*, vol. 11, no. 2, pp. 65–76.

Perusco, M 2010, 'Bible bashing the homeless, Abbott style', *The Sydney Morning Herald*, https://www.smh.com.au/politics/federal/bible-bashing-the-homeless-abbott-style-20100215-o2tj.html

Phillips, B, Gray, M & Biddle, N 2020, *COVID-19 JobKeeper and JobSeeker Impacts on Poverty and Housing Stress Under Current and Alternative Economic and Policy Scenarios*, viewed 22 February 2021, https://csrm.cass.anu.edu.au/sites/default/files/docs/2020/8/Impact_of_Covid19_JobKeeper_and_Jobeeker_measures_on_Poverty_and_Financial_Stress_FINAL.pdf

Pope John Paul II 1991, *Centesimus Annus*, viewed 18 November 2020, http://www.vatican.va/content/john-paul-ii/en/encyclicals/documents/hf_jp-ii_enc_01051991_centesimus-annus.html

Poppendieck, J 1999, *Sweet Charity? Emergency Food and the End of Entitlement*, Penguin, New York.

Saunders, P 2011, *Down and Out: Poverty and Exclusion in Australia*, Policy Press, Bristol.

Schoenfeld, E & Mestrovic, S 1989, 'Durkheim's concept of justice and its relationship to social solidarity', *Sociological Analysis*, vol. 50, no. 2, pp. 111–127.

Sennett, R 2003, *Respect in a World of Inequality*, W. W. Norton & Company, New York.

Shapiro, D 2007, *Is the Welfare State Justified?*, Cambridge University Press, New York.

Smith, S & Lipsky, M 1993, *Nonprofits for Hire: The Welfare State in the Age of Contracting*, Harvard University Press, Cambridge.

Tronto, J 2015, *Who Cares? How to Reshape a Democratic Politics*, Cornell University Press, Ithaca.

Walker, R 2014, *The Shame of Poverty*, Oxford University Press, Oxford.

Wright, E 2013, 'Transforming capitalism through real utopias', *American Sociological Review*, vol. 78, no. 1, pp. 1–25.

Young, I 1986, 'The ideal of community and the politics of difference', *Social Theory and Practice*, vol. 12, no. 1, pp. 1–26.

Index

Note: *Italic* page numbers refer to figures.